Authoritative Governance

Authoritative Governance

Policy-making in the Age of Mediatization

Maarten A. Hajer

OXFORD
UNIVERSITY PRESS

OXFORD
UNIVERSITY PRESS

Great Clarendon Street,
Oxford ox2 6DP

Oxford University Press is a department of the University of Oxford.
It furthers the University's objective of excellence in research, scholarship,
and education by publishing worldwide in

Oxford New York

Auckland Cape Town Dar es Salaam Hong Kong Karachi
Kuala Lumpur Madrid Melbourne Mexico City Nairobi
New Delhi Shanghai Taipei Toronto

With offices in

Argentina Austria Brazil Chile Czech Republic France Greece
Guatemala Hungary Italy Japan Poland Portugal Singapore
South Korea Switzerland Thailand Turkey Ukraine Vietnam

Oxford is a registered trade mark of Oxford University Press
in the UK and in certain other countries

Published in the United States
by Oxford University Press Inc., New York

First published 2009
First published in paperback 2011

British Library Cataloguing in Publication Data
Data available

Library of Congress Cataloging in Publication Data
Data available

Typeset by SPI Publisher Services, Pondicherry, India
Printed in Great Britain
on acid-free paper by the MPG Books Group

ISBN 978-0-19-928167-1
ISBN 978-0-19-959567-9 (pbk.)

10 9 8 7 6 5 4 3 2 1

Acknowledgements

This book has benefited from the many exchanges with academic colleagues, students, policy practitioners, and journalists over the past years. While most thinking, reading, and writing was done in an '*a deux*' with my laptop, it is over the many, often very informal, exchanges that one starts to appreciate where the strengths and weaknesses of a more complex argument like the one in this book really are. I feel privileged to have been able to tap all the arguments, thoughts, and reflections of those meetings and would like to thank everybody that thus, often perhaps unwittingly, contributed to my thinking and writing.

Some people and institutions deserve to be mentioned explicitly. First of all, my academic home institute, the University of Amsterdam, that granted me a year-long sabbatical after completing my term as Head of Department. Then the Wagner School of New York University, where I spent a substantial part of my sabbatical. I would like to thank Dean Ellen Schall, Rogan Kersh, and Tyra Liebmann for their hospitality.

At the University of Amsterdam I supervised a group of talented graduate students; the exchanges with some of them contributed directly to the work presented here. I should mention Christian Bröer, Kateryna Pischikova, Katharina Paul, Justus Uitermark, Marcel Maussen, and Imrat Verhoeven. Research assistance was provided by Chantal Laurent and Sander van Haperen.

Over the course of writing this book I benefited from the many intellectual exchanges in the international academic network, especially those with Kathrin Braun, Brian Burgoon, John Dryzek, Frank Fischer, John Forester, Archon Fung, Herbert Gottweis, Yrjo Haila, Paul 't Hart, Patsy Healey, David Howarth, Judy Innes, Sheila Jasanoff, Aletta Norval, Susan Owens, Bron Szerszynski, Jacob Torfing, Douglas Torgerson, Mark Warren, and Dvora Yanow. Special thanks to those colleagues who later on read and commented on part of the manuscript or the papers that were directly related to the research: John Dryzek, Archon Fung, David Laws, Tim Marshall, Aletta Norval, Mark Warren, and Elisabeth Wilson.

Acknowledgements

In particular I would like to express my gratitude to those colleagues with whom I co-authored papers or articles on topics related to the book: David Laws, Anne Loeber, Justus Uitermark, Hendrik Wagenaar. Here the discussions, and the drafting (and redrafting) of pieces led to that wonderful sense that what you publish eventually is truly a collaborative work, and a better one because of the collaboration that created it. David Laws, in his characteristically polite but persistent way, made invaluable suggestions to carve out the argument even better at a stage at which I was ready to follow the dictum 'publish and be damned'. Among the co-authors I should, however, reserve a very special word of thanks for Wytske Versteeg, who was first a talented MA student-assistant in my 'Deliberative Policy Analysis' class, then became my research assistant, and then quickly my co-author. Her comments always pushed me to think the arguments through both more carefully and more radically, with this book as a result.

At Oxford University Press I should thank Dominic Byatt, not least for his patience.

Earlier versions of two chapters were previously published as journal articles. Chapter 3 on the murder of Theo van Gogh is a modified version of 'Performing Authority' published in *Public Administration* (2008, no. 1); an earlier version of Chapter 4 was published as 'Rebuilding Ground Zero' in *Planning Theory and Practice* (2005, no. 4). I thank the editors and publishers of the two journals for their permission to reprint these papers in the amended form here.

Contents

List of Tables

List of Figures

Introduction

The meaning of a murder

On the morning of 2 November 2004 I was making my way through the morning rush hour, jostling with thousands of 'Amsterdammers' on bikes of all possible variations, when I suddenly saw police officers running across the street. Some were just in shirt–sleeves, despite the chill of the November morning. I stopped pedalling and let my wheels roll. Thirty metres down the road I saw men and women crying; others merely gazing blankly as traffic passed. Their faces expressed perplexity, astonishment. Others simply stood there, in shock. People covered their mouths with their hands, or held their heads in disbelief. There seemed to be a centre to the situation. Just ahead, a body lay in the road. 'It's Van Gogh', a woman said, and I immediately knew she meant Theo van Gogh, a local filmmaker. Thoughts ran through my head, but none made sense. Van Gogh lay dead, killed, it must be. But who would actually kill Van Gogh? The *bête noire* of the Amsterdam cultural scene was sometimes an annoying, even tedious, character, but he was very much a peripheral figure. A jester, not a crook. Then it hit me: *Submission*, a twelve-minute film Van Gogh had helped make. It attacked the suppression of women in Islam, with very direct visual images. It was controversial; it must have offended many Muslims. Yet I could only guess what the meaning of the murder was, what its meaning *was to become*.

It was a perplexing experience of uncertainty that started right at that moment and actually lasted for a couple of days. There was one fact: Van Gogh was dead. But beyond that all was open. What would happen in the next hour, the next day, the next week? People would start to give their accounts of what had happened. First via eyewitnesses, but most likely the discussion would gradually shift as people tried to make sense of what it all meant. Some would blame the murder on the government.

Had it not failed to see the threats? Van Gogh was a fierce social critic, and his opinions were not always subtle. Another object of his scorn was, I reflected, Job Cohen, the mayor of Amsterdam, whom he accused of being soft on the Moroccan youth that he and many others blamed for causing havoc in Amsterdam neighbourhoods. This had been a major topic in the newspapers over the preceding weeks. If the murderer turned out to be of Moroccan descent, Van Gogh supporters might claim that the Cohen administration was responsible. What would happen if the murder was claimed as a defence of Islam? What if Van Gogh was killed because he blasphemed?

I continued past the crowd and made my way into the city centre. I did not know what was to come—this overwhelming sense of uncertainty was all there was. So, what would the murder mean for the city? Would events turn against the government? What if the murder unleashed a confrontation between accusers and accused later that day? Would the government be able to control, perhaps even guide, the political dynamics triggered by the events? Governments at times need to be prepared to be authoritative, and they have all sorts of means to control and maintain public order; but would the government be able to control the meaning of the murder? What means did it have at its disposal in such symbolically complex situations, anyway? What could it do, what would it do, and with what effect?

Governance as the authoritative enactment of meaning

The murder of Van Gogh caused a moral shock in the Netherlands, its ripples reaching other countries (cf. Buruma 2006). At the University of Amsterdam the murder of Theo van Gogh affected our academic work. Just like American intellectuals who had felt the urge to help understand the situation directly after 9/11 (cf. Mollenkopf 2005; Sorkin and Zukin 2002), Dutch political scientists wanted to contribute to the effort to understand the event. How could we make sense of the animosity that was suddenly out in the open—in the Netherlands, where people always pride themselves on 'our' tradition of tolerance and openness. Could I, perhaps, help people to gain a better sense of the role of government in such a symbolically complex situation?

In Dutch society, the political turmoil that followed the murder of Van Gogh became connected to a more general feeling that, at the beginning of the twenty-first century, politicians had lost their connection to 'the' people. In the Netherlands it was the flamboyant dandy-politician Pim Fortuyn who first exploited the political opportunity raised by this feeling of disconnection. Out of the resulting fragmentation, Fortuyn created a personal, populist genre that was hitherto unknown to the Netherlands (cf. Corner and Pels 2003). He too had suffered a violent death. In the years after Fortuyn was murdered in May 2002, both his style (a strange mixture of playfulness, common sense, and critique of governmental dullness and alleged incompetence) and his message (a rehabilitation of common sense, a call for bold measures, in particular against migrants from Islamic countries) were picked up and became part of political discourse. Next to the message there was the direct manner: the development of 'personality politics'—cutting out any intermediary structure, of party, association, or union—strongly depended on the interplay with the new centrality of the media in politics. It led commentators to pine for a supposed past in which politics was about content, not style and form. That 'golden age' was portrayed as an era in which politicians were assumed to be authoritative figures speaking for a constituency, not political personalities frantically searching for ways to appeal to their public via statements in the media. This new politics came with the risk of a 'dumbing down'; a politics driven by an incident-prone media logic that would, according to observers, destroy the politics based on a commitment to reasoned elaboration and organized representation to deal with public problems.

The concerns over 'dumbing down' and a loss of authority of the political sphere are widely echoed in the media, but are shared too by political analysts around the world (e.g. Postman 1985; Putnam 1995, 2000; Hay 2007). Whereas I argue in this book that the 'dumbing-down argument' is lacking in nuance, it cannot be denied that political leaders must be performers in order to be persuasive in our mediatized environment. But what does this mean for the authority of governance?

Authority has never been self-evident, nor has there ever existed a 'golden past' when politics would have been about just about content, not style. Even our familiar political institutions (which I will refer to as 'classical-modernist', cf. Chapter 1) are particular (re)presentations of democratic legitimacy, as becomes clear in the story about the origin of the modern parliament narrated in Chapter 2. The authority of democratic institutions as symbolized by those people elected to hold office is not a given, but something that needs to be secured, attained, or, as I will call it here, enacted. Thus, the point is not that politics now is all about performance whereas it used to be habitual; the argument is that our mediatized society requires a different, arguably more complicated, way of performing politics to be persuasive and engaging; it calls for new political responses and new political repertoires.

In order to be persuasive, leaders have to perform in situations that are partly beyond their control. Contemporary political conflicts are expressed in many different political arenas: arenas that often not so much pre-exist as rather emerge in the course of the conflict. The mediatized age has reordered the political landscape. The media's wish for decor, for plots, for cliffhangers, or for framing policy in terms of conflict, changes the conditions under which politics is made, and affects how politics is conducted. Moreover, in the age of mediatization new actors get easy access to the stage. All sorts of entrepreneurs can make claims, and these self-imposed leaders are now often staged as spokespersons and can, in that capacity, severely challenge political and administrative leaders, despite the fact that they might lack a clear institutional base or a concrete following. In a situation of making claims and counter-claims, politics is about who can make his/her claim authoritative *in the scenes and at the stages that matter* in the age of mediatization.

My analytical question is: how does authority shape up in this mediatized environment? The analysis of the politico-administrative response to the murder of Theo van Gogh first brought out the crucial role of political discourse and political drama. In the ten days following the Van Gogh murder, Amsterdam and the Netherlands were lucky enough to see how the local political leadership found a response that was at least adequate. Yet the research also elucidated to what extent this was based on improvisation and the circumstance that those in charge brought a experiential habitus with them that allowed them to perform in certain ways in the first place. But beyond the case of the Van Gogh murder a whole set of questions emerged. Ultimately, it led to the research project that this book gives an account of, and which focuses on one leading question: how is authoritative governance possible in today's politics?

Dislocations in politics

This search for an understanding of how authoritative governance is possible almost naturally led to some thinking 'out of the box'. I connected public administration to symbolic analysis; the analysis of public policy to the analysis of political communication and performance theory. For me, the wave of unrest in Western European cities acted as an intellectual catalyst. It showed the urgent need of gaining a better understanding of the particular dynamics in which politics is made nowadays. The murder of van Gogh in 2004 was followed by unrest in other European cities: riots in the Parisian *banlieues* in November 2004; the July bombings in London of 2005; the outcry over Danish cartoons of Muhammad in 2004–5. Each of these incidents in its own way showed the exposed flank of the academic study of politics and policy-making. The deeply felt hostility of certain groups of the population that was expressed in the Parisian *banlieues* or in the London bombings; the realization of the bizarre but truly 'glocal' interaction between global signifiers ('Islam') and a set of localized protests—in the supermarkets and squares of the Arab world, in the streets of Africa (where more than 200 people were killed during the demonstrations following the publication of the cartoons in Denmark), or in the Western media; it all implies that we need to gain a better sense of the dynamics of meaning in order to be able to suggest what might constitute authoritative governance in today's politics and to what extent this can be explained in terms of good political performances.

In trying to answer the authority question, there was no need to restrict the study of governance to situations having to do with the issue of integration or (Islamist) terrorism. Analytically, the crucial point in this book lies in instances where political or institutional authority becomes unhinged, even if it is only for a moment. Such moments, in which political routines seems to be lifted from their solid institutional hinges, and where things occur that seem to disrupt a symbolic order, I will call moments of 'dislocation', drawing on Howarth (2000: 111). Dislocations can be found in other domains as well. In situations where there is a moral outcry, a moment of broadly shared emotionality, or a feeling that trust was breached, legal rights might be entirely clear, but it is neverthe-less inconceivable that an appeal to those rights would suffice to decide the rights and wrongs of the case and win the political battle. Quite the contrary: political leaders who think they can draw upon their *de jure* authority in such situations can end up in trouble. But what is required instead? How can one handle such situations authoritatively?

This book presents three situations of dislocation that allowed me to study the phenomenon of authority of governance in detail. First the Van Gogh case (Chapter 3), then the rebuilding of Ground Zero after the attacks of 2001 (Chapter 4), followed by the British response to the BSE crisis (Chapter 5). The BSE case proves particularly instructive, as it constituted a situation in which a government had almost completely lost the trust of the public; in 1996 it emerged that the government had concealed knowledge that led to the death of hundreds of citizens. In dealing with such cases a high degree of political performance is called for, and analysing such events in detail may reveal how the enactment of politics matters.

The enactment of politics

The focus on the enactment or performance of policy situations implies certain assumptions. This book starts from the premise that political situations are often far more open than is appreciated. Taking conflict-ridden political situations as my empirical focus, I aim to bring out what means are used in such situations to create or suggest stability or continuity, or on the contrary to create commitments to do things in a different way. I think this is important, as much academic thinking on public policy-making, politics, and political theory works from the assumption of stability: it assumes continuity in the 'cast' of political actors; in the 'setting', that is, the polity and its accepted political arenas; in a shared understanding of the scripts, that is, clarity of political cleavages, a basic, mutual, understanding of tactics and expectations among political opponents. In a similar vein, it is often assumed that political actors share a commitment to articulate conflicts within the confines of existing political institutions. Yet politics in our age characteristically goes beyond the confines of the constitutional spaces of politics; new media technologies have created a range of powerful new political stages, and political actors are creative in connecting what they say to where they say it, mobilizing other, non-constitutional sites to get their message across and dominate the politics of meaning.

Governance, in my view, is and has always been first and foremost about the authoritative enactment of meaning. Once meaning is given, policies will follow, albeit obviously not autonomously and effortlessly. Ontological and epistemological convictions (cf. e.g. Hajer 1995, 2003a; cf. also Yanow and Schwartz-Shea 2006) ensure that I pay a good deal of attention to the contingency of political moments and the sequential logic of political events that, from one moment to the next, create and re-create meaning and, ultimately, create political facts. With the emphasis on this discursive work comes the return of the actor, although obviously in settings that exert influence themselves. The presumption then is that situations are constantly negotiated, and that those who are able to impose their interpretations of reality on others gain substantial control over political debates, no matter what their institutional position is. It is (yet another) call to open up the institutions that represent power, and investigate empirically how and why institutions (and the protagonists that are their 'face') are authoritative in some situations, and what explains their failure in others.

Given this emphasis on the role of political performance, it will not come as a surprise that I suggest we can make sense of policy-making in our age by employing a perspective analysing governance as political drama. It implies that I seek to make sense of the realities of governance by paying particular attention to what political leaders and administrators do, very concretely, in identifiable and observable settings. The analytical focus in this book is less on what happens behind the scenes; instead, it is on what the public can see. No political scientist would argue that what happens behind the scenes, in the corridors of power, is not important of course; there are all sorts of power that stem from acts and thoughts that we as the public cannot observe. Yet underlying this analytical focus is the conviction that the performative dimension is of increasing importance in a mediatized political culture and deserves more attention. Moreover, when it comes to authority it is the particular quality of the performance that matters, no matter what happens behind the scenes. It is through the presentation of the political self that meaning is given, roles are defined, and narratives of conflict or cohesion are promoted.

The central concept of the 'enactment' of politics holds that, when people act, they bring events and structures into existence and set them in motion, producing constraints and opportunities that were not there before they took action (Weick 1988: 306). Employing a term like 'enactment' means constantly trying to relate discursive work (wording, i.e. invoking categories, metaphors, analogies) to situations (settings, stagings); to relate situations to discursive signifiers. It is through this discursive and dramaturgical work that political actors *perform* or *enact* a situation, either reconfirming an existing and powerful way of seeing, or breaking away from it and rendering other perspectives in crisis.

This book, then, is an attempt to identify mechanisms, modes of interaction, and new political repertoires that can help us to understand the dynamics of contemporary politics and policy-making. It can be seen as a development of my earlier work on discourse (e.g. Hajer 1995, 2003*b*; cf. also Hajer and Laws 2006; Hajer and Versteeg 2005). Yet it is substantially new, in that the enactment of politics is here elaborated to include not only a discursive, but also an explicitly *dramaturgical* dimension. This brings in a—hopefully more subtle—treatment of the role of the setting in which discursive work gets done, elaborating also on the concept of 'practice' in the earlier texts.

Using this dramaturgical dimension of politics as an analytical frame is easily misunderstood. First of all, there is a widespread idea that political 'performance' should be seen as a form of 'deceit': political performances would 'hide' the true politics, and a 'critical' agenda of policy-making and politics should therefore look 'behind' the performance in order to expose the true politics (e.g. by doing political-economic analysis of the 'outcomes' of politics, monitoring uneven development and levels of inequality, or, alternatively, by trying to find out what goes on 'behind the scenes'). This scholarship is and remains crucial, and has, incidentally, shown a remarkable professionalization both in terms of data and methods. Hence my research project does not aim or pretend to render this scholarship irrelevant. Yet in our day and age, in which the power and speed of communication is so pervasive, we also need a better understanding of the politics of performance itself. Performances matter, they make a difference, and while some performers most certainly will try to deceive others, it is a trivialization of the subject to suggest that political performances are only about deceiving publics or 'simply' playing a role. As critics of rational actor theory have pointed out, human beings are neither able nor willing to calculate their interests and adopt a role that serves those interests. In practice, politicians need to act not on the basis of rational calculation but out of a feel for the game that they have accumulated over time and in environments inside and outside of politics (Bourdieu 1998). As I will elaborate in Chapter 2, to see politics in terms of performance or 'enactment' implies that it is through the staged interaction that meaning is created in the first place.

A second potential misunderstanding of this book's focus on performance lies in the reading of 'performance' in terms used by scholars of public administration. As is widely known, in 'public admin' performance connotes the degree to which governments achieve goals; it is about efficacy. It should be obvious by now that I will not be employing the term in that more traditional public admin meaning.

The perspective on performance presented here can be summarized as follows. I not only argue that politics has never existed without performances, but go one step further to suggest that particular presentations of politics could and should be valued positively. After all, persuasion is crucial to the establishing of any democratic commitment, any connection between politicians and the citizens they are supposed to represent. The failure to establish this connection in a durable way is, of course, what preoccupies politicians in our age. Using 1993 data, Manuel Castells pointed out how political leaders *all across the Western world* suffered under very low approval ratings (1997: 344). The tendency in these figures has most certainly not changed for the better since (cf. Stoker 2006; Hay 2007). While it is undisputed that policy content matters, it does not explain the very negative relationship between those in power and those who put political leaders in power. Just by way of illustration, in 2008 Dutch politics the economy was doing well, unemployment was very low, people were very happy about their private lives, yet they were pessimistic about the state of the country, and very negative about the political leadership (Dekker and Steenvoorden 2008). Here it seems that political performance may play a role.

The analysis of political performances, which of course goes back to the classical study of rhetoric, gets a new lease on life in an era in which the media have become such a crucial dimension of the political game. Looking for 'interesting' news stories, the media highlight incidents and crises, not the 'non-event' of political stability. The media *frame* politics in terms of conflict, and hence this is how people perceive it. In such situations the volatility of the connection between political leaders on the one hand and the public(s) on the other becomes painfully clear.

Reflecting on the changing nature of the political, Dick Pels observed how: 'Increasingly, positions of political power are dependent upon public trust, belief and confidence (and upon those who are able to manipulate these volatile variables), and hence upon a recognizable political style that weaves together matter and manner, principle and presentation, in an attractively coherent and credible political performance' (Pels 2003: 57). If that is the new art of politics, then we must understand it so as to know how political actors negotiate such situations effectively. The new agenda, then, is not only about content but also about a style that is seen as trustworthy in a seemingly unstable situation; it is not only about responding to the incident but also about how to avoid throwing out the baby with the bathwater, that is, rescuing the valuable parts of a tradition of policy-making in a situation that suggests that a governmental response was 'utterly' inadequate. In this book I introduce the term 'politics of multiplicities' to refer to the mechanisms that haunt policy-makers in the new mediatized environment. It understands the authority problem of politics in terms of the struggle to conduct politics at multiple sites, relating to a multiplicity of publics, and communicated through a multiplicity of media. *What is crucially new nowadays is that political actors must constantly reckon with the fact that what they say at one stage to one particular public will often, almost instantaneously, reach another public that might 'read' what has been said in a radically different way and mobilize because of what it heard*. It is a situation in which they cannot control streams of communication, in which messages are constantly refracted and utterances are constantly picked up out of context and often turned against those who uttered them. If 'This is not what I meant' is one of the most frequently heard expressions in politics today, this is just a telling indication of the complicated politics of meaning in today's governance.

The all-too-obvious struggle of public office-holders in a mediatized environment calls for an answer to the question of what it is that makes particular claims authoritative. Yet while there is satisfaction to be gained out of the illumination of particular mechanisms that explain the fate of authoritative governance, there is in fact a second motivator underlying this whole endeavour. I also undertook this study to see if it was possible to connect an authoritative governance in the age of mediatization to particular forms of deliberative governance. I will leave that difficult question for the very end of the study, but I hope that the book as a whole will contribute to reflection on what democratic governance could look like in an era marked by fragmentation, instability, and volatility.

Harold D. Lasswell once formulated the inspiring aim for academics studying policy-making: to contribute to the mobilization of collective intelligence for collective problem-solving (cf. Torgerson 1985, 1986). It is a major task in an era in which demagogy and simplifications abound. In this book we investigate whether particular performances of politics can facilitate that other tradition: that of policy-making by reasoned elaboration. How do we create a reasoned and shared position on the way in which we should go about addressing pressing public problems? What has become apparent in much writing on the subject is that we have only limited creativity in thinking critically about how to handle situations in which the soft underbelly of governance is exposed, that is, in which emotions run high, people strongly claim a superior right to speak over others (e.g. as victims), or even claim a right to take things into their own hands (e.g. as wrongly accused, or as deeply insulted), and various groups invariably have a crack at political leaders and policy-makers. All too often 'fragmentation', 'volatility', and 'crisis' are invoked to suggest that in such periods 'management' has to prevail over democratic deliberation. Situations that are open, where it is unclear if they are going to result in turmoil or will slowly wither away, do not seem to go well with a commitment to democratic governance. But is that necessarily so? Are there political repertoires that do not revert to the managerial reflex?

The structure of the book

By invoking the notion of a 'mediatized politics' I want to underline the enormous impact of the media on current politics and policy-making, indeed, the way in which those elements have often become impossible to distinguish from one another. But I do not argue that the growth of media influence is the prime driver of the instability of the political landscape, or that the role of the media would be sufficient to explain the prominence of conflicts, crisis, and incidents in today's politics. Without playing down the impact of the media and their practices, it still is a secondary, not a primary cause of the change. I argue that to really be able to understand the context in which political authority has to be achieved nowadays, we need to dig deeper and engage in the political-sociological changes that have occurred. This is what we will do in Chapter 1, elaborating on my earlier concept of the 'institutional void'. Subsequently we will turn to the significance of mediatized politics and spell out the particulars of political performances. This leads to an elaboration of the earlier conceptual framework in Chapter 2, where I distinguish between two prime dimensions of performance: discourse and dramaturgy. This framework will then be employed to analyse the three cases mentioned above.

An essential aspect of this approach is to work through detailed case studies in which the dynamic process over the control of meaning is acted out. The first case examines the handling of the aftermath of the Van Gogh murder which has taken so much of my attention over the past years. The murder marked the return of political violence to the streets of a city and country that have a worldwide reputation for tolerance and conviviality. This case, researched with Justus Uitermark, first of all raised the question of how to perform authoritative and democratic governance in a situation in which the political leadership itself was blamed by some for the murder. The case also prompted a more fundamental rethink of what a resilient democratic governance requires.

A second approximation is made through the analysis of the case of rebuilding Ground Zero, which shows the discursive politics that frustrated the initial attempt to impose a 'business as usual' approach to rebuilding on the World Trade Center site. It narrates the discursive interplay over the meaning of the site and shows how this influences the ideas of what should be built and within what limits, and it points to the crucial interplay of discourse and setting in a mediatized political environment. It also illuminates how difficult it is to keep a planning process going in a good democratic spirit.

The third and final case unravels the British institutional response to the BSE ('mad cow disease') crisis of the 1990s. As British readers in particular will probably remember, this was a crisis in which the government was found out to have known much more about the risks of eating beef than it had shared with its citizens. The domain of food safety became an exemplar for the new Labour government that wanted to show its commitment to a 'new governance' which would centre on transparency and taking citizens seriously. Drawing on research started with David Laws and then developed with Wytske Versteeg, the case study narrates the establishing of the new Food Standards Agency which was developed in a way very much congruent with the principles of a deliberative democracy. It is a case study in the enactment of deliberative governance, and shows how the British government sought to regain authority but based on new principles. The study contains crucial lessons for how new deliberative democratic practices depend on a repertoire of political performance.

The three cases all have their own political dynamics, and each of them sheds light on a particular element of today's political situation/predicament, but the focus on politics as performance runs through all three.

In analysing governance as political drama this book hopes, first of all, to gain a place in a tradition in political science that takes seriously the role of language and dramaturgy, of discourse and settings. That literature is subtle but has somehow always remained peripheral in the discipline. It includes Murray Edelman's *Symbolic Uses of Politics* (1964) and *Constructing the Political Spectacle* (1988), Merelman's work on political dramaturgy (1969), Goodsell on political architectures (1988), and Gamson on *Talking Politics* (1992). The present book is a call to take more seriously what Carl Friedrich already said about authority: authority is a quality of communications, not of persons (1958: 35–6). I hope it will be seen and appreciated as a further development of my previous work on political discourse (1995). The analysis of how politics is performed in times of crisis can, in my opinion, contribute to an understanding of both the resilience and the vulnerabilities of current political institutions.

A second dimension that is characteristic of the book is its focus on governance. My interest has always been with the interaction between state and society, with government as actor in an effort to make public policy work. The book aims to shed light on the art of governance in a period characterized by growing fragmentation in which many of the well-rehearsed and well-institutionalized approaches to governance fail.

The third dimension, finally, is the book's engagement with the literature on media and politics. It came as a surprise to me to see how the literature on governance and that on media and politics are really quite separate. As the argument unfolds in this book, it will become increasingly clear that I see this as a serious flaw. Rethinking strategies of governance needs to fully incorporate an understanding of what a mediatized politics implies. At the same time, however, there is a need for those working in media studies to rethink their understanding of contemporary politics. Too much of it is based on the classic idea of politics as having a clear centre, whereas a new authoritative politics will have to be able to inform decisions at various levels, in various spheres, and not at one focal moment, but much more in a stream of continuing events.

Perhaps it is important to state at this point that this is far from a pessimistic book. In it I will note various elements of a new repertoire that can cope with the instability and ambiguity that surround many policy issues today. By considering how amplification and argumentation interact, we can see how the new mechanisms at times do indeed produce the feared 'dumbing down', but at other times allow for sound deliberation and a considered choice of what course of action to undertake.

1

The Authority Problem of Governance

On 12 October 2007 the Norwegian Nobel Committee announced that Al Gore, the former vice-president of the United States, would receive the Nobel Peace Prize for 2007. More precisely, the prize would be shared by Al Gore and the Intergovernmental Panel on Climate Change (IPCC), 'for their efforts to build up and disseminate greater knowledge about man-made climate change, and to lay the foundations for the measures that are needed to counteract such change' (Norwegian Nobel Committee 2007).

In academic circles the Nobel Committee's choice was met with a tongue-in-cheek cynicism that quickly put Al Gore on par with Mother Teresa. In the meantime, the media remained uncertain of what to make of the choice. 'Mother Teresa not only talked the talk, but she also walked the walk for her Nobel Prize', read a letter to the editor in the *New York Times* (Steiner 2007). Al Gore, the former VP, whose political career was over, was to be the 2007 laureate. And for what? For making a movie? So it would seem.

The unease generated by honouring Gore seems to reflect a widespread fear that politics is 'dumbing down'. Our new 'mediatized politics', so the worry goes, does not only imply a growing sensitivity to forms of political 'spin' (McNair 2003). It also leads to a preoccupation with personalities, with style, and with events that make for colourful presentation in the media (cf. Postman 1985; Franklin 1994, 1998; Blumler and Gurevitch 1995; Putnam 1995, 2000). Through this frame, the decision of the Nobel Prize Committee appears as yet another illustration of the drift towards superficiality in contemporary politics. The fact that Gore won an Oscar ('Best documentary') in the same year that he won the Nobel Peace Prize, almost certainly an unprecedented double, only deepens such concerns. The Norwegian Nobel Prize Committee highlighted a different facet, however. It referenced Gore's efforts to disseminate knowledge about man-made climate change. Even this can be reinterpreted. His message caught on, but at the cost of the quality of information. Could it be more telling that, not long thereafter, a British judge would rule that *An Inconvenient Truth* could only be shown in schools if preceded by a statement that not all facts as presented in the film were uncontroversial?[1] Seen through this 'dumbing down' frame, selecting Gore for the Nobel Peace Prize is 'yet another' indication of the advance of populist mediocrity and the waning appreciation for the value of reason, deliberation, and scientific expertise.

The predilection with stardom and the tendency to personify is hard to deny. We have become all-too-familiar with the phenomenon of 'celebrity politicians' (cf. e.g. Street 2004, 2005). And, admittedly, it was Al Gore, not the IPCC, that initially received attention in the press coverage of the announcements of the 2007 Nobel laureates.[2] Yet is this reading of the situation convincing? The Nobel Prize Committee did not give the prize to Al Gore alone; it chose to give the prize to both Al Gore and the institutional body of the IPCC. Even here the 'dumbing down' frame has a response: 'IPCC? Did you know that they take a vote on the texts they publish?!' Yet this question suggests that those most worried about the dumbing down may not be all that fact-regarding themselves.

The IPCC is an institution *sui generis*. Launched in 1988 by the WMO and UNEP in Geneva, the Intergovernmental Panel on Climate Change managed to forge a global consensus on the science of climate change. What started off with fierce debates on the essence of global warming among scientists from the South and the North ended up as a series of IPCC reports which came up with a policy-relevant assessment of the contribution of man-made emissions to climate change, acknowledging uncertainties (Petersen 2008). What is more, the IPCC began to point out what the repercussions of climate change might be for the world community. Scientists from a wide range of disciplines developed a common methodology and a set of technological tools that allowed them to overcome the lack of consensus that had marked debates in the 1980s. This was a remarkable achievement. The IPCC provided probably the most

---

[1] In order for the film to be shown, the Government must first amend their Guidance Notes to Teachers to make clear that: (1) The Film is a political work and promotes only one side of the argument. (2) If teachers present the Film without making this plain they may be in breach of section 406 of the Education Act 1996 and guilty of political indoctrination. (3) Nine inaccuracies have to be specifically drawn to the attention of school children (source: *www.newparty.co.uk/articles/inaccuracies/gore-html*).

[2] A query on LexisNexis for *International Herald Tribune/Wall Street Journal/New York Times/ Guardian/Global News* wire shows on '(gore AND nobel AND prize) from 3/4/2007', 215 items; '(IPCC AND nobel AND prize) from 3/4/2007', 54 items (3/4/2007–3/4/2008).

complex 'science for policy' vehicle to be created to date, not only bringing together the academic disciplines needed to understand global warming, but speaking and reporting to the 113 governments that were involved in the UN climate-change initiative as well. Whatever the merits, in a historically unique institutional effort the IPCC somehow found a way to make an authoritative claim on what surely rates as one of the most complex and fundamental policy challenges of our time. In this sense, the announcement of the 2007 laureates might be seen as reassuring to those concerned about a continued dumbing down in our politics.

An intriguing question that remains is how did Al Gore end up becoming a media personality and a Nobel Prize Laureate. This was, after all, the same Gore who, as a politician, had earned a reputation for being dry and stiff. Was it the fact that he was a politician whose time was past? Did losing an improbable presidential election to George W. Bush in 2000 somehow give him new authority? It was certainly an epic moment, that cast a long shadow over whatever Gore would do next. The 2007 Nobel Prize went to a new Al Gore, however, the creator of, and lead actor in, an Academy Award-winning documentary. Yet here again, the basic facts of the script in *An Inconvenient Truth* (2006) are not what immediately captures the imagination. The film basically shows the former vice-president on a global tour with a PowerPoint presentation (*sic*!). Al Gore was presenting more or less the same message he had first presented fifteen years earlier; this is, in actual fact, the story that *An Inconvenient Truth* narrates. Its storyline shows how Gore has been campaigning for attention to climate change ever since he first became acquainted with the science. What, then, explains why his claim was suddenly more authoritative? While the content might have remained more or less stable, Gore found a new way of saying what he thought needed to be said. This new place and new way to speak created the audience for his message. Seen in this light, he reinvented his performance into one that resonated more deeply with the public.

It seems that it is not *what* Gore said that explains his new status. It has more to do with other factors, such as *how* he said it, where and when he said it, and to whom. Al Gore tinkered with the way in which to convey his message. This was what the Norwegian Nobel Committee appreciated. Even in its brief press statement the committee took time for the following observation (Norwegian Nobel Committee 2007):

> Al Gore has for a long time been one of the world's leading environmentalist politicians. He became aware at an early stage of the climatic challenges the world is facing. His strong commitment, reflected in political

activity, lectures, films and books, has strengthened the struggle against climate change. He is probably the single individual who has done most to create greater worldwide understanding of the measures that need to be adopted.

In tinkering with his message Gore was experimenting with the conditions of the age of mediatization in which *An Inconvenient Truth* was made. Eventually he found a way to resonate with key audiences. Yet how did this work? What we see is more than a set of strategic choices about message style and presentation techniques. Gore's performance blurs familiar genres. The message is not initially central; rather, the focus is on the presentation of self in historical context: 'Hello, I am Al Gore, and I used to be the next President of the United States.' Once the narrator is cast, we see how he presents a story, supported by an—admittedly, pretty slick—PowerPoint presentation that amplifies his message. He employs the genre of science and scientific expertise. Graphs, figures, and presentations of paleontological findings are crucial components of the argument he delivers. Gore presents no new facts, but something in what he says is new. He 'performs' the case for action on global warming using presentation tools that give the science of climate change a dramaturgical effect. To tell a story that can persuade a diverse audience, Gore uses different 'takes'. At one point in the film he explains his passion about climate change in terms of personal experience: he recalls a month spent in hospital fearing that he might lose his son. This gave him the strength and perseverance to act on what he saw as most important—life itself. These melodramatic references aim to create a credible claim by appealing to both head and heart, each in its own terms. The most remarkable moment is when we see Gore step, clumsily, almost pathetically, into a small construction crane to put the rise in CO_2 concentrations over the past 150 years into graphical historical perspective. Another is when he shows images of what rising sea-levels might do to the coastal regions of various continents. In arguing his case, he finds ways to amplify it.

Gore and his team had done their best to stage him as a man on a mission—a man beyond self-interest, concerned about the future and in touch with the future generations. We see him in shots taken from pop culture and celebrity life: Gore on the move, slumped in the back seat of a car, pounding away on his Apple laptop. We see him meet crowds of smiling—even cheering—mostly young faces in locations around the globe. The connection to the past remains as the film also dwells on his former status as statesman. He has been there, he has met the powerful players. This new life is a choice. A key feature of Gore's new mission is his effort

17

to use new paths to convey what he thinks needs to be said. The IPCC still spoke to conventional political institutions; Al Gore found a way to speak 'an inconvenient truth' to society at large.

Yet somehow all the efforts that went into making the film and staging Al Gore do not seem sufficient to explain these effects. Again, there was more going on. The release of *An Inconvenient Truth* (in May 2006) was quickly followed by the publication of the 'Stern review' by the British government. Could this have added legitimacy to Gore's claim? The report, commissioned in July 2005 and published in October 2006, added something significant to climate-change discourse. It employed the authoritative logic of 'cost–benefit analysis' to add a new frame for the problem of climate change.[3] It was no longer a question of melting ice-caps and polar bears on drifting floes; climate change was also a case of 'market failure'. Before the Stern Report, those who favoured policies to curb CO_2 emissions were nearly always rebutted with the claim that such steps 'would cost the economy billions of dollars' (to further blur the line by quoting a fantasy vice-president from another climate-change movie—*The Day After Tomorrow*, whose release preceded *An Inconvenient Truth* by two years). The Stern Report employed the argumentative logic of cost–benefit analysis to argue the opposite. Indeed, at the presentation of the report to the press, the then UK chancellor of the exchequer Gordon Brown described climate change in precisely these terms, as 'the world's largest market failure' (Jordan and Lorenzoni 2007: 310). And of course, all the discursive takes were interlaced with mediatized images and footage of 'evidence' or illustrations of climate change, from the melting glaciers to the lonely polar bears apparently having difficulty in coping with drifting ice, as well as with the experience of hot summers and torrential rains which were then mediatized as facts of climate change.

Different languages appeal to different publics. While Gore and Tony Blair campaigned on public stages with drama and an almost Messianic zeal, the Stern Report stood out for its non-drama. Climate change was a matter of facts and cool calculation. The report suggested seriousness, if not rigour. In its 700 pages we get a detailed account illustrating how swift action on climate change can save us billions of pounds in the long run. Of course, as Douglas Torgerson has rightly pointed out, this 'matter-of-fact', 'the-figures-speak-for-themselves' approach is itself a particular presentational style (Torgerson 2003; Ezrahi 1990). Even in non-drama argumentation and amplification are intertwined, as in the way the Stern

---

[3] It was criticized by other economists. For Stern's reply see Stern 2006.

Report was consistently referenced as authored by 'Sir' Nicholas Stern, 'an eminent economist' or 'a former chief economist of the World Bank'.

The making of an 'authoritative claim'

I draw on the example of Al Gore and the IPCC at some length as it illustrates the new ways in which authoritative claims are sometimes made in our day and age. After all, this was not an acting prime minister explaining the course of action that needs to be taken to the parliament to which he/she is accountable. Gore's success was about new discursive practices. It was about defining the problem in such a way that a particular course of action was seen as almost inevitable. Politics was made using other repertoires on different stages than we usually take into account. To make sense of it, we need to understand more generally how dramaturgical techniques and mechanisms work and how they play out in our politics today. How do argumentation and amplification interact in some settings to produce reasoned elaboration and in others to produce a dumbing down?

This book addresses one question: *how is authoritative governance possible in our day and age?* How should we conceive of governance in an era in which elected or appointed political and administrative officials have far less control over the situation than before, if only because the problems they face span governmental jurisdictions or because the actors whose cooperation is needed for effective action cannot be ordered but have to be persuaded?

The term 'authoritative' may initially cause some confusion, as authority quickly merges into the 'authorities', that is, those with the assigned power, an account that may even resonate with medieval notions of god-given power. This perspective on authority would certainly be in conflict with the current governance literature, with its emphasis on collaboration and creating a sense of a shared problem (Kooiman 1993; Kjaer 2004; Rhodes 1997). Authority in this sense would require obedience even when it conflicts with one's own judgement. Such a suppression of argumentation is of course detrimental to both reason and politics (cf. Raz 1979: 3; Warren 1996: 51). This particular tradition of thinking about authority, of which Arendt (1961) is probably the most prominent member, is less helpful for our purposes. If we want to think about the authority of governance as a collaborative endeavour we need to find a way in which authority can be combined with interaction and a shared problematization of assumptions and predispositions.

To make this shift, I draw on an alternative conceptualization of authority. It was Carl Friedrich who asked whether authority and reason are antithetical and concluded that, upon reflection, this reading confuses power and authority (1958: 29). He and others have recaptured a sense of authority, that 'rests on the ability to issue communications which are capable of reasoned elaboration' (ibid.). Friedrich starts from authority's etymological origins (*auctoritas, augere*), which stress the importance of reasoning for authority (ibid.; cf. Friedrich 1972: 47–8). *Augere*, or to augment, leads to an *auctoritas* which supplements 'a mere act of the will by adding reasons to it' (1958: 30). He cites Mommsen, who translated this to mean advice that cannot be disregarded. This may be the root of misunderstanding, as it raises the question *why* can this advice not be disregarded. Take the example of the expert and the layman. Can expert advice not be disregarded because it is the expert speaking to the layman? Is it the arguments and reasons that the expert can give that make the layman accept his claim? Or is it something in the way an expert speaks to a layman that lends authority to this communication? Or is it a combination of the above?

Friedman, also starting from Latin origins, reminds us of the influence of the 'auctor' as one of authority's etymological roots:

> The Latin 'auctor'…points to both senses of the English 'author': (1) a writer, and (2) an actor in the sense of the person responsible for an action or for starting a line of action.…From this perspective, a person with authority has been understood to be someone to whom a decision or opinion can be traced back as the source of that decision or opinion or else as someone who carries forward into the present, continues or 'augments' some founding act or line of action started in the past. However, it is equally important not to ignore the notion of an 'auctor' in the first sense of a writer, witness or someone who gives an account of something. (Friedman 1990: 74–6)

So an author is someone who begins something, gives an account of something, is a source. The question then is if this more open idea of authority can be applied to settings in which different actors have to come to 'joint authorship' as a basis for authoritative governance.

We know of the traditional way of thinking about authority. An individual can be put 'in authority' through a proper and generally accepted procedure, after which people will defer to him or her because they subscribe to these procedures. The most well-known examples of this type of authority are probably the 'rational-legal' and the 'traditional' forms of authority identified/described by Weber (1978). Yet someone can also be regarded 'an authority' because he or she has demonstrated superior powers of judgement or special knowledge (Friedman 1990: 79); this comes close to

Weber's 'charismatic authority'. In the climate-change case, for example, the IPCC was put 'in authority' by the UN but—given the political controversy surrounding climate change at the time—this institutional fact was not sufficient to be respected as 'an authority'. In bringing together all the relevant science on the theme, it strove to create an 'epistemic' authority based on involving the best people with expertise on the subject and on using of peer review as an institutionalized form of 'virtual witnessing' (Edwards and Schneider 2001: 233). But this did not, in and of itself, produce an immediate acceptance of its statements as authoritative claims. The IPCC had to establish its authority through an extended contest: until rivals could no longer successfully challenge its claims. Then the IPCC became the authority in the climate-change case. But was this process purely an argumentative one of responding to counter-claims with reasoned rebuttals?

What seems more likely is that the development of authority was also supported by the particular way in which this process was conducted. There was, as Friedman puts it, a 'performative' element to authority (Friedman 1990: 79). The IPPC might have been given the status of 'being in authority' by the UN General Assembly, but there are situations in which those who have politico-administrative functions cannot rely on the rational-legal authority they derive from the institutional position they have been given. In addition to this *de jure* authority, they have to create *de facto* authority by acting out their role in a sequence of concrete situations. This was the situation that the IPCC faced. Consider the procedural structure of IPCC, for instance. We know the IPCC assessment reports are compiled and reviewed at various stages by leading scientists from relevant disciplines, and that the exact wordings of the politically far more important 'Summaries for Policymakers' (SPMs) also have to be agreed upon by delegates from all the participating countries. Whereas some criticize this method as allowing politicians to finally decide about what constitutes 'scientific consensus', it is also clear that this very act of translating/expressing science into summary statements crucially contributed to the political importance of the assessment reports, apparently without sacrificing their content (Schrope 2001; Edwards and Schneider 2001). In other words, the claim was regarded as authoritative because of the way in which it was made, where it was made, and by whom it was made. Understanding authority, then, always demands an analysis of the relation between the maker of a claim and the public(s) that need to be persuaded. Authority is always a relational notion. And here the IPCC tinkered with its procedural logic to take into account the fact that 'simply' speaking in a scientific language might not be the best way to structure the interface between the scientific community and the political bodies that would work with the IPCC reports.

Authority here stems from a particular practice of reasoning, which developed over time. The success of the IPCC fits with Carl Friedrich's (1958, 1972) account of the process through which authority is gained. While his writings on the topic are not without ambivalence, he theorizes how authority is always related to the person who speaks and the very way in which the message gets expressed (cf. also Herbst 2003):

> [Authoritative] communication[s], whether opinions or commands, are not demonstrated through rational discourse, but they possess the *potentiality of reasoned elaboration*—they are 'worthy of acceptance.' Seen in this perspective, authority is a *quality* of communication, rather than of persons, and when we speak of the authority of a person, we are using a shorthand expression to indicate that he possesses the capacity to issue authoritative communications....The capacity of men to speak in meaningful terms, to say the things which may be thus elaborated, varies enormously. This capacity, I think, is implied when we speak of some of them as authorities. (Friedrich 1958: 35–7, italics in original)

Hence Friedrich not only explicitly links authority to communication; he also appreciates the fact that authority is bolstered by communications that allow for reasoned elaboration. The actually existing, though not necessarily employed, 'potentiality of reasoned elaboration' is what determines genuine authority. Authority, then, is not about submission, not about acquiescence, or about 'clenched fists in pockets' (Roberto Michels, quoted in Herbst 2003: 481); it is achieved through communication; it is about the development of a way of seeing things that can be, and indeed is, taken up by others and which results in the acceptance of a particular line of thinking and acting. Finally, finding a way to speak in meaningful terms is here taken to mean speaking in different languages to different publics (science, politics).

This notion of authority moves away from a foundational understanding of authority and elaborates a discursive model of authority, as Warren (1996) notes. It is a way of thinking about authority that helps us understand its dynamics outside the context of fixed institutions. Viewed in these terms, the IPCC is an example of the new 'ad hoc' policy-making practices that, when initiated, characteristically lack any pre-given authority. Whether they can really contribute to helping to address the policy problems depends heavily on their abilities to *generate* authority.

To sum up, authority is a quality of communication and is therefore contingent. It is something that can be won and lost. If we examine governance in these terms we may, first of all, distinguish certain 'repertoires' of governing that might differ in terms of their capacity to generate authority. My claim here is that, in contemporary policy-making, we experience how even familiar and strongly ritualized forms of governance can lose their communicative capacity to generate authority.

On the other hand, new ways of making authoritative claims have also emerged. Arguably it was the combination of multiple ways in which the climate-change case was communicated—the scientific overview; the attempts to come to interdisciplinary scientific understandings; the political translations of the IPCC process; the economic cost–benefit analysis of the Stern Report; the personalized and more popular expressions by Al Gore—and the discursive linkage to reported or even experienced 'real' events of a changing climate, that made the claim for action on climate change authoritative for various key publics and thus turned things around politically. In such cases it is not just the discourse that matters; we can also see the significance of the particular way in which the political acts were performed, including the selection (or indeed invention) of apt stages for these performances. This is what making a DVD or making a report is about, and it is in this combination that we may find what it takes to act authoritatively on some of the public problems that we face.

Climate change, one of today's most pressing public problems, made it to the top of the agenda because of a *combination* of efforts to give meaning to an issue potentially too big to handle. The mechanisms that are behind such claim-making are at the heart of what we need to know if we want to understand how authoritative governance is possible in our day and age, and—following Friedrich's definition of authority as the potentiality of reasoned elaboration—how particular performances contribute to either a dumbing down or, on the contrary, create the basis for a subtle deliberation on the definition of a problem, its impact on different groups, and on possible solutions.

The authority of classical-modernist government

Even though we now have begun to establish a communicative understanding of authority, it is obvious that the authority of governance as we know it has always been firmly supported by the standing political institutions. Institutions like parliament, bureaucracy, and scientific expertise lend their weight to the words of the administrative leadership. They, too, communicate meaning. Yet there is nothing 'natural' about 'our' political institutional arrangements. The institutions of policy-making and politics have their own particular history and are themselves the product of the (settlement of) conflicts of a particular period. In this book I refer to these institutions that we inherited from the twentieth century as 'classical-modernist'. My claim is that the authoritativeness of classical-modernist government is related primarily to those political conflicts that dominated the past and is far less established in other fields.

Let us first consider what made classical-modernist governance stand out. Analytically we can identify seven principles of classical-modernist governance. Together these seven principles, which emerged over the last few centuries, help to explain the authority of classical-modernist government in the late twentieth century.

First of all, in the classical-modernist conception democratic institutions are based on a territorial order. What distinguishes one polity from the other is its territorial base. The Peace of Westphalia (1648) is the undisputed starting-point of this territorial ordering of politics. It codified the relationship among states and provided the foundation for political leaders to speak with authority for the people of a given territory.

A second principle derives directly from the principle of territoriality: democratic institutions are nested: they are conceived of as a series of *matrouchkas*. Like the Russian dolls, levels of government are look-alikes that fit inside one another (i.e. local parliament fits into regional, which fits into national, which fits into the supranational). This also gave each a sphere of authority and defined the relations among these spheres. Of these, the nation-state was the crucial level for politics. The Westphalian order of nation-states defined the principle of national sovereignty and the right to self-determination together, creating an effective sphere of domestic political authority. Twentieth-century politics added the sphere of international politics, which was followed by the institutionalization of a range of supra- and transnational organizations like the European Union, ASEAN, or NAFTA. These principles of territoriality and nestedness gave the classical-modernist order much of its clarity. It allowed for the system of rules and procedures laid down in constitutions, in national laws, and in other legal documents such as international treaties. All in all, this institutionalized a system that created positions of *de jure* authority and differentiated, in strict judicial terms, which locus of authority was superior.

The third principle is that, in the classical-modernist order, political leadership gets its mandate through elections and universal suffrage. In this electoral politics there is a pre-given public that elects its leaders who will ensure that its ideas, interests, and value-preferences are represented in the councils of representative democracy.

The fourth principle of classical-modernist governance is the sharp, Weberian, distinction between politics and bureaucracy. The authority of the political leadership is facilitated by a sectorally organized bureaucratic 'intelligentsia', politically controlled by a democratically elected body (albeit sometimes elected only indirectly). These administrative units, in turn, derive legitimacy from their relationship to political leadership and from their bureaucratic professionalism. Administrators are accountable to representative democratic councils that act as an imagined 'whip' at their back: administrators know that politicians might lash out to regain control of the situation if this is required.

The fifth principle is a positivist model of 'science-for-policy'. The political administration could do its work particularly well because it was based on the assumption that science could speak 'truth to power', to use Wildavsky's famous phrase (1979). Policy experts had the ability to systematically order knowledge about means and ends, interests, and various forms of scientific expertise for political deliberation. The science-for-policy model grants authority to the expert-professional based on the conviction that scientific methods can, if operated well (i.e. by standards controlled and developed by the scientific community), bring out universal laws in social life that are culturally neutral and objective. Scientific research would thus help to create a controlled environment for policy interventions, bracketing all sorts of unwanted (political) interference and reducing uncertainty. There is, after all, 'no Republican way to build a road', as Woodrow Wilson proclaimed in 1886.

Sixthly, over time public participation gained a place in classical-modernist governance. After the 'shout in the street' of the 1960s (Berman 1983), provisions were made to give citizens the possibility to participate in policy-making. These provisions were mostly given a legal status in the 1970s. Yet they had the character of 'one-off', 'add-on', and 'single level' participation. That is to say, participation was possible in the lead-up to taking one particular decision, it was added on to the policy-making process that remained intact, and it was always focused on one, mostly lower, level of government (e.g. municipal, state).

The seventh principle is that media, from newspapers to radio, to television, fulfil the 'messenger function' of reporting to the public what happens in the political domain. Media function as 'mass media', and work with parliamentary reporters who have the assigned task of keeping the public informed about debates in parliament, new legislation, and so

on, thereby helping to create the mechanism according to which politicians can be held accountable and through which these politicians can
reach the public.

These seven principles created an institutional base for the authority of
the classical-modernist system of governing. With hindsight we can see
how the strength of the classical-modernist arrangements was boosted by
the remarkable effectiveness of these institutions in providing economic
development, social welfare, and education. What is more, these institutions bring out the characteristics of the particular political conflicts that
dominated that period (cf. Hobsbawm 1977; Joll 1978; Manin 1997), and
it is for those conflicts that they are best suited.

There is another reason for the success of classical-modernist politics.
These institutions shaped politics in a historically unique situation that
I call 'territorial synchrony' (Hajer 2003*a*). Over the late nineteenth and
twentieth centuries societal developments occurred primarily within the
territorial domain of the national polity (i.e. the nation-state). Historians
of the welfare state and of international relations have shown how the
nation-state became the primary level of political integration in the mid-
nineteenth century (Ewald 1986; Zürn 1999). Economic historians have
described how the primary level of economic integration shifted from the
local to the national in the late nineteenth century (Reich 1991). The classical-modernist political order allowed for the accommodation of many
different interests and was the basis for the tremendous political project of
creating the welfare state on the national level. This can in itself be understood as a political means to produce both economic success and 'social
peace' and some sense of cultural coherence (Williams 1961).

The apex of classical-modernist politics came in the second half of the
twentieth century when this synchrony was at its strongest. In the post-
war period the practices that reproduced the stable political order worked
in their mature form. This is the era of multi-party democracy, the welfare state, and mass consumption. Social conflicts were managed through
constitutionally defined political processes, with mild redistribution of
the surplus wealth that was created. This knife cut two ways: economic
growth allowed for the social peace and cultural adherence that enhanced
political stability, and the political institutions of the nation-state allowed
for the development of modern capitalist economies (Lane 1979). It was
a relationship of mutual gain, as nation-states provided the much-needed
protection and legal-administrative 'level playing-field' upon which business could flourish, while economic life provided the taxation base to pay
for the growing demand for welfare-state arrangements. And this ability

to manage public affairs conferred a naturalness—i.e. expressing a natural order—on the classical-modernist institutions, which, in turn, meant that the authority of these institutions was not seriously questioned.

Problems for the classical-modernist order

The above discussion suggests that the authority of classical-modernist governance is best understood against the backdrop of a historically contingent 'territorial synchrony' of political institutions, cultural adherence, and economic development. Yet this territorial synchrony is now waning and, consequently, the power of classical-modernist institutions is put to the test. In his *The Work of Nations* (1991) Robert Reich eloquently describes how the economy is slipping away from the nation-state. Manuel Castells's (1996) influential metaphors of the 'network society' and the 'space of flows' have guided a wealth of empirical work that illuminates how social and economic processes and cultural adherences now stretch across territorial spaces (cf. Hannerz 1996 and Appardurai 1996, 2006). This sense of a break from the unity of national politics, economy, and culture is also observed in the domain of political communication. Bennett and Entman (2001) describe how the singular public sphere of the late twentieth century has been fragmented by developments in the communication technology that replace 'mass media' with a pluralization of channels targeted to specific groups, with the effect that citizens no longer share 'common mediated political experiences', making it more difficult for politicians to represent the public. Moreover, in the field of political philosophy Birtek describes how national identities wither as affiliations make way for affinities, raising questions about the very assumption of a pre-given public with stable preferences (Birtek 2007).

In terms of governance, this loss of territorial synchrony constrains the effectiveness and the legitimacy of the classical-modernist institutions. They now have to operate without the implicit support of aligned socioeconomic processes and cultural adherences. The unity of political centre, public, and problems is lost, and this makes it difficult to find the potential for reasoned elaboration. The loss of authority that classical-modernist institutions experience is paradoxical, of course, as they have co-produced the opening up of socio-economic and cultural processes that have driven the decline in their authority. Individualization and globalization are products of the decades of success in modernist policy-making that produced mass education, development, and expanding markets. So first the stability of the classical-modernist order formed the precondition for the tremendous success in generating education and wealth, and then education leads to people taking their lives in their own hands (Beck's 'individualization'; cf. Beck and Beck-Gernsheim 2002). This unintended consequence was felt as citizens started to challenge classical-modernist forms of authority, whether this meant no longer deferring to expertise or questioning political leadership. Moreover, the comforts provided by sustained economic growth did not only create an appetite for ever more wealth among those fortunate enough to live in the OECD countries. It also had appeal for others who did not live under the comfortable 'cupola' of classical-modernist institutions. Mass migration is, in this sense, also an unintended by-product of modernization, and with the same effect: it contributes to the break in the territorial synchrony of political institutions, socio-economic processes, and aligning cultural adherences at the level of the nation-state.

The cartoon in Figure 1.1 illustrates the kind of problems these developments have created for the classical-modernist order. What the British cartoonist Polyp captures is how a statement that would have been authoritative in the 1960s now backfires. 'Governments', 'heads of industry', the

www.polyp.org.uk

Figure 1.1. Authoritative governance as a challenge (reprinted with permission from Polyp.)

rhetoric of officialdom ('official statement', 'no significant risk'), the attack on the (anonymous, yet presumably independent) critic ('irresponsible scaremongering'), and the downplayed risk that previously would have suggested total certainty ('not a single fatality'), no longer reassure. After Harrisburg, Bhopal, or BSE (to name just a few mediatized mishaps) the meaning of such rhetoric is reversed: it now connotes arrogance, insensitivity, and an inability to learn.

Like all successful models, the classical-modernist order gained a quasi-natural authority. Over time, the socialized expectation became that politics made through the institutional moulds lent it authority and legitimacy. Even while the nation-state remains the primary locus of legitimate political power and authority, there is a broad recognition that states often lack the power to solve pressing policy problems on their own. This may be rooted in 'simple' discrepancies between the geographical reach of political institutions and the scale of public problems. Many of our most serious public problems transgress political boundaries, and effective mitigation requires political collaboration, both among governmental agencies and with NGOs of various kinds. The governance of international financial markets, global environmental change, migration, and terrorism, to name just a few major contemporary policy issues, are tasks for politics that a single nation-state cannot meaningfully address on its own.

A triple deficit

The erosion of classical modernism is more than a matter of territorial discrepancies, however. Over the last decades of the twentieth century a triple deficit in the authority of classical-modernist institutional politics became apparent:

1. *An implementation deficit*: policy may be politically agreed upon but that does not mean it gets implemented. Nearly all policy sectors have examples where politicians decided on plans or measures that just did not fit the practical realities and which led to policy evasion or even non-implementation. Implementation cannot always be decreed; or, put differently, it helps if actors in a given policy field have a sense that the policies address the problems they are themselves concerned about, and if solutions are adapted to local circumstances.

2. *A learning deficit*: it is still popular to think about policy-making in terms of a policy 'cycle'. First you conceive of policy, then you determine policy,

and then you implement it. Characteristically we see a hard distinction of (*a*) administrative policy analysis, (*b*) political decision-making, and (*c*) administrative execution. Yet this distinction presupposes more knowledge on part of the government in the period of policy-making than is realistic. The practical realities always pose new problems. While various strategies are available for improving the knowledge 'input' in the policy-analysis stage, the true challenge seems to be how to permanently enhance the learning capacity. This requires a different organization of policy-making that would allow for much more, and much more regular, interaction with actors from the field in which the policy is supposed to generate its effect.

3. *A legitimacy deficit*: the primacy of politics presupposes that the council of elected representatives confers legitimacy on the decisions it takes. Yet when policy problems do not respect the territorial scales, this system breaks down. Elected representatives and appointed officials react by starting to negotiate solutions among themselves, but this undercuts the legitimacy of the decisions they reach. This is particularly true in situations where civil servants take on this role (as, for instance, in the extensive regulatory deliberations in the European Union).

New strategies have emerged and been tried in response to the experience of these deficits. We see similar moves towards collaboration between state agencies and societal actors in different fields of public policy. Such steps open a potential reordering of political space and pose the question how authority is brought about in such situations.

Network governance as alternative

Policy-making on issues such as climate change, migration, international crime, HIV/AIDS, or ecological sustainability is not a matter of 'survey, analysis, plan'; the varied search for effective and legitimate solutions involves interactions among researchers and practitioners searching for efficacy and salience in a non-orchestrated and dispersed process of trial and error. At times the interaction around particular public problems produces new forms of politics, in which the public is defined anew and a new authority seems to become established.

I use the concept of 'network governance' to refer to the approach to public problem-solving in which we no longer simply rely on the state to impose solutions, but instead conceive of problem-solving as a collaborative effort in which a network of actors, including both state and non-state organizations, play a part (Hajer and Wagenaar 2003; Kjaer 2004; Sörensen and Torfing 2005).[4] A crucial feature of this network-governance approach is the appreciation of interdependence: most of the time, actors do not turn to governance out of conviction but because 'old' classical-modernist strategies have failed them or new arrangements are thrust upon them.

The *Brent Spar* case will go down as one of the key examples of the often unappreciated limits of classical-modernist policy-making. In this case, a powerful multinational (Shell) had been given permission to scuttle the *Brent Spar*—an oil-storage buoy—by the British government, which held territorial authority over the waters in which the buoy would be sunk. The government's formal decision followed an extensive technical review, first by Shell experts and then by marine scientists from the Fisheries Research Service, all in a formal process to determine the 'best environmental option'. The routine classical order of this process was upended when Greenpeace intervened and adeptly shifted the stage by occupying the buoy and mounting a media campaign—including footage of the occupation—that challenged the British regulatory decision. The campaign triggered a consumer boycott and Shell's share price began to fall. In this new 'policy' context, Shell came to appreciate the wisdom of decommissioning the *Spar*, rather than sinking it (see Holzer 2001 for a full account). The case stands as an example of the sort of disruptions, frustrations, and unexpected turns that help to explain the interest in network governance as a strategy of policy-making outside the well-ordered system of the classical-modernist institutions (cf. Rhodes 1997; Pierre 2000; Dryzek 2006; cf. Heclo 1974).

What the *Brent Spar* did for Shell and the United Kingdom, deadlocks in infrastructure development (Pressman and Wildavsky 1984) and other policy domains did for other Western governments. Ignoring the public's ability to act outside of the classical-modernist institutions proved costly again and again, both in terms of time and money. In many places network governance was embraced as the alternative that could organize a

---

[4] I have started to prefer 'network governance' to the more general term 'governance'. In much of the literature 'governance' is then pitted against 'government'. This is, however, often confusing, as governance is often also used to refer to the general acts of governing. Also, it is in this latter meaning that the term was used in modern political science. Using 'network governance' instead helps to avoid this conflation of meanings.

31

search for solutions that interdependent parties could live with. The idea of a network-governance alternative emerged from repeated confrontation with the triple deficit outlined above.

The confrontation with implementation, learning, and legitimacy deficits led to an active search for alternatives. This is what continues to push the network-governance alternative. Nearly always network governance is born out of a combination of three factors: (1) a frustration with the classical-modernist organizational practices; (2) an awareness of interdependence; and (3) a willingness to explore trajectories of 'mutual gain'. In network governance, actors organize around particular problems and collectively seek to find ways to address them in a mutually agreeable way.

Network governance has liberated considerable creativity for problem-solving. International agencies now use NGOs to monitor treaty compliance; government agencies realize that they need interest groups to secure implementation; business and industry invites NGOs to the table to avoid the high costs of having to redesign products when fear or a controversy arises later on (e.g. with GMOs in food products). Environmental groups lobby industry to make 'greener' products, in the awareness that competition among firms may be more effective than focusing on state-imposed rules and regulation only. Yet can network governance be authoritative in addressing the public problems of our time? And, if so, how can authority be produced, what forms might it take, and what will such developments mean for the relationship to the formal classical-modernist institutions?

Many obstacles prevent us from gaining a full view of these challenges. For one thing, the academic discipline of political science that might help provide this perspective is itself implicated in the development of the classical-modernist institutional arrangements. Academic discourse has been intertwined with the development of a particular set of institutions, raising the risk of reification. Just as modern sociology was tied to the development of industrial society and the welfare state (cf. Lenzer 1975; Dahrendorf 1988; Beck 1992; Heilbron, Magnusson, and Wittrock 1997), and thus had difficulty disentangling itself from these institutions, modern political science and policy analysis have facilitated the stability of classical-modernist political institutions in Western nation-states during the post-war era (cf. Dryzek, Farr, and Leonard 1995; Goodin and Klingemann 1996). In this sense, academic disciplines are vulnerable to naturalizing institutions that they have helped to create, stabilize, and promote, a priori refuting the possibility that these institutions could ever be reinvented.

This highlights the risk of conceiving of these dynamics in evolutionary terms. Language that speaks of 'generations' of governance institutions, or even employs the idea of 'eras', would suggest a quasi-natural process in which classical-modernist institutions wither away as they are outperformed by alternative arrangements that are better adapted to current problems. Such language then contributes to the effect that it describes. It is far too early to suggest that the days of the classical-modernist political order are numbered. It might not 'deliver' to the extent or in the way that it did in the past, but this does not imply that it will become obsolete. Moreover, evolutionary arguments (tacit or explicit) fail on logical grounds if we insist on the contingency of policy situations and the crucial role of political performance. Anticipating this move, we can conceive of classical-modernist politics as a particular institutional *genre*, a particular and recognizable way of organizing politics. The task of analysis is to work against the naturalism with which institutions are always imbued, and show why particular configurations are authoritative in particular situations instead. This is an important task, as any form of organization is inscribed with power relations. Any institutional arrangement implies a 'mobilization of bias' that will benefit some courses of action at the costs of others, or, I think more fundamentally, some ways of conceiving the world at the costs of others. This is often referred to as the difference between 'politics' (the activities in the given order of political institutions) and 'the Political' (referring to the myriad ways in which this symbolic order is created or challenged, whether this is by invoking/refuting particular classifications or by claiming authority for the handling of a particular problem) (cf. e.g. Mouffe 2000).

Policy-making and the institutional void

It has become an established fact that much policy work nowadays takes place *next to* or *across* established orders. This shift in topography changes the conditions in which authoritative governance must be achieved considerably. Policy-making nowadays is most often a complex negotiation among actors with disparate backgrounds and divergent goals. The weakening of the state goes hand in hand with the growth of a civic politics and the emergence of new citizen-actors and new forms of mobilization through new sorts of coalitions. The spill-over of jurisdictional mismatches and this growth of a civic politics—in which state agencies take part in governance rather than drive political developments—together shift policy-making to an 'institutional void' *where there are no clear and generally accepted rules and norms according to which politics is to be conducted and policy measures are to be agreed upon.* There is no classical-modernist order to revert to; in its place comes a complex negotiation about how to understand the problem and what can be done about it, and about how to come to agreements in the first place. In the institutional void, politics is about the authoritative allocation of meaning in its broadest possible sense.

The notion of an institutional void helps us grasp the politics of the 'in between', to which participants bring their expectations of rules and norms and for which there is no given or agreed-upon standard of behaviour against which the participants can evaluate one another. The institutional void should be understood as a social-scientific concept that highlights the dependency of contemporary politics *on the enacted interaction*, on the way in which the political process is conducted 'in vivo' among its protagonists.

The claim that policy-making is now conducted in an institutional void should not be misunderstood to suggest that state institutions and international treaties are 'suddenly' meaningless.[5] It is not as if some new 'order' appears. Nor do I mean to suggest that the whole classical-modernist political machinery comes to a standstill. It continues in other domains and practices, including its representation as institutions of authority in the media (compare Rhodes 2005 on 'the Westminster smoke screen'). Yet the institutional void poses a predicament for the authority of governance. How should situations be handled when there is no clear hierarchy among participants, when no single actor can make the policy choice or even decide how a joint decision is to be reached? How should such a group deliberate when there is no shared understanding of what the problem 'really' is? What is more, how can participants agree on a political strategy if there are no constitutional rules and norms that tell them what constitutes a legitimate decision?

---

[5] I derive the term 'void' from art theory, where it was invoked to refer to a generation of postmodern artists that played with the 'modern' expectations of the audience (e.g. Jeff Koons with his work *Ushering of Banality*). Arguably a key to their success was the way these artists upset the expectations of various audiences by causing friction between what people saw and the discursive rules with which people approached the work of art. This created a new, and essentially open, basis for judging what beauty or quality was. A range of exhibitions employed the term 'void' to refer to this type of intervention. Judging from the responses to earlier papers in which I employed the term, many people interpreted 'institutional void' as institutional 'emptiness'. However, my point is that there are no rules that bind all participants. Hence it is a lack of rules that function *institutionally*.

Under conditions of institutional void, the very way in which agreements are to be reached becomes part of the political negotiation. The particular way in which this is done is what gives these negotiations the quality of reasoned elaboration described above.[6] Today's politics is, more often than not, a matter of negotiated governance: deliberations among a diverse group of people with distinct backgrounds and interests. Rod Rhodes describes politics in terms of 'differentiated polities' (Rhodes 1997), capturing the conditions in which 'there is not one point of contact' and fragmentation and specialization lead to a loss of central steering capacity and an increase in complexity, confusion, and uncertainty. As 'networks are pervasive', governments have to learn the skills of indirect management and 'the challenge is diplomacy in governance'. James Rosenau, following this line, argues that if a state wants to be effective nowadays it cannot simply assert its authority; it expresses it in relation to other distinct 'spheres of authority' (Rosenau 2007). Rosenau has in mind the important roles that well-established NGOs and 'intermediary organizations' play, the way their support has become necessary to address key policy problems effectively, and the way these organizations share the burden of organizing the legitimacy of policy measures. He seems to suggest that actors such as NGOs 'have' authority within a distinct sphere, and describes how, without a political centre, protagonists that each relate to a particular public must work together to create a basis for authority that will allow them to explain to these distinct constituencies why a particular line of action is elaborated, but he fails to theorize what authority means. John Dryzek (2006) pushes this line of thinking to argue for 'discursive political institutions' that could be seen as the conglomerate of meetings and statements of a coalition of actors that collaborate to discover solutions for situations that they each find problematic.

In a situation of institutional void, political actors will often find themselves working in new, ad hoc circles. This reinforces the importance of Friedrich's observations on how authority works. Authority might, in this view, emerge from participants' efforts to negotiate trust and credibility sufficiently to jointly author a framing of the problem and a proposed solution. Authority is then derived from the particulars of the group, the way it conducts politics, that particular way it communicates, and the particular way it stages its activities. Similarly, since moral authority

---

[6] I also use the concept of 'institutional ambiguity' to refer to situations in which there are one or more clearly defined ordering systems and it is at least unclear whether any system is accepted and which of these systems can overrule which of the others.

cannot be assumed (as this would require a coherent community to back it up, cf. MacIntyre 1981), leadership and a sense of joint purpose have to be acquired, or, as I would prefer to say, enacted, in the political interaction itself. This challenge is complicated by the fact that the joint work in the ad hoc setting does not replace the political work in the established classical-modernist institutions. Characteristically, network governance involves a continuous back and forth between improvised settings of negotiation and established settings of accountability, in which all actors must be able to show how they addressed their shared goals and their distinct ends. To appreciate the challenges this implies, we have to come to grips with one last feature of the new politico-sociological landscape—the contours of mediatized politics.

Governance and mediatized politics

The literature on governance, which claims to give the best insights into the new reality of governing, fails to systematically take into account the impact of the media. Most authors acknowledge that the mass media are important for contemporary governance, but this importance is most often mentioned only in passing (but cf. Crozier 2007, 2008; Bang 2003; Helms 2008).[7] There is surprisingly little attention paid to the impact of media on the making of public policy.[8]

Politics now takes place in what some call a 'mediated' age (Bennett and Entman 2001) and others have called a 'mediatized politics' (Meyer and Hinchman 2002) or 'mediatization' of politics (Crozier 2007). For all the difference among the authors in media studies and political communication, there is an observed trend towards the interpenetration of media and politics.[9] My claim here is that the analysis of the mediatization of politics helps to formulate the true challenge for authoritative governance.

---

[7] There is one notable exception to this: US foreign policy-making, and in particular the war against Iraq, has been analysed as a case of mediatized politics (Bennett, Lawrence, and Livingston 2006; Entman 2004; Norris, Kern, and Just 2003). Yet this has not led to the development of a theoretical framework that convincingly reconceptualizes the relationship between media and politics beyond that particular case.

[8] Of the standard works on governance, Kooiman 2003 probably gives the most detailed account of media influence; Rhodes has paid attention to the media strategy of the Blair government in various publications.

[9] The term 'the media' will be used for lack of a better term, but is in a sense misleading. It brings with it a false suggestion of unity, as if the media would form a homogeneous institution, thus hiding the fragmented, heterogeneous reality.

Politics and media have become more and more entangled, so much is clear; but there is no consensus about the implications of this development. Some authors fear that the 'colonization' of politics by the media democracy will cause citizens to see politics only as an aesthetic phenomenon. Their idea is that the theatricality, personification, and suggestive power of image distracts from is/ought questions and that market logic replaces knowledge with entertainment (Meyer and Hinchman 2002). Others, however, emphasize the enabling and potentially democratic effects: a politics of personal style could broaden the platforms for engagement and participation and limit the risk of authoritarian governance by 'lowering the political hero to the level of the common citizen' (Meyrowitz 1985; cf. Street 2004; Van Zoonen 2005). Still others state that any separate conceptualization of the political realm and the media makes no sense, as the two are too densely interwoven: communication and governmental action elide into each other (Corner and Pels 2003: 5; Crozier 2007).

For all the variation, the literature on media studies and political communication clearly reflects a break with the classical-modernist logic: it suggests a move away from a functionally differentiated order in which media would fulfil the 'function' of reporting on what happened in the political domain.

But there is a second inference from the literature, one that is more relevant here: governance is mediatized itself. In the above discussion I established that authority should always be understood in terms of the communications it involves. Logically, to understand how governance can be authoritative in our age we need to see how the communication over public problems takes place, and hence we need to establish an understanding of the mechanisms that are at play in the mediatized world of governance. Bennett and Entman observe that 'many polities have reached a point where governance, along with a host of related processes such as opinion formation, could not occur in their present forms without various uses of media' (2001: 1). In *Governing with the News: The News Media as a Political Institution*, Cook argues that news media in the United States have become part of government (2005: 86).[10] Cook states that: 'Journalists can create importance and certify authority as much as reflect it, in deciding who should speak on what subjects and under what circumstances' (p. 87). In making news, 'reporters do not only reflect authority; they reinforce if

---

[10] Conceptually it would have been more appropriate to say that the media have become part of the new system of governance.

not confer it as well' (p. 92). What is more, they have substantial influence in disqualifying leaders and administrators. It is what Susan Herbst refers to as 'media-derived' authority (Herbst 2003).

Yet it is not only that media need politics for news; those active in governance often need the media to reach their target audiences, even if these audiences are inside the organization. There are many examples of this practice, whether it is the minister who inspires his civil servants via public speeches, or chiefs of police who want to be seen to defend their officers in a televised debate. Graber speaks of 'external message paths' in this context (Graber 2003). Cook argues that news-making and policy-making become blurred as actors use both in their attempt to dominate the allocation of meaning. Referring to the work of Doris Graber, he notes that nowadays:

> The news is valuable as a way to communicate—internally to the agency as a whole and externally to constituents—what the agency is doing. Since...each form of communication has biases, costs, and benefits, officials can and do view communicating through the news as one alternative to other forms of less public communication that have their own pros and cons. Rather than see officials as thinking 'Should I make news today?' Graber views them as asking 'How best can I communicate what I need to communicate to the audiences that matter most for the success of my policy?'—the answer to which may be 'the news.'...newsmaking and policymaking are increasingly intertwined to the point of being indistinguishable. Thus, what we see as an effort to make news may be understood by an official as an effort to shape policy. (Cook 2006: 167)

Consequently, the divide between news-making and policy-making becomes blurred and news-making practices become a key form of external and internal meaning production.

Mechanisms of mediatized governance

The interpenetration and interdependence of media and governance leads to a readjustment of the theory and practice of governance. Some authors have taken this so far that they conceptually transcend the difference between media and governance. Crozier has developed a notion of 'recursive governance' based on the idea that information flows are the essence of governance, thus fundamentally breaking away from the notion of a policy process (Crozier 2007, 2008). Bang (2003) conceives of governance as a communicative relationship, beyond hierarchy and organizational order. Yet this jump—conceiving of governance as information streams—risks losing sight of the particular, context-specific mechanisms by which governance and the media influence each other when politics is actively played out by identifiable actors in concrete settings. As the media work with particular organizational formats, governmental actors may be inclined to try and link up to those formats in order to be able to reach their target audiences. Several mechanisms can be distinguished that act as a mould for political communication and thus steer policy-making processes. Not all of these mechanisms are necessarily new; I discuss them, nevertheless, as they help to understand the challenge of a mediatized politics for authoritative governance. In the first instance my focus is on more traditional media such as newspapers, radio, and television.

First of all, media operate through the mechanism of narrative and story-telling. This narrative dimension to news influences how dilemmas of governance become represented in the media. Cook quotes a famous memo from within the world of NBC News: 'Every news story should, without any sacrifice of probity or responsibility, display the attributes of fiction, of drama. It should have structure and conflict, problem and denouement, rising action and falling action, a beginning, a middle, and an end. These are not only the essentials of drama; they are the essentials of narrative' (Cook 2005: 99). Once this mechanism is recognized by policy-makers it starts to affect their behaviour. Now there is nothing wrong or threatening as such in appreciating the narrative character of understanding for policy-making (White 1999). But in a media landscape dominated by competition this easily leads to sensationalism. Graber notes that:

> To get and retain coverage, agencies have to adapt their information strategies to satisfy the media's need for exciting stories. The consequences can be unfortunate. If important stories that the agencies wish to publicize lack drama, agency personnel may withhold them, depriving the public of essential knowledge. Alternatively, officials may feel forced to dramatize stories excessively or to emphasize the wrong facets of the story. Officials may even create dramatic events solely for publicity purposes. (Graber 2003: 247)

Secondly, and closely related, there is the predilection to frame policy realities in terms of conflict. Conflict fulfils a central role in the media's representation of political realities. Conflict is built into the system of news-making, argues Cook: 'Above all, for any news medium, whatever the source does must be packaged into a narrative. Not only must the story have protagonists and antagonists in conflict, but the sources' actions must move the story along to a new episode. In the absence of such movement, journalists tend to conclude that "nothing happened" and there is therefore no news' (Cook 2005: 89). This predilection with conflict then runs counter to the predominantly analytical and conceptual way of thinking in circles of public policy-makers.

Thirdly, media, and television in particular, love drama. To the extent that matters can be portrayed in dramatic terms, there is a higher likelihood that media will be willing to report on policy-making. It is not policy deliberation that is interesting; it must be an event, a clash, a walk-out. In a type of analysis that political scientists know from the literature on agenda setting (Cobb and Elder 1972), Hilgartner and Bosk (1988, as quoted in Johnson-Cartee 2005: 68) argue:

> Public arenas place a premium on drama. Social problems presented in a dramatic way have a higher probability of successfully competing in the arenas: a) saturation of the arenas with redundant claims and symbols can dedramatize a problem; b) repeated bombardment of the public with messages about similar problems can dedramatize problems of that class; and c) to remain high on the public agenda, a problem must remain dramatic; thus, new symbols or events must continually renew the drama or the problem will decline.

Narrative, conflict, and drama determine whether public policy facts have 'news value'. No representation without dramatization.

The media are a crucial part of the new topology of politics. Media practices undoubtedly come with a strong bias, yet it does not automatically follow that the mediatization of politics leads to a disempowerment of politics. Mechanisms such as the ones mentioned above are both constraining and enabling for governance. What is clear, however, is that the intensified interaction between politics and media implies a new ordering, with new modes of preferred behaviour, new power relations. It is not immediately clear if this will always work to the detriment of an authoritative governance. It is clear, though, that policy-makers will be less successful if they do not relate to these specific features of a mediatized politics.

What is more, this new interaction between politics and media seems not to sit well with the notion of a deliberative policy process which, after all, is characteristically searching, taking twists and turns (Forester 1999). Deliberative modes of governance, to the outsider, often appear messy and unstructured. This is the logical consequence of taking turns and organizing policy processes in such a way as to allow a variety of actors to act on and respond to newly gained insights (cf. Hajer and Wagenaar 2003; Hajer, Sijmons, and Feddes 2006). It appears to resist powerful mediatic representation which requires people to 'stay on message'. At the same time work in media studies and political communication suggests that the growing interdependency of media and politics offers a powerful incentive to take the mechanisms of a mediatized politics into account, something which we can now also trace in the daily practice of governance (cf. Uitermark and Duyvendak 2008).

Moreover, new communication technologies increasingly define the political experience and literally mediate the way in which public policy is regarded by citizens. Bennett and Entman argue that media images hold more significance for the authoritative allocation of values than underlying facts (Bennett and Entman 2001; but cf. Domke, Perlmutter, and Spratt 2002). This is well understood, and there is an understandable worry about a shift in public policy-making from content to communication. There are many cases where spin and impression-management have played a significant role in the debates on public policy choices, the case for the war against Iraq being the most obvious and most troubling example. Yet we should analyse what explains the vulnerability of the system for such practices rather than take it for granted that mediatized politics necessarily come with such perverse effects. This might then also open an appreciation of the potential virtues of a mediatized politics, as in the case of Al Gore's campaign on climate change. It is much more interesting to figure out how particular effects are brought about, and also search for examples where the same mediatized political environment is put to good use, that is, has helped to find solutions for pressing public problems in a democratically legitimate way.

Fortunately there are several authors who do suggest how a mediatized politics can be acted upon. For one thing, the suggestion that politicians and government officials are powerless in the mediatized environment is a false one. Schudson (2002: 251) describes news-gathering as 'an inter-institutional collaboration between political reporters and the public figures they cover'. Organizational studies consistently argue that 'official sources dominate the news' due to the centrality of reporter–source relations (ibid. 258). Whereas the media logic has a structuring influence on today's policy-making (Castells 1997; Cook 1998/2005; Sparrow 1999), the relationship between reporters and government officials could be characterized as a situation of interdependence.

Now, a crucial move is to refrain from thinking about a mediatized politics with a passive, recipient 'audience' in mind. The role of the various audiences in reading the media is more active than the term 'audience' would suggest. According to Newton (2006), media effects are mediated and diluted by variables like social networks, personal knowledge, values related to class, education, relations, and religion, and distrust of the mass media to such an extent that an overly pessimistic assessment is unfounded. Audiences have developed new forms of visual and emotional literacy, allowing them to 'read' political characters and 'taste' their style, to judge their claims of competence and authenticity (cf. also Van Zoonen 2005). Likewise, Corner and Pels (2003) suggest that a dumbing down is not the inevitable outcome of the career of the image and the narrative, arguing that under 'new conditions of mediated visibility and "thin" solidarity, a politics of personal style may generate democratic effects, by expanding the platforms for engagement and citizenship' (2003: 10). They proclaim a new centrality for the political actor as someone 'whose performance is continuously judged in terms of authenticity, honesty and character' (ibid.). Authoritative governance depends on the quality of communication which encompasses more than reason-giving alone.

If Wolfsfeld (2001) argues that news media are almost forced to show politics in the format of a sequence of 'exciting episodes', he suggests that this requires a change in the habitus of political elites that comes with its own costs and benefits: 'Political leaders are forced to adapt to this constructed reality, and this in turn has a significant impact on the political process itself. The need for a quick, well-packaged response becomes a central priority. Other, often equally important issues are ignored' (2001: 248). Yet the potential positive effect is that citizens become engaged in the political process (cf. Street 2004); the negative is that a wave characteristically focuses on a narrow bit of the issue at stake. Elaborating on the scholarship mentioned above, we can examine cases where authoritative governance was to be achieved in mediatized conditions.

Governance and the politics of multiplicities

This chapter sketches the political sociological context for contemporary governance. My principal argument here is that authority is so difficult to achieve because administrative and political elites have trouble developing communication that allows for a reasoned elaboration. Authority of the parliament and the sovereignty of the state were always based on the 'power to define' and to make its 'definitions stick', as Bauman has argued (Bauman 1991; cf. Hajer and Laws 2006). Arguably this still is the case. Yet in today's political landscape definitions are far more difficult to control. The sites where the fight over meanings take place have proliferated, and the degree of control of authorities over political meaning has shrunk significantly.

So far I have described the move from a functionally differentiated organization based on division of tasks and with a clearly demarcated system of communication, towards a situation of institutional void, in which more and more comes to depend on the concrete enactment of politics and in which politics is mediatized. Here any medium not so much represents politics as re-presents it: trying to be authoritative now has to be accomplished in settings that have their own formats and rules. All these formats and rules are part of The Political—have political effects.

Hence the thesis here is not that politics is now conducted in the sites of the media; the argument is that politics is mediatized, by which we mean that any medium used has a political effect. There is one complication of this new mediatized politics that I have not addressed so far. What becomes more and more apparent is that the relationship between (1) political decision, (2) public problem, and (3) political public is unstable. My take on this is to speak of a politics of multiplicities. Let me explain. Politics and media struggle with the lack of a unified political centre. First, there are multiple *sites* at which politics is to be conducted; obviously not all sites are equally important, and some are more meaningful than others, but there is no easy way to spell this out beforehand. Politics is conducted at a multiplicity of interconnected sites, each with its own characteristics, the interrelationships of which need to be spelled out. If it appears that there is a political centre, this is because it is successfully staged as such. We will come back to this aspect later on.

Secondly, today's politics is hampered by a multiplicity of *publics*. There is not one coherent public, let alone one—presumably passive—audience. The recent reappraisal of the work of John Dewey speaks precisely to this point. How people engage in politics depends on the forms and designs of political practices through which a public gets its expression. Or, as Alan Irwin recently argued in an important article on recent practices of public participation, 'there is no direct or context-free access to "the public"' (Irwin 2006: 36). The public is not 'out there' waiting to be heard, it is constantly formed by the way in which it is allowed into, or forces itself into, the political process (cf. Gomart and Hajer 2003). This is true both for those cases in which a group manifests itself concretely and for those in which the public is generated indirectly, as for instance via the usage of opinion-poll data or via the statements of self-proclaimed leaders who argue that they speak for a group. Politics in the age of multiplicities is, in this sense, often very different from the politics of the twentieth century. Apart from the predominant parliamentarian politics, twentieth-century politics was always based on either representation of groups through leaders of formal organizations (with memberships, membership contributions, statutes, etc.) or through social movements (which had an alternative but very visible mode of expression, e.g. through mass demonstrations, campaigns, or manifestations). The politics of multiples, however, is based on affinities, on stories and images that have a strong mobilizing effect. What is more, political activism might begin in government policies that people do not agree with, and that make activists out of seemingly apolitical citizens. The publics that then manifest themselves are not constitutive of governmental activity, as is assumed by the classical-modernist order and its related notion of legitimacy: they are the product of it (Hajer 2003*b*). These new political actors do not show up in surveys or membership counts. Today's polity is one of 'citizens on standby' (ibid.): people with many political skills but who are not necessarily interested in employing them. Showing up in surveys as 'not interested in politics', they can transform overnight into active and capable publics if something occurs that they feel is unjust. Schudson (1998) speaks of 'monitorial citizens' in this regard:

> Picture parents watching small children at the community pool. They are not gathering information; they are keeping an eye on the scene. They look inactive, but they are poised for action if action is required. The monitorial citizen is not an absentee citizen but watchful, even while he or she is doing something else. Citizenship during a particular political season may be for many people much less intense than in the era of parties, but citizenship now is a year-round and day-long activity, as it was only rarely in the past. (Schudson 1998: 311)

Citizens appear as a rapid-deployment force that can mobilize and make itself felt when need be. Yet they don't show up on the political radar of surveys and opinion polls, as their activism is not based on deeply felt beliefs but on concrete negative experience. They may also miss the possibilities for the 'one-off, add-on, single-level' form of participation. It is less predictable when they will 'switch on'.

This focus on multiple and highly dynamic publics moves away from a notion of politicians acting on a stage in front of an audience of voters. The very idea of active politics for a presumably passive audience of spectators is out of sync with our politics of multiplicities. Bernard Manin concludes that 'the electorate appear, above all, as an *audience* which responds to the terms that have been presented on the political stage' (Manin 1997: 223). This is not because the public is necessarily or essentially passive—as the term 'audience' in Manin's book deliberately expresses—but because of the particular practices through which polit-ics shapes up. Of course, Manin's book is devoted to the principles of representative government and perhaps the employment of this meta-phor is somewhat more legit-imate within that confined constitutional space. Yet if we broaden our scope and think about politics in terms of governance, we most certainly have to refrain from this idea of an active political centre in front of a passive mass of spectators. The reality of gov-ernance is one in which societal actors, often in unexpected and original ways, find their route into the policy-making process, and at least claim to represent a public so as to lend more legitimacy and political weight to what they bring in. Characteristically, we see media performances of actors claiming to speak for a public (the self-proclaimed leader) or actors claiming to know what the 'real' public thinks (the pollster). It then often comes as a surprise if subsequently a citizen group springs up to argue a case that was not represented through the forms that were monitored by the political leadership. Hence the notion of a politics of multiplicities and its notion of multiple publics refers to the characteristic instability of publics and the way in which political publics are products of the prac-tices and storylines that create them in the first place.

Thirdly, multiplicity relates to the mediatized political environment characterized by news 24/7 and where media include many new web-based variations. Media were always part of politics, as there was always a need for intermediate technologies, however primitive, to transmit news from the people to the political centres and vice versa. Yet the new mediatized environment is one in which news is a competitive commodity and where the array of publics gets its reports from their own preferred stations, chan-nels, news-sites, or weblogs. This again suggests a multiplicity, this time of *media*, which makes it far harder to fulfil the task of creating a bond between those governing and those governed. It also brings about a reacti-vation of the citizen, as they now themselves create messages, whether it is via contributions to *YouTube* or by sharing photographs or videos that regis-tered improvised performances of politicians or recorded dubious actions on part of state officials. The media is no longer confined to the group wearing badges indicating that they are registered journalists; in the politics of multiplicities nearly everybody is empowered to register and contribute.

Above I presented three components of a politics of multiples. Yet the politics of multiplicities refers to the combined effect of these multiples, the multiplication of those multiples. The condition of the politics of multiplicities is that everything that is said to one audience, in one particular context, and in reply to one particular concern, is potentially relayed to other audiences that understand the message with a different frame of mind or where the message gets repackaged to suit another purpose. *What seems to be crucially new nowadays is that political actors must constantly reckon with the fact that what they say at one stage, to one particular public, will often almost instantaneously reach another public that might 'read' what has been said in a radically different way and mobilize because of what it heard.* This is the true break with the previous idea of political communication. Communication is no longer about the construction and distribution of a message; it now is about messages that are constantly changing meaning as instant receivers repackage them and reconnect them (cf. also Crozier 2007: 6).

Ever since Aristotle, political observers have been aware that, in order to be effective, politicians need to understand, capture, and learn to express themselves in a mode of expression that resonates with those upon whose support their power depends. In this chapter I have established that authoritative governance works on a similar basis: it requires the capacity to issue communications that allow for a reasoned elaboration, and this, in turn, requires actors to be able to express themselves in a language that resonates with key publics.

Libraries have been filled with (auto)biographies and analytical studies on how political leaders have taken up this task. Political leaders had to be able to speak different languages and know which language to speak and when. Yet in an era of the politics of multiplicities these skills are no longer enough. Technological developments in the media, from the multiplication of attention for political leaders to the dissemination of pocket-size technologies that register what politicians do wherever they are and allow for instant sharing of that registration, create the preconditions for a politics of multiplicities. Add to that the new topology of politics in which politicians no longer have a stable cultural bond with the publics involved, and we realize the substantive tasks facing those trying to solve public problems in a democratically responsible way.

The politics of multiplicities suggests that authoritative governance is to be organized in a world of hyper-realities in which politicians will often have to respond to incidents and images and to the meanings that other politicians or opinion leaders read into particular incidents, stories, and images. Politics then risks becoming nothing more than a matter of damage control, marked by exclamations like: 'That is not what I meant!' or 'You quote me out of context!' These are the expressions characteristic of the fatigue and frustration of political leaders caught up in the politics of multiplicities. It is not as if this stands in the way of managing to address the 'real' problems that supposedly lie 'behind' this room in which mirrors reflect various fragments of a problem. Fiske (1996: 2) observed that with 'media events' it is no longer meaningful to differentiate between the 'real' event and its mediated representation. This firing of claims and interpretation at a range of stages, uncontrolled, with all sorts of distortions, reflections, and refractions, and twists and turns in the meaning of what is said, is, whether we like it or not, part-and-parcel of contemporary policy-making and governance. It is the multiplicity of sites of production of meaning, the constant diversion, the rerouted messages, and the refracting that accompanies this process that create a structural instability in the political space.

To gain a better sense of why authoritative governance is so difficult to achieve nowadays, which 'repertoires' work, and why, we have to conduct empirical research. We must take these logics of multiplicity into account and try to see how they affect the process of policy-making and governance if we want to understand what it requires to be authoritative in early twenty-first century politics.

2

A Framework for Analysis

We live in a world which has developed elaborate institutions that turn political conflicts into issues of public policy. This is a major achievement. It is all so common and accepted that we no longer ask a fundamental question: how is it possible to take authoritative decisions on public policy? Why would people, educated to be free and independent, accept decisions taken that may restrict them in substantial ways? There are lots of answers, of course, but most of them are very rationalist or abstract: enlightened self-interest, the power of the sword, the anticipated reaction, routine. Such accounts seem to miss an important dimension. In *Negara: The Theatre State in Nineteenth-Century Bali*, the anthropologist Clifford Geertz presents his celebrated account of the political order at Bali (Geertz 1981). In his study Geertz reminds us that 'state'—the 'master noun' of political discourse—comprises at least three etymological themes: 'statecraft', 'estate', and 'stateliness'. Why is it, Geertz wonders, that modern studies of the state always tend to focus on the first theme, that of statecraft or governance (1981: 121)? Geertz concurs that the two other, more symbolic, dimensions of 'estate' (in the sense of ranking, status) and 'stateliness' (as dignity, presence) are at least as significant for understanding authority and power. Why do we not examine the effect of these more symbolic dimensions of governance?

It is an intriguing question. The obvious answer is that we tend to overlook the symbolic because the symbols are so familiar to us. We take them for granted. And, of course, because our mechanisms of differentiation and ordering are less lavish and conspicuous than their highly ritualized counterparts at Bali. Not to address the symbolic in the case of Balinese rule would probably strike all of us as absurd. Even today Bali overwhelms with the beauty and skilfulness of its ritual performances, the persistence of its daily ceremonies; it appears as part of a cosmic order that somehow survived the imprint of modernity. Here the symbolic ordering is all-pervasive and the social power of the symbolic can be felt, and the functioning of the state cannot be regarded merely in terms of statecraft. If we look carefully, governance in our age turns out to be full of ceremonies and rituals too. Yet they are easy to overlook and, what is more, we do not regard them as crucial aspects of our theories of governance. As Gusfield and Michalowicz (1984: 418) point out: 'Modern life is viewed as being dominated by a secular, matter-of-fact, rational culture and social organization in which human responses are governed by attention to means and ends.' All preoccupations with efficacy and efficiency, means and ends, costs and benefits, try to blend out the role of symbols, rituals, and drama as functional elements of a way of governing. Modern organizational Weberian logic prides itself on the strength of impersonal, rational proceduralism. Yet a trained eye sees how our politics is full of symbolism too, with subtle mechanisms of inclusion and exclusion, micro-enactments of power and symbolic markers of decision-making and legitimacy. Being all-too-familiar, it easily escapes the eye.

Our political analysis tends to focus on strategy not ritual, interests not performance. When we do discuss the symbolic order of politics and the aspects of politics as performance this is often seen as either trivial or, alternatively, as deceit, as the intentional and strategic effort to control an interaction, and hence as something that we have to look 'beyond'. To be sure, such an analytical approach would recognize that politics is staged, but it would argue that the 'real' politics takes place *behind* the performance. We have developed detailed analytical techniques to study that 'which does not meet the eye'; predictions of behaviour, strategic choice, real interests, and hidden power structures. We are also very sophisticated at analysing in detail the logic and rationality of arguments made in politics as well as in the instruments politics has on offer to influence the societal state of affairs. Yet Geertz was right in pointing out that all this focus on statecraft comes with the risk that we fail to see how the symbolic and the performative are unavoidable dimensions of the dynamics of politics even if you operate in rational proceduralism.

There is, of course, a political-science scholarship that has appreciated the symbolic dimensions as a 'real' political factor in itself (Arnold 1935; Goffman 1959; Edelman 1964, 1988; Burke 1969; Merelman 1969; Goodsell 1977; Goodin 1978; Gusfield 1981; Kertzer 1988; Yanow 1996). Moreover, March and Olsen explicitly criticized the treatment of the 'symbolic' as window-dressing in their influential work on the new institutionalism of the 1980s (1984, 1989). Yet despite the obvious quality of this work, it has not secured a stable place in the analysis of politics and policy-making. My claim here is that an appreciation of the symbolic and the performative in politics is crucial to an understanding of how an authoritative governance is at all possible in an age of multiplicities. These factors determine how politics 'meets the eye', thus influencing what people expect from a government and what they accept as authoritative from those who (try to) govern.

The story of the parliaments of the French Revolution

In Chapter 1 I suggested that there is nothing 'natural' about our political institutional arrangements. Nevertheless, the spaces of parliament are the undisputed central site of politics in modern democracies. Parliament occupies a prominent role in the public imagination as the symbolic site where public decisions are made. Parliaments deliberate in public, decide in public, and can subsequently be held accountable by the public. The coming of the mediatized politics has not changed this. We watch the important debates, we listen to the daily reports. While parliament is the unrivalled symbolic centre of politics, we know that all sorts of decisions are taken elsewhere (Pressman and Wildavsky 1984; Mazmanian and Sabatier 1989; Beck 1986). All sorts of sociological or political-economic studies have shown how relative the power of parliaments is, but they remain the cornerstone of the mediatized representation of politics. It is an indication of their continued symbolic: the physical space of parliament is the apex of public deliberation, the culmination point of public decision-making.

This symbolic power of parliament is undisputed, yet there is nothing natural about it. Parliament is the product of endless tinkering, of hard, discursive work. Its symbolic power was acquired over time. What is more, its institutional authority is conditional. If parliamentary politics is enacted well, it will be widely recognized to be the legitimate setting of binding decisions. The whole context—its architecture, its structured procedures, its rules of deliberation—then lends its weight to the legitimacy of what gets decided in the parliamentary setting. Yet the persuasive power of the parliament is fundamentally contingent and conditional. There is something which we may call a dramaturgy of political power that is crucial to its authority. We elect actors in a complicated, very precisely laid-out procedure, and we follow clear rules as to how decisions are to be taken. There are operational procedures that assign roles and places to various actors, there is a '*mise-en-scène*', and there are routines that make sure that the public can see the performance of political decision-making. We teach our children about these rules in schools, we watch them in action on television. The legitimacy of the decisions taken in parliament partly derives from this established dramaturgy. But that dramaturgy is not fixed. If actors perform a parliamentary setting in the wrong way, its power may shrink.

Parliamentary proceedings appear so natural to us that one might easily forget that they are themselves the product of endless thinking and rethinking of how political decisions are best taken. What now appears a natural procedure is in fact a dramaturgy of political decision-making that was established after many rehearsals and try-outs. This is beautifully narrated by the political theorist Jean-Philippe Heurtin in his study on the parliaments of the French Revolution. Heurtin shows how the French revolutionaries constantly changed the shape and organization of the parliament, in an attempt to make the spatial organization fit the spirit of the Republic. He reconstructs no less than seventeen different models of the ideal parliament between 1789 and 1795 alone (Heurtin 2005: 760). In their search for the optimal *mise-en-scène* the revolutionary elite constantly tinkered with the design of the parliament. For instance, Antoine C. Quatremère de Quincy was worried in 1789 about the acoustics, as: 'The man obliged to raise his voice is in a forced state, and thereby prone to violence; and this situation can be felt by those listening to him...In a chamber of this kind the speech soon becomes an exclusive privilege of men whom nature has endowed with a powerful voice' (quoted in ibid. 758). As the parliament had moved to a new space in the Tuileries in May 1793, Danton qualified the room as 'real mute' exclaiming: 'It would be appropriate that the legislators of the French Republic deliberated in a room where the reason could be heard by human organs' (quoted in ibid. 757). The search was for a space that would allow everyone into the conversation and contribute to the public deliberation.

What Heurtin brings out is that this tinkering with the form of the parliament was not 'merely' a matter of changing the material 'outside' of politics. Quite the opposite, it involved changes in the cognitive make-up of democratic politics of the revolution itself. Changing the shape of the parliament, changing the place of the rostrum, reorganizing the place of the public—here the very conceptualization of what it meant to be a council of representatives, what it meant to control the power of the executive, how accountability to the public was 'shaped' and moulded, were all at stake. The French revolutionaries are shown to have been very perceptive about the effect of the spatial layout of the parliament on the sense of working in the public interest. This led to a critique of the rect-angular shape of the parliament space at one time, as it prevented all members of parliament from seeing each other and seeing the president. Jean-Antoine-Nicolas de Condorcet was most explicit as he called for a chamber that would enable 'members to exercise mutual censorship, useful to the maintenance of order and silence' (ibid. 758).

Parliaments, argues Heurtin, should be seen as 'moral architectures'. In the revolutionary spirit the circle was preferred to the rectangular form as the circle expressed values such as equality, accord, unity, and indivisibil-ity (ibid. 760). It helped to solve the acoustical problem and had the extra advantage that it would help solve the problem of order and silence, as all members could use 'that useful censure of looks' to discipline others. But in this design there was no rostrum, as it was envisaged that members would speak from their place. This fact, along with the circular shape, would be prone to lead to antagonistic forms of behaviour as the respect-ive members would literally face each other. An alternative was found in the semicircle, which had as an extra virtue that it would allow for a 'grand and noble' staging of both the president and the speaker who could stand behind a rostrum. In the end the semicircle was completed in January 1798, and basically remains the shape of the French Chamber of Deputies today.

The struggle of the French revolutionary government speaks to a cru-cial issue in our politics today. The French Revolution was a moment at which there was nothing natural about the idea that parliament was the site where the public interest would get its expression. It still had to be invented and its legitimacy still had to be conquered. They were tinkering with the very way in which this public interest should be found. Heurtin points out that this was not 'merely' a matter of representation or adding up various individual insights and opinions. The parliamentary moment was one in which something new was created *through* and thanks to the carefully staged exchange. In that sense the parliament was the moment of the 're-public': the public got its new, collective expression. Or, as Heurtin puts it: 'It is through speech that the empirical people become The People as the source of sovereignty' (ibid. 768). Heurtin analyses the search for the best revolutionary parliament in terms of a search for a 'grammar' that would help create a sense of collectivity, that could support the sense that the parliament was working to define the public interest and would be seen to do so in a responsible spirit.

Heurtin's study here serves as a reminder that the classical-modern way of staging political decisions has itself very particular historical roots.

Those of us lucky enough to live in modern Western societies do not know better, having grown up with the stability of a well-codified and well-rehearsed enactment of political decisions. Heurtin in fact describes the early days of what was to become the climax in the dramaturgy of classical-modernist politics. The parliament was and is the apex of nation-state politics, and the rites and rituals that belong to it together constitute the dramaturgy of contemporary politics. Over the course of the twentieth century it was even employed as model to give shape to new international organizations such as the United Nations and the European Union. Parliament is the symbolic centre of democratic politics, at which we carefully stage 'the decisive act', the moment at which the collective will achieves its expression in order for those belonging to the 're-public' to be able to see, experience, and accept the decisions taken. Parliamentary practice is well institutionalized and well rehearsed. It is a crucial technology of politics which in part draws its power from the way in which it stages this moment of collective decision-making.

The question now is whether this particular staging of politics can still hold on to its symbolic power. After all, in the light of the analysis of institutional void and a politics of multiplicities presented in Chapter 1 we expect a discrepancy of the existing political order and the problems that emerge on the public agenda, as well as a dispersal of politics which would be to the detriment of the idea of unity of political time and space. Writing about the emergence of social dramas, Jeffrey Alexander states that: 'When society becomes more complex, culture more critical and authority less ascriptive, social spaces open up that organizations must negotiate if they are to succeed in getting their way. Rather than responding to authoritative commands and prescriptions, social processes become more contingent, more subject to conflict and argumentation' (Alexander 2004*a*: 544).

In the twenty-first century we see shifts in the dramaturgy of power, with new forms of expression, new frames, and new coalitions but also a multiplication of the settings via which politics is conducted. This multiplicity does not 'suddenly' render the classical-modernist order irrelevant, but the primacy of the national Houses of Parliament is no longer automatic. Parliaments find themselves in competition with other sites at which politics is conducted, and the particular way in which parliamentary political power is enacted starts to count again. Just as the French revolutionaries needed to find the right way of expressing the difference from the '*ancien régime*', so our politicians need to find new ways to express their politics so that it matters. McLeod (1999) pointed out that the traditional view is that ritual, drama, and symbols have less of a role as societies grow more complex, yet here, with McLeod, I take the opposite view, suggesting that 'the more complex and larger the units of society become, and the more diverse the population, the more important rituals...become in the political process' (McLeod 1999: 363).

Analysing governance as performance

A performance perspective on governance holds that policy-makers and politicians are seen as constantly and actively trying to create order and structure in potentially unstable situations (cf. Hajer and Laws 2006). This might be regarded as attempts *to perform a policy situation*: policy-makers and politicians use all the tools that are available to them, from the power of narrative to the employment of the very context in which they speak. Obviously their power to structure and 'manage' the situation is limited and dependent on the behaviour of others and the conditions under which all these interactions take place. Starting from the presumption that political realities are intersubjectively negotiated, it is better to avoid speaking of 'government' as a static, dead entity, but rather to look for situations where governance is *de facto* 'performed' or 'enacted' in the activity of governing (cf. Butler 1999). Empirically we can then examine how governing takes place vis-à-vis a particular problem or situation. Understanding governance thus comes from studying the contextualized interaction of actors as a series of 'performances', drawing on the combined analytical vocabularies of discourse analysis and dramaturgy.

To 'enact' is to give meaning to a situation, but not simply by giving an opinion, or stating what one thinks is the case. When people act, Karl Weick argues, 'they bring events and structures into existence and set them in motion' (1988: 306). In this sense, structures of power depend on their enactment for their effect. To employ terms like 'enactment' or 'performing' means to constantly try to relate categories to situations and situations to categories. While a discourse analysis would primarily identify how certain terms (concepts, classifications) dominate a political debate over a period of time, attention for performance or enactment implies a more precise focus on how people use particular terms in particular situations. It is an approach to politics in which we take into consideration what actors say and what actors do. This empirical focus on how actors perform a situation is the logical consequence of an anti-essentialist stand: what actors do in a particular situation matters, and political realities might be different because of it. We can analyse what language they employ (deliberately or inadvertently), and what acts or situations ('scenes') we can discern through which political realities come to be. We can look at the very way in which people seek to construct the situation as 'routine' or what others do to suggest precisely the opposite. Political identities, the meaning of a particular event, or a conflict between two antagonistic parties, are not represented in discourse but are 'performed, enacted and embodied through a variety of linguistic and non-linguistic means' (De Fina, Schiffrin, and Bamberg 2006: 3).

A performance perspective implies that we analyse how political figures are called upon to give meaning, sometimes quite literally, as in situations of crisis when political leaders face a battery of microphones and the question: 'What is the meaning of this?'[1] Yet policy situations can also be performed in a far more continuous way, by constantly employing a particular vocabulary and writing particular expectations, role assumptions, and possibilities into a situation (cf. Butler 1999).

One important form of interaction, then, is when an actor can make others see the world according to a preferred frame and thus generate the legitimacy for a preferred course of action. To achieve this all sorts of dramaturgical tools can be mobilized, and in this sense the analysis has a keen eye for the strategic action by individual actors and the dynamics that unravels in the course of their interaction. Yet it is not as if politics has in my perception suddenly become a fully free and open affair in which actors can change situations as they see fit. It remains true that people make history, but not under conditions of their own choosing: we can observe regularities or patterns in the way in which governing takes place, for which we would employ terms like 'institutionalization' or 'practice'. In other words, there are many elements that lend stability to a political situation and thus contextualize the strategic behaviour of actors, sometimes facilitating what they want, sometimes standing in the way of a course of action or a line of reasoning.

This attempt to connect the influence of what political actors do to the situational logic was conceptually systematically elaborated by Kenneth Burke (1945/1969) in his so called 'Pentad' (cf. Czarniawska 2004 for an accessible introduction) differentiating between scene, actor, agency, act, and purpose. Burke introduced the concept of 'scene–act ratio' connecting scene to act. He argued that a scene could be 'a fit "container" for the act, expressing in fixed properties the same quality that the action expresses

---

[1] Sometimes literally so, as we will see in Chapter 3.

in terms of development' (1969: 3). From a poststructuralist perspective, Burke's work on the dramaturgy of politics has always been regarded with some suspicion as it overemphasizes the stability of the relationship between act and scene. Burke conceives of the relationship between form and act as more or less constant; the scene–act ratio is seen as an institutionalized relationship. In arguing that scenes have to be regarded as 'fit containers' for certain acts, Burke meant that the quality of acts could not be understood without understanding the setting within which the acting took place.

The performance perspective is more dynamic. I regard the performance perspective presented here as an elaboration of my earlier work on discourse analysis of politics. To be sure, that was written in the same vein: it had a focus on discursive practices in which language is uttered, not on the linguistic representations *per se*. But now we add much more precise ways to analyse the context in which discourse production takes place, and under what conditions it becomes effective. While it is common to see 'discourse' and 'practice' as inseparable twins, I actually want to open up the concept of practice. All too often the concept of practice is implicitly used as an *explanans* while in actual fact the working of practices is in itself to be explained. By approaching the context in which people make their utterances in terms of performance and dramaturgy, we may be able to take a further step in our interpretive understanding of political processes and governance. The performance perspective does not assume the impact of context, whether it is a macroeconomic situation or the particular position from which a person argues, but searches for traces of that context in the interaction. Here discourse is not seen as being determined by settings, nor is it considered meaningful to try to establish the scene–act ratio of practices of governance in general. What we can do, however, is analyse the way in which scenes and acts interrelate to produce particular political realities. Similarly, we can bring out how the context of political action is 'mobilized' in a particular situation. Every act takes place in a particular 'contexture' (Lynch 1991) that influences the quality of that act. By situating an exchange in a particular 'setting' we can influence both the meaning and the influence of what is said.

The performative dimension of language

Performance, of course, is not a new notion for social-science research. Arguably the classical Greek study of rhetoric was based on the appreciation of how orators could 'perform' politics through the way in which they made certain statements. Yet if we move closer and examine the scholarship of the twentieth century, one notices how the celebrated studies are marked by the presuppositions of the classical-modernist way of thinking. That is true for Burke with his strong emphasis on the stability of the 'scene' in which people acted. But it is also evident in what is probably the most celebrated text on performance and language: J. L. Austin's *How To Do Things With Words* (1962). Austin first pointed out the performative dimension of language: to say something is an act. Exploring the interconnections between the philosophy of language and the social sciences, Austin proposed the term 'performatives' for utterances that constitute an action and argued that, in order for speech acts to succeed, they must meet certain criteria. These conditions form what Austin called 'felicitous performatives':

> The Austinian conditions for a happy performative
> (A. 1) There must exist an accepted conventional procedure having a certain conventional effect, that procedure to include the uttering of certain words by certain persons in certain circumstances, and further,
> (A. 2) The particular persons and circumstances in a given case must be appropriate for the invocations of the particular procedure invoked.
> (B. 1) The procedure must be executed by all participants both correctly and
> (B. 2) Completely.
> (T. 1) Where, as often, the procedure is designed for use by persons having certain thoughts or feelings, or for the inauguration of certain consequential conduct on the part of any participant, then a person participating in and so invoking the procedure must in fact have those thoughts or feelings, and the participants must intend so to conduct themselves, and further,
> (T. 2) Must actually so conduct themselves subsequently. (Austin 1962: 14–15)

Looking at these conditions one is struck by the central role of convention, permanence, and replication. Austin always assumed a shared repertoire or register of occasions in terms of which an utterance can and is to be understood. In the first instance this seems to undercut the relevance of the Austinian perspective for us. After all, the crucial aspect of the politics of multiplicities is that this shared system of meaning can no longer be assumed. However, in a thoughtful piece David Laws (2009) has reconceptualized Austinian thinking on performance and speech acts for contexts of institutional voids. He takes the example of a policy conflict over radioactive waste-disposal, with participants from a diverse group of organizations including activists, industry, state ministries, hospitals, unions, and amenity groups. A meeting is called to discuss what action should be taken and by whom. Participants in the meeting will inevitably ask themselves: 'What sort of occasion is this?' and 'According to which conventions will this meeting be conducted?'

His point is that in contemporary politics the answer to these questions cannot always be found in the register of political practices known to them. More precisely, actors lack a shared register, and different actors most likely will understand the practice in terms of *their own* register. Intrigued by the functioning of contemporary 'deliberative institutions', Laws suggests that today's participants may often be struggling with a corollary to the conditions that Austin saw as key to 'felicitous performatives':

> (A.1') What is the 'accepted conventional procedure having a certain conventional effect' in which I am participating? or 'What convention do I feel is appropriate?'
> (A.2') What do 'particular persons and circumstances' suggest about the conventional procedure that is being invoked? Do they fit with my ideas of what an appropriate procedure would be?
> (B.1') What procedure are we executing? Do we agree? Do we know how to do it?
> (T.1') What thoughts and feelings about the conventions are suggested by the actions of other participants? How do they match with my thoughts and feelings of what would be required by the conventional procedure I believe is appropriate?
> (T.2') What rules of conduct are we acting on or should we adopt? (Laws 2009)

So, whereas Austin suggested that speech acts perform by referring back to conventions familiar to us all, Laws points out that in the unsettling situations of today's multi-party, multi-level deliberative governance (cf. Dryzek 2006) people first need to agree on a provisional sense on what convention(s) are to prevail. Policy-making depends on speech acts in which people inter-subjectively negotiate a situation and through which political power gets its expression. But how to make sense of this interaction analytically? In what follows I will provide an analytical framework for the study of policy dynamics through the lenses of discourse and dramaturgy, respectively. To be sure, I see the two as intimately related and will analyse discourse in terms of practices. Yet in order to gain a more advanced understanding of the way in which political realities are produced, I will here introduce the two dimensions of a performance perspective: discourse and dramaturgy.

The politics of discourse

We know that governance draws on talk, but how can we analyse the effect of the words we use? How can we analyse how language sometimes acts as a structure, and comes with its own particular bias, allowing some ways of thinking into the discussion while organizing others out, to paraphrase Schattschneider (1961; cf. Hajer 1995)?

The recognition of the importance of language as 'systems of signification' in policy and politics has given rise to a rich and varied literature, ranging from narrative analysis to discourse analysis, from the study of the role of metaphor to the study of frames and reframing, over the last few decades (e.g. Czarniawska 2004; Hajer and Wagenaar 2003; Roe 1994; Schön and Rein 1994; White 1999; Yanow 1995). Many of those authors take at least some of their inspiration from the pioneering work of Murray Edelman within political science. Edelman argued early on that 'language styles' were probably 'a more sensitive and useful index of political functions in the modern state than the conventional division into executive, legislative and judicial actions' (1964: 134). To him it was obvious that political language should be regarded as political reality in itself (Edelman1988: 104). For later scholarship the question was much more about what mechanisms could explain how certain political languages come to occupy a central role, whereby some analysts focused on the identification of broader, well-structured categories of thought (cf. also Fairclough 1992; Laclau 1996; Norval 2007; Howarth 2000), and others specialized in the analysis of detailed interaction patterns (Potter 1996; Gumperz 1982). While in the first type of discourse analysis the aspect of strategic action seems lost, the latter is so focused on the interaction that the relationship between the detailed interaction and the broader societal developments is often elided.

Earlier I defined discourse as an ensemble of ideas, concepts, and categorizations through which meaning is allocated to social and physical phenomena, and that is produced in and reproduces in turn an identifiable set of practices (cf. Hajer 1995: 44). Yet work over the past few years has increasingly illuminated a weakness in this definition.[2] Ideas, concepts, and categorizations are all rational, cognitivist concepts. In empirical analysis I always found that less cognitive categories, like

---

[2] Particular reference should be made to the Ph.D. work of Justus Uitermark that successfully develops my discourse-analytical approach to analyse integration policies in the Netherlands.

storylines, metaphors, or images, played a key role. It therefore makes sense to rephrase the definition of discourse to include 'notions' as a term referring to such less-cognitive vehicles.[3] Here I will refer to discourse as an ensemble of notions, ideas, concepts, and categorizations through which meaning is ascribed to social and physical phenomena, and that is produced in and reproduces in turn an identifiable set of practices. 'Ideas' then refers to explicit assumptions and causal reasoning, 'notions' refers to less causal forms of commitments, for example things reiterated through stories, metaphors, or catchphrases. Notions, ideas, concepts, and categorizations structure our language and create a pattern in a discussion among actors. Discourse analysis is the method of finding and illuminating that pattern, its mechanisms and its political effects.

It is important to distinguish discourse from 'discussion': following the definition above, the analyst might trace different, competing discourses in a particular discussion. Moreover, we could try to see how governance is practised by existing 'discourse coalitions', whereby discourse coalitions are made up of the ensemble of particular storylines (see below), the actors who employ them, and the practices through which the discourse involved exerts its power. Discourse coalitions are not primarily made up of particular persons (let alone with a coherent set of ideas of beliefs that is not specific to context), but of the practices in the context of which actors employ storylines and (re)produce or transform particular discourses. This is important, as it helps to come to terms with the fact that some actors might utter contradictory statements (for the analyst typically posing 'inconvenient facts'), or indeed help to reproduce different discourse coalitions.

Illuminating discourse(s) allows for a better understanding of controversies, not in terms of rational-analytical argumentation but in terms of the particular argumentative logic that people bring to a discussion. Characteristically, an interaction will be found between interests and meaning-making discourses, that mutually influence and constitute each other and thus generate a particular argumentative logic. For instance, despite the very high economic stakes involved, the planning process for the redevelopment of Ground Zero was not only about money and fixed interests—the political process was also about the different meanings that people attached to the building-site and the ways in which these related to their reflections on the state of society in general and that of politics in particular (cf. Chapter 4).

---

[3] I have to thank Justus Uitermark for making this explicit.

Let me lay out the basic elements of the analytical framework. I distinguish between two central linguistic mechanisms: storylines and metaphor. During the analysis one examines statements. These often have the form of a narrative: people tell facts in a story. One quickly becomes aware that in any field there are a couple of such stories that fulfil a particularly important role. For instance, the process of rebuilding Ground Zero was often described as a way to show the world that America would not accept the terrorist attack on democracy: 'We must rebuild as a democracy.' This is an example of a *storyline*: a condensed statement summarizing complex narratives, used by people as 'shorthand' in discussions. Here the storyline 'We must rebuild as a democracy' guided the political process as it initially legitimized an open and inclusive debate on what to do with the site, thus also keeping the claims of those who have legal rights to build at bay. As the exact meaning of the storyline is ambiguous, it can allow people with conflicting interests to join the process. This is also why a storyline is also often found to 'guide' a policy process over a period of time: it allows actors to develop the story, to change it according to new insights or to fill in the blanks over time.

Secondly, the use of metaphor: metaphors bring out the 'thisness' of a that or the 'thatness' of a this (Burke 1969: 247), or as Lakoff and Johnson wrote in their classic *Metaphors We Live By*: 'The essence of metaphor is understanding and experiencing one kind of thing in terms of another' (Lakoff and Johnson 1980: 5.). Metaphors abound in politics, and the mechanism implied is well understood. The 'war on drugs' invokes 'war' to show serious commitment on the part of the political leadership; the 'greenhouse effect' comes with the association of humidity and emphasizes how global warming can make us suffocate, and thus should create political support for action, etc. The political mechanism of metaphors is to focus, simplify, compress, and appeal.

Linguistic signs have the 'ability...to point to aspects of the social context' (De Fina, Schiffrin, and Bamberg 2006: 4). Discourse analysts refer to this as processes of *indexing*: audiences 'have knowledge about forms of language typically used by speakers of different identities in particular situ-ations. These connections are then available to be used as resources that take on meanings associated with typical users and situations—they *index* these situations' (Kiesling, in ibid. 265; italics in original). These meanings are not static or determined beforehand, but can only be settled by studying the context within which the language is used; the context alters the meaning of the indexical expression (Potter and Wetherell 1987: 23). Here I will use the terms indexing and indexicality to describe how performances are (un)consciously scripted and staged in a way that draws on previously existing knowledge or experience of audiences, stimulating them to understand the performance as 'such-and-such an event'. This can be done by spatial setting or by the employment of certain metaphors and storylines that effectively highlight certain elements of a situation, thus framing an interaction. It is obvious that this is a highly political activity which is likely never to result in a constant meaning or referent. Indexicality basically explains the political effect of what I previously also called 'emblems': certain elements that become a marker and indicator of a particular identity or political position.

Storylines and metaphors fulfil a particularly significant role in political processes where policies have to be determined in a group of actors that do not share the same frame of reference. In such settings metaphors and storylines are the vehicles for trust and consensus. But they derive their political effect from the fact that different actors can have a (slightly) different reading of a particular statement. Much communication, in particular among people of widely differing backgrounds, is based on interpretive readings, on thinking along, on measuring statements in terms of whether they 'sound right'. This is why the concepts of storyline and metaphor are crucial devices. It should not be taken to be a cynical approach to politics ('It is all based on misunderstandings!'): it can be shown that people who *can be proven not to fully understand one another* nevertheless together produce meaningful political interventions. The multi-interpretability of metaphors and storylines is a vital aspect of their political efficacy.

These linguistic mechanisms are important but are sometimes made into a fetish: analysts are carried away by the metaphors they have found (cf. e.g. Inns 2002 and Cornelissen, Kafouros, and Lock 2005 on metaphorical analysis). In a performative understanding the focus is on discursive practices in which language is uttered, not on the linguistic representations *per se*. This can be done in two ways: first by looking at the relationship of what is said to the 'practice' in which it is said; and secondly by showing how people, by saying something, position a new event in a historical context.

First, the discourse-analytical approach works from the awareness that language does not simply 'float' in society but should be related to particular 'practices' in which it is employed (Hajer 1995; Forester 1999; cf. Wittgenstein's concept of 'language games'). 'Practices' then come to fulfil the crucial role connecting actors to the context of their action, and it is our chosen task to explain how discourse and practice interact. From a discourse-analytical perspective the argument is not that there is no strategic behaviour as such (which would be an odd position for a political scientist to take anyway) but that strategic action (including the employment of a metaphor) is contextualized and partially dependent on its particular situatedness for its effectiveness. For example, certain statements work well in a street rally ('No shelter for drug addicts in our street!') but not at the negotiation table ('A deprived neighbourhood that suffers under so many problems already is hardly the place for such a facility'/'This is probably the one single neighbourhood where children can still play unattended in the streets and park. It is poor planning to jeopardize this by siting this public facility here when there are so many other possible locations').

Secondly, actors perform politics through what they say via the way in which they connect a new situation to previous events. The sociolinguistic term *intertextuality* points to the fact that a particular statement (sociolinguists would say 'text') can derive its power from the way in which it refers to other texts: 'both the meanings of individual words...and the combinations in which we put them are given to us by previous speakers, traces of whose voices and contexts cling inevitably to them' (Tannen 1989, as quoted in De Fina, Schiffrin, and Bamberg 2006: 11). Words and stories travel in time, and we can examine how some interlocutors effectively leave their markers in a story. Hence when analysing governance as performance we should keep an eye open for how actors create historic 'chains' of meaning, linking the past to the present and the present to the past. We use the term *citation* to refer to the *in situ* mobilization of historical events to understand or actively frame a new situation. 'Watergate' (Irangate, 'Bannergate') is probably the most-employed political citation in American politics. It gives meaning to a new event by evoking the shared emotions belonging to the Watergate affair (cf. Schudson 1992; Alexander 2003). We will often find that actors refer to a historic situation or event to create legitimacy for what they propose to do.

On the other hand, particular concepts can get reproduced in established routines, hence not depending on active agency. Or, as Price and Shildrick put it: 'Performativity is...not a singular "act" for it is always a reiteration of a norm or set of norms, and to the extent that it acquires an act-like status in the present, it conceals or dissimulates the conventions of which it is a repetition' (1999: 241). A discourse-analytical perspective allows for (insists on!) the inclusion of the analysis of the various practices in which a particular way of reasoning has become 'stored'. Indeed, there is, as we will see in the case-study chapters, ample reason to pay attention to the power of what we may call 'stock texts' and 'stock practices': routinized ways of reasoning and acting that often cast a long shadow over a struggle to try and understand a new political situation. However, feminist theorists like Judith Butler have pointed out how such a 'stylized repetition of acts through time' (1999: 179) might reproduce relationships in society, but in this very reproduction also provides possibilities for contestation and change. We will here use the notion of *positional statements* to refer to claims that contest the conventional repertoire and—if not rebutted—create new discursive realities. Positional statements create a space for change by suggesting a new definition for experienced realities.

Thus, we can also assess the influence of metaphors, storylines, and discourses over time. Earlier I coined two terms to facilitate this assessment: *discourse structuration* occurs when a discourse starts to dominate the way a given social unit (a policy domain, a firm, or a society, depending on the research question) conceptualizes the world. If a discourse solidifies in particular institutional arrangements—say, a measuring system for air pollution—then we speak of *discourse institutionalization*. We thus have a simple two-step procedure for measuring the influence of a discourse: if many people use it to conceptualize the world (discourse structuration) and if it solidifies into institutions and organizational practices (discourse institutionalization). If both criteria are fulfilled, we argue that a particular discourse is dominant.

Measuring discourse structuration and institutionalization is something that suits research that extends over longer periods, of say up to ten to fifteen years. Yet it is also important to be able to trace the effect of what people say through a string of meetings, and how meanings and coalitions evolve through a sequence of interrelated events. An analysis of governance as performance will have to pay attention to the diachronic perspective in which one examines how particular ways of seeing are taken up or lost, routinized, or altered, and how this has to do with the particular places at which things are said (see below). I analyse dis-

Table 2.1. Concepts of discourse (as presented and elaborated in Hajer 1995, 2003*b*, 2006)

Discourse
Refers to bias, *markers*, *structures*, and *patterns* in a discussion.
- *Discourse*: an ensemble of notions, ideas, concepts, and categorizations through which meaning is allocated to social and physical phenomena, and which is produced and reproduced in an identifiable set of practices.
- *Metaphor*: understanding and experiencing a particular thing/event in terms of another.
- *Storyline*: a condensed sort of narrative that links an event to one or more discourses and thus provides the basis of 'discourse coalitions'.
- *Discourse coalition*: the ensemble of particular storylines, the actors that employ them, and the practices through which the discourse involved exert their power.

(Continued)

Table 2.1. (Continued)

- *Practice*: operational routines—mutually accepted rules and norms that give coherence to social life.
- *Discursive affinity*: arguments that may have very different roots and meanings but that together uphold a particular way of seeing.
- *Emblematic issue*: a specific policy problem that captures the imagination at a particular moment in time and fulfils a key role in the general understanding of a much larger problem complex (metonym).
- *Discourse structuration*: a discourse dominates the way a given social unit (a policy domain, a firm, a society—all depending on the research question) conceptualizes the world.
- *Discourse institutionalization*: a discourse solidifies in particular institutional arrangements—say, a measuring system for air pollution.
- *Indexicality*: performances are scripted and staged in a way that draws on previously existing knowledge or experience of audiences, stimulating them to understand the performance as 'such-and-such an event'.
- *Intertextuality*: a particular statement refers to other texts to enhance the power of the statement.
- *Citation*: the *in situ* mobilization of historical events to understand a new situation and/or to exert influence.
- *Performativity*: a reiteration of a norm or set of norms.
- *Positional statement*: a claim that, if not rebutted, creates a particular discursive reality.

course as inherently dynamic and context (or 'setting')-dependent, which makes the approach markedly different from a conversational-analytical perspective in which one would focus empirical research strictly on what is said.

From discourse to dramaturgy

Although the literature manifests a strong awareness that people do things with words (Austin 1962), we sometimes forget that settings do things with people too. Or, to quote Murray Edelman: 'Although every act takes place in a setting, we ordinarily take scenes for granted, focusing our attention on actions' (1964: 95). Whereas discourse analysis analyses the political dynamics of what people say, the dramaturgy of politics analyses how they say it, where they say it, and to whom they say it. The dramaturgical perspective has a long history in the social sciences. It is one which highlights the importance of *interaction* in the creation of meaning in the world. As Edgley (2003: 147) puts it: 'Whether a person is aware of the dramaturgical principle or utterly oblivious to it, it is how people interact with others that is the source of the emergence of meaning in their lives. In this sense, dramaturgy represents a radical insistence on the primacy of acts over everything else (Mead 1938).'

Including the dramaturgical dimension presumes that we approach political (inter)action as contextualized in time ('sequence') and place ('staging'), and that we make explicit who speak and to whom ('dramatis personae'). 'Performing involves the demonstration and enactment of power. It concretizes ideas regarding the struggle between protagonists and antagonists and reveals to audiences ways they can achieve or pre-serve desirable power relations' (Benford and Hunt 1992: 45).

Elaborating on Burke (1969), Lynch (1991), and Benford and Hunt (1992), we can define the following basic concepts. First, *scripting* refers to those efforts to create a setting by determining the characters in the play and to provide cues for appropriate behaviour. An obvious differ-ence between theatrical drama and social drama is that scripts are more often disrupted by actors in social life (cf. Alexander 2004*b*: 92). This is arguably even more true for political drama, which is why I integrated the notion of '*counter script*' to refer to the conscious activity of antagonists who try to alter the effects of particular stagings of politics, to twist the meaning of what is said by giving it a new contextualization or intro-ducing a new antagonism. Second, *staging* refers to the organization of an interaction, drawing on existing symbols and the invention of new ones as well as on the distinction between active players and (presumably passive) audiences. Third, *setting* is the physical situation in which the interaction takes place, and can include the artefacts that are brought to the situation. Once polit-ics is conceived of in dramaturgical terms, the *mise-en-scène*, or setting of the stage, is an obvious intervention in the play of politics: 'In the drama, the opera, the ballet, in the display of paintings and in the performance of music setting is plotted and manipulated, just as it often is in the staging of governmental acts' (Edelman 1964: 96). Drama can be manifested in the sequential ordering of political moments or in the staging of a particular political act. *Performance*, then, is the way in which the contextualized interaction itself produces social realities like understanding of the problem in hand, knowledge, decisions, and new power relationships.

By analysing political processes as a sequence of staged performances we might be able to infer under what conditions a variety of voices emerges in political discussions, how the different contributions can be related to one another in a meaningful way, how conflicts are expressed, and under what conditions such statements can be made with influence on the actual decision-making. If seen from a dramaturgical point of view, politics is a sequence of staged events in which actors interact over the meaning of events and over how to move on.

Table 2.2. Concepts of dramaturgy

Dramaturgy
Analyses policy-making as a sequence of staged performances.
'Although every act takes place in a setting, we ordinarily take scenes for granted, focusing our attention on actions.' (Edelman 1964)

- *Performance*: the way in which *the contextualized interaction* itself produces social realities like understandings of the problem at hand, knowledge, new power relations.
- *Setting*: the physical and organizational situation in which the interaction takes place, including the artefacts that are brought to or found in the situation.
- *Scripting*: the efforts to create a particular political effect by determining the characters in the performance (the 'dramatis personae', the protagonists and antagonists) and to provide cues for appropriate behaviour.
- *Counter-scripting*: efforts of antagonists to undo the effect of scripts of protagonists.
- *Staging*: the organization of an interaction, drawing on existing symbols and the invention of new ones, as well as to the distinction between active players and (presumably passive) audiences (*mise-en-scène*).

Discourse and drama in a mediatized polity

In order to be effective for the purposes of analysing governance, I will also have to develop this analytical vocabulary to connect to the political sociological argument of Chapter 1. My argument there was that it is the politics of multiplicities—in which the institutional void and the mediatizedness of politics stand out—that troubles the attempts to come to authoritative forms of governance. But how does this relate to the analytical language introduced above?

A first—straightforward, but nevertheless important—analytical point relates to the understanding of actors and audiences in politics. Given its background in theatre studies, performance theory or dramaturgy quickly assumes a differentiation of actors and audience. This is, of course, part and parcel of the theatrical metaphors we are employing here. It is also one that often gets imported into political scientific analysis, for example in Manin's notion of an 'audience democracy' (1997). Yet in today's politics the differentiation of 'actors' and 'audience' is problematic. First of all, there is no one single audience any more: there are multiple public spheres, as we established in Chapter 1 (cf. Fraser 1992). Politicians have to reach out in different directions to make contact with their key audiences.

Also, the assumption of a passive attitude on the part of the audience does not hold. 'Audience as mass' has made way for 'audience as agent' (Holbert 2004). The hypersensitivities of politicians have resulted in a permanent 'performance monitoring' through techniques such as opinion-polling or focus groups, the results of which are then quickly fed back and translated into adjustments in the script. The constant tinkering with discourse and dramaturgy makes the public a co-determinant of politics. But there are two other ways in which the concept of 'audience' no longer suffices to describe today's publics. On the one hand the public now also actively co-produces politics, by recording and filming it—including when this is inconvenient—and on the other, it actively frames and reframes its claims, by readjusting its agenda and even by inserting 'counter scripts' (compare Shellers 2004's notion of mobile publics). Such acts on the part of the public do have real effects: they often provide new discursive understandings and change the political dynamics.

Furthermore, today's political drama takes place before a multiplicity of publics. This is a reality that is being responded to already. Hence where political scripts are consciously made, they now often include cues meant for different publics. A bizarre example is what is now known as the mechanism of the 'dog whistle', which refers to coded statements in a general address which are targeted and understood by a particular audience without others than those intended noticing. More common is the situation where political actors are seen to speak to a particular public but are aware that they are watched by a 'secondary public'. In such cases the 'real' localized event might in actual fact be part of a scripted staging to reach the—hidden—secondary public. It is what communication scientists refer to as a 'pseudo-event'; an event primarily planned for the purpose of being reported or reproduced to other publics (Boorstin 1961). Yet the true multiplicity comes out when the message is read and responded to by a third public and then changes the meaning of the first act, a nice example being the wholly unexpected agency of Paris Hilton after a McCain campaign ad in which he compared Obama to 'celebrities' like Paris Hilton or Britney Spears in the run-up to the 2008 US presidential elections. It reframed the situation, as a surprisingly articulate Hilton ironically recombined elements of celebrity live (a pool, global travelling, body culture) with the presentation of an alternative-energy strategy. Her message was interwoven with suggestions that fitness mattered and that it was McCain who was perhaps not fit to lead. The politics of meaning then quickly comes to resemble a ball in a pinball machine, rapidly and sometimes erratically bouncing from left to right and from top to bottom, while those trying to stay in control are only in the possession of the flippers—pretty meaningless devices if the ball is out of reach.

The framework outlined above also refers to the sociolinguistic research on indexicality which analyses how particular statements may be used to signal particular relationships. With the growing importance of television, the very staging of a statement, that is, the conscious choice of 'decor', a set, is increasingly mobilized to achieve that effect of index-icality, thus amplifying the impact of what is said. The most notorious example of indexicality in recent political history is undoubtedly the case for the war against Iraq made by Colin Powell to the UN Security Council on 5 February 2003. In his 2003 UN presentation of the 'evidence' of Iraqi deception, Colin Powell deliberately drew a parallel with Adlai Stevenson's presentation of evidence to the UN Security Council during the Cuban Crisis in 1962. Or in the words of his advisor: 'that 'Stevenson moment'...was the effect they were after', an effect to be attained not only by the terms employed ('an accumulation of facts'), but also by the way in which maps and photographs were used (DeYoung 2006, quoted in Stark and Paravel 2008: 52). While the staging of the speech made a clear reference to the successful performance of the Kennedy Administration at the time of the Cuban Crisis, thus hinting at a similarity between the latter and the war against Iraq, it was as if the US intelligence services had not made any progress in terms of satellite photography in the four decades since 1962. However, in their reference to the 'Stevenson moment', Powell and his staff were clearly aware of the influence that key images and camera footage can have on the way in which political decision-making is portrayed and evaluated. Although it would be too simplistic to state that images actually drive public opinion—as is often thought—they do influence people's information processing. They alter the way in which audiences frame and value news events, but this occurs in a complicated interplay with individuals' existing predispositions and values (Domke, Perlmutter, and Spratt 2002).

Mediated politics frees political drama of its unity of action, time, and place; politics is given a fourth dimension of circulating images and illustrated storylines. The political drama often becomes a 'flow' of statements and events, something that can also cascade out of control as it did in the case of the 'mission accomplished' banner marking President Bush's premature victory celebration after the invasion of Iraq. In the words of Angus:

> Media continuously translate each other; thus they constitute an *environ-ment*, rather than *a* simple plurality. Post-modern society is constituted by a media envir-onment characterized by the continuous circulation of signs and messages. The distinctions which are representational distinctions become insufficient to grasp the 'simulation' of signs by the media. They are not copies of 'real' relationships, but the simulation of media events that produce real relationships. (Angus 1989: 342, quoted in McLeod 1999)

The difficulties in controlling the meaning of events are aggravated by the fact that, in addition to the traditional 'constitutional stages', like parliament or official press conferences, 'non-constitutional' stages like public manifestations or television talk-shows have grown in importance in the past decades. And typically, political discourses shape up, shift, and change in a continuous interaction between these stages.

This dramaturgical reality of a mediatized politics has significant consequences for the way in which governance needs to be performed in our time. It is not as if actor and (target) public(s) relate directly towards each other. Media effects are taken into consideration when the way in which political messages are delivered is drafted. As Cook (2005) points out, it no longer makes sense to conceptualize the media as an institution that 'represent' the political; they are now part and parcel of governance, they are a political institution themselves. It also implies that, if we want to understand the dynamics of governance, we need to understand the specific mechanisms that characterize the media as a site of discourse-production and dramaturgy. We know that this is fundamentally a two-way process. As outlined in Chapter 1, media have preferred ways of conveying news, using conflict frames, bringing antagonists to counterbalance protagonists; they like 'news' in the sense that they prefer stories that are unfinished ('cliffhangers'), and so on. This gives a powerful new life to established dramatic techniques such as cognitive simplification, the time–space compression of decision-making, the format of antagonism which pits protagonists against antagonists. Mediated politics opens up the solidity of classical-modernist governance and re-creates politics as a story with twists and turns ('stay with us!'; cf. Alexander 2004*a*, *b*). Political actors, on the other hand, actively seek to influence the meaning of the event, selecting their most effective storylines for further use in media performances.

It is now understandable why crises and incidents can gain such a prominent position in our perception of politics and governance. Media are attracted to a crisis frame, and politicians see how media are a crucial vehicle for their continued credibility and the legitimacy of their work. They cannot ignore presentations suggesting incidents, even if they do not agree, and respond by buying extra expertise in political communication. This is an obvious reaction, but the dramaturgical effect is delimited by the fact that it is still administrators and political leaders who will actually have to deliver.

Together with Justus Uitermark I developed the notion of 'performative habitus' to account for the fact that political actors develop certain discourses and dispositions over the course of many years that help or hinder

Table 2.3. Additional concepts

- *Pseudo-event*: an event planned primarily for the purpose of being reported or reproduced, with an ambiguous relation to the underlying reality of the situation and intended to work as self-fulfilling prophecy (Boorstin 1961).
- *Constitutional stages*: parliaments, official press conferences, official gatherings of political leaders in NAFTA, EU, or ASEAN, etc.
- *Non-constitutional stages*: public manifestations, television talk-shows, visits, interviews.
- *Performative habitus*: embodied dispositions, developed over the course of many years that help or hinder actors to respond tactically to a given situation.
- *Situational credibility* (cf. King 1987: 10): the way in which the credibility of an actor is dependent on the combination of his/her performative habitus and the setting in which he/she operates.

them to respond tactically when they need to act in highly contingent and stressful situations (Hajer and Uitermark 2008). Thus, a large part of the behaviour of administrators in the initial phases of crises can be understood as responses that derive from their embodied dispositions and that develop in relation to the forces immanent in the settings in which they operate. The notion of 'performative habitus' can help us to understand how administrators respond tactically in emotionally loaded exchanges. It highlights the role of dispositions that have been shaped over many years of symbolic labour and that allow politicians a level of agency and tactical intelligence in particular settings. The concept of performative habitus transcends the dualism between the model of the politician as a rational actor in pursuit of predefined goals and models of the politician's actions as being determined by a pre-given 'personality' or by the context in which he performs (cf. Marcus 2000: 'Emotions in Politics'). As will be shown in the case studies which follow, the situational credibility of a politician or administrator depends on the combination of his or her performative habitus and the particular setting in which he or she has to perform.

The approach

The idea of studying governance as political drama and performance fits a tradition of thought that goes back to Aristotle and Pericles discussing the preconditions for deliberation in governing and Aristotle's differentiation of logos, ethos, and pathos in political rhetoric; Edmund Burke pointing to the fact that parliaments should be seen as a 'theatrical exhibition hall for dramatic talents' (Hindson and Gray 1988); Rousseau, who suggested that the authoritarian aspects of institutions would influence the cognitions and attitudes of those involved in the deliberation; and John Stuart Mill, who subsequently criticized Rousseau's ideas on the mandated representative as this form would delimit the quality of the deliberation, something which was later reiterated by Kenneth Burke (1969). It reminds us of the famous statement made by Winston Churchill, who argued that the Lower House should be rebuilt in exactly the same shape rather then extended, because the sight of a very crowded place would signify the great importance of the discussion at hand. All of these are examples of reflections appreciative of the fact that political deliberation cannot and should not be regarded only in terms of what is being said, but should always take into account where things are said and how they are said as well. 'We don't start from certain words, but from certain occasions or activities', as Wittgenstein put it (cf. Norval 2007: 1).

Politics always implies performance. My point here is that in situations in which there is an absence of clear and generally accepted rules and norms, and where the very locus of politics is unclear, the performative becomes the dominant force. When politics and policy are made in unstable settings, performing co-determines which rules are followed in the process, which definition of reality is followed, what temporal-spatial frame is seen as 'appropriate', and what constitutes legitimate intervention. The very variability of the setting and staging of politics calls for more explicit attention to be paid to the dramaturgical side of political processes (Hajer 2003a). This understanding of politics as performance recovers a sense of politics as an artistic endeavour. Politics is an art, and the analysis of politics as performance brings out the skilful way of engaging a public, of making politics like good theatre, that is, as an experience that is created and made possible by those who were part of it, including those who were not necessarily on the stage.

The previous chapter sketched the new political sociology of the politics of multiplicities: a politics without a logical centre and a politics struggling with the lack of broadly accepted political routines. The politics of multiplicities is also a politics where many pressing problems escape the logic of predefined polities, where civil servants sometimes unexpectedly find themselves in the spotlight of the media, whether they like it or not, where politicians need to create their support in unconventional ways, and where new actors may walk onto the stage unannounced, unexpectedly, and often without respect for long-standing institutions. The condition of multiplicities is not the end of politics; it calls for its reinvention. It most certainly calls for new skills and new action patterns, and it is this dynamics that we want to uncover and understand.

In this chapter I have tried to bring together scholarship from a range of disciplines to develop an analytical language that gives us a handle on the political dynamics in the era of multiplicities. In the following chapters I will present the analysis of three distinct cases: the political handling of the murder of filmmaker Theo van Gogh in Amsterdam; the rebuilding of Ground Zero in New York; and finally, the handling of the aftermath of the BSE crisis in Great Britain.

Although each case has its own context, they share a common denominator. In each case the established, classical-modernist way of governing is challenged and the political dynamics seem to threaten the established categories. In discourse-theoretical terms we understand this as a 'dislocation'. Dislocations are defined by Howarth as 'events that cannot be symbolized by an existent discursive order, and thus function to disrupt that order' (Howarth 2000: 113), events that 'disrupt and destabilize orders of meaning' (ibid. 132). In cases of dislocation there is no authoritative system to routinely differentiate among claims. Initially, the event defies interpretation because of its extraordinary nature. Yet, for precisely this reason, it invites all sorts of attributions of meaning and provides opportunities for discourses that allow alternative or radical interpretations. Simply put: if established discourses cannot accommodate the event, new ways of seeing the world conquer discursive space.

In Chapter 1 I argued that classical-modernism or network governance should be regarded as *genres*, particular sets of practices through which governance is performed. It is through empirical research that we can see how existing genres of governance become challenged, to what extent they are able to 'survive' a dislocation and what difficulties are encountered in cases where alternative ways of organizing governance are introduced. In the remainder of the book I analyse three cases where such a dislocation occurred. I see these dislocations as moments in which the authority of the established classical-modernist discursive order was at least temporarily disrupted and new repertoires and recombinations were sought for. Analytically the question is what political dynamics we see at these moments of instability and what this tells us about how an authoritative governance is possible in our age of multiplicities. To guide this analysis I work with six propositions.

The *first proposition* is that the relationship between (1) political decision, (2) public problem, and (3) the public is unstable. In this situation governance is first and foremost a matter of the enactment of meaning whereby authoritative governance assumes the potentiality of reasoned elaboration, and thus the possibility of communication both among those active in governing and with the multiple publics that might be affected by their decisions.

The *second proposition* holds that an analytical distinction between political action and media representation is inappropriate. Politics and media are fundamentally intertwined. Politics is best understood as a sequence of enactments, taking place at many different places, including constitutional and non-constitutional stages, through which meaning is given to societal events.

The *third proposition* holds that incidents and crisis situations ('dislocations') fulfil a crucial role in a politics of multiplicities; it is through the enactment of those foregrounded situations that political repertoires are tested, rethought, and renegotiated. The loss of contextual supports and taken-for-granted routines ('institutional void') implies an increased importance of the concrete political acts of individual actors. Conflicts and incidents are therefore pivotal in the (re)production of authority.

The *fourth proposition* holds that there is no essence, no necessary evolutionary shift from one type of governance to the next. Hence, *even if* the limits to the classical-modernist genre of governing are exposed, alternative forms of governance will only succeed in impacting on political decision-making routines to the extent that they are able to find answers to the crucial questions that prevail during the period of dislocation. The actual occurrence of such a shift will depend on the ability of actors to develop and institutionalize new definitions of the meaning of 'the' situation; it depends on how the dislocation is performed.

The *fifth proposition* holds that the performance of a dislocation can be understood by seeing governance in terms of a political performance, differentiating between a discursive and dramaturgical dimension (see above). When media and politics can no longer be meaningfully distinguished as separate realms, style becomes more important. Whether or not a particular style is effective in establishing authority depends on the 'match' with the particular stages at which politics gets enacted.

The *sixth proposition* is that authoritative governance and deliberation are not each other's opposites. Following deliberative rules can result in authoritative decisions. Yet having the same insight is not the same as reaching a joint agreement. Lacking the symbolic and procedural props of the constitutional classical-modernist institutions, deliberative forms of network governance will only result in a resilient policy solution if the process of deliberation *performs* a shared policy commitment. In order to gain authority, network governance requires more than following the often-reiterated deliberative rules of conduct (force of the better argument, inclusiveness, reciprocity, publicity, accountability); it will gain (or decrease) in authority depending on its response to (expected or unexpected) policy drama as it unfolds. Staging, (counter-) scripting, and dramaturgy in general crucially influence *whether* a public is formed through deliberation and *how* this occurs. It is not the controlled moments of quiet rational reasoning that are crucial, but the way in which reasoned elaboration is experienced which can be enhanced through the sequence of, often emotional, exchanges and enactments.

The emphasis of the analysis thus comes to lie with the study of the particular enactment of politics at particular moments, studying four elements of the political act: what actors say, how they say it, where they say it, and to whom they say it. The challenge is to combine the appreciation of the ways in which established discourses and settings pre-structure social realities with the obvious possibility for individual actors to act on a particular situation. Discourses come with particular 'subject positionings' (Davies and Harré 1990; cf. Hajer 1995), and it remains hard for actors to liberate themselves from these preconceived action patterns. Similarly, people are socialized in a particular way of conducting politics, and one may assume a certain 'dramaturgical loyalty' (Goffman 1959). Hence the emphasis on performance is not to be taken to suggest that actors have total freedom to act as they wish.

Obviously access to the crucial 'means of symbolic production' is unequally divided. In that sense there is a political economy to the politics of performance which needs to be kept in mind. The power of routinized ways of operating are a case in point, but the possibilities to be creative with the staging of politics, the ways in which different actors differ in terms of access to crucial stages, or the way in which some actors just do not have a choice among the genres available, all influence the way in which political conflicts are enacted and how particular points of view come to be expressed.

At the same time this performance perspective on governance allows us to substantially break away from a rationalist bias in policy analysis, to focus on how politics is experienced and how it is literally given shape. Studying politics as performance enables us to trace how a claim comes to be seen as authoritative in a sequence of enactments, and we may be able to understand why. It connects discourses to actions, strategies to structures. A performance perspective allows us to analyse governance in terms of the *genres* that politicians and administrations employ as well as in terms of the *repertoire* of genres that they master and (can) bring to bear in the situation. Here the analytical task is to illuminate the forms of argumentation that are surfacing, showing how politics was enacted, explaining authority not only in terms of the substance of what is said but also the way in which it is said, and the particular setting in which things are said.

3

Performing Authority After the Assassination of Theo van Gogh[1]

Maarten A. Hajer with Justus Uitermark

Introduction

On 2 November 2004 an Islamic extremist assassinated Theo van Gogh, filmmaker and *bête noire* of Amsterdam's intellectual elite. A year earlier Van Gogh had collaborated with Ayaan Hirsi Ali in making the movie *Submission*, which sought to demonstrate that the Qur'an considers women to be fundamentally inferior to men. Ayaan Hirsi Ali, according to *Time Magazine* one of the world's hundred most influential persons of 2005, is a Somali refugee and former Muslim campaigning against Islam in the name of women's emancipation, and at the time an MP for the Dutch right-wing liberal party VVD.

The murder was exceptionally violent and shocked the country. The assassin, Mohammed Bouyeri, a 26-year-old Dutch citizen of Moroccan descent, shot Van Gogh seven times before cutting his throat and stabbing a note onto his chest. It contained an extensive death-threat to Hirsi Ali, while two other politicians were explicitly mentioned: Jozias van Aartsen, the leader of the VVD party and patron of Hirsi Ali, and Job Cohen, the (Jewish) mayor of Amsterdam. Soon thereafter other politicians were reported to be on a 'death list', among them Ahmed Aboutaleb, the alderman for diversity in Amsterdam, a practising Muslim of Moroccan descent.[2]

---

[1] We thank Marieke Wagter for her work on the digital media analysis and Wytske Versteeg for general assistance in the research project.

[2] Dutch local government is made up of a mayor appointed by the queen, and aldermen appointed by the coalition parties after the elections. Together they form the executive ('B&W'), which is accountable to the City Council.

The violent act added fuel to the already heated debate on the integration of ethnic and religious minorities. In the ten days after the murder a number of mosques were daubed with racist symbols, an Islamic school was burnt to the ground, and churches were vandalized. Even though the number and intensity of incidents soon decreased, what remained was the sense that there was 'trouble in Paradise', as the *Financial Times* put it on 4 December 2004 (Kuper 2004). The Netherlands was portrayed as a country in moral shock.

The meaning of a murder

The assassination of Van Gogh took place at 8.50 a.m. on a Tuesday morning. As the news spread, the struggle to capture the meaning of the event started. This politics of meaning preoccupied the country for days and weeks to come. For instance, a day after the murder Amsterdam alderman Aboutaleb faced as his opening question on national television: 'What is the meaning of the murder?' (*Twee Vandaag*, 3 Nov. 2004).

Initially the debate was preoccupied with the question of whether 'Jihad had now come to the Netherlands'. This framing of the murder was strongly reinforced by television images of a day-long siege of an apartment in which members of the terrorist 'Hofstad' group (to which Mohammed Bouyeri was found to belong) were hiding. Yet while the terrorism issue was a concern to national politics, the Amsterdam government was under siege because of its insistent multicultural policies. Critics were quick to point out that this murder showed, once again, that 'multiculturalist' policies were naive and outdated. That criticism put the pressure directly on those public officeholders whose storyline had been for years that their task was to 'keep things together' ('de boel bij elkaar houden'): Job Cohen and Ahmed Aboutaleb. Both had long-standing reputations as defenders of an approach to ethnic diversity based on mutual adaptation and empathy. Job Cohen gained this reputation by involving religious and ethnic organizations in decision-making processes, Ahmed Aboutaleb established his image of a defender of multiculturalism in a previous job as director of Forum, a national, government-subsidized institute for multicultural development. Aboutaleb and Cohen publicly symbolized what was pejoratively labelled the 'soft approach', portrayed by political opponents as merely 'having tea with various social groups'.

Initially the antagonists were several right-wing MPs and media commentators who argued that the assassination was a 'wake-up call': these 'anti-multiculturalists' (cf. Uitermark 2005) had always argued that extremist Islam posed a serious threat to Dutch society. The storyline of the 'dead end' of multiculturalism and the threat of an 'Islamization' of Dutch society had been rehearsed in the years before by a range of intellectuals and politicians, most notably by the populist politician Pim Fortuyn, who was shot dead in May 2002. The murder of Van Gogh only served to strengthen their conviction.

After the assassination of Van Gogh, the anti-multicultural camp was reinforced by a new actor in the symbolic struggles over integration: a group that became known as 'the Friends of Theo'. Theo van Gogh was a radical hedonist and had been part of a group of writers, filmmakers, and journalists like Max Pam, Theodor Holman, and Gijs van de Westelaken that operated at the margins of the Dutch cultural elite. Being well connected, they had a very high presence in the news media in the immediate aftermath of the assassination. With utmost determination they continued Theo van Gogh's battle against 'political correctness' and especially the alleged tendency of multiculturalists to downplay the black sides of Islam, targeting Mayor Job Cohen very directly. In public performances, protagonists and antagonists tried to script and counter-script the meaning to the murder, using all the available stages.

We examine the enactment of authority in five settings that had most prominence in the media coverage of the ten days after the murder (and indeed echoed in the media in the weeks thereafter).

Setting 1: The press conference

Following the murder, the mayor, chief of police, and chief prosecutor (the so called security 'triangle') were immediately called on to coordinate the security policy. Operating from the safe and secluded space of the coordination bunker underneath City Hall, their task was to figure out what had happened, if the murder was an act of an individual or a terrorist cell, and to determine the security risks. Yet the authorities also felt the pressure from the media and realized they 'needed to be seen' as actively and authoritatively working on the case. They therefore decided to organize a press conference only three hours after the arrest, being fully aware of the risks of openness in this early stage when not all information was available or verified.

Table 3.1. The Van Gogh murder: chronology of events

2 Nov.	**8.50: Murder**—Van Gogh is torn from his bicycle while cycling to his studio, shot and stabbed.
	9.30: Arrest—the murderer is arrested after a fire-fight in which a policeman shoots him in the leg.
	13.00: Press conference—by the mayor, chief of police, and chief prosecutor; announcement by Mayor Cohen of 'Lawaaimanifestatie' (manifestation of noise) at Dam Square to protest against the murder.
	18.00: *NOS Journaal* —(national television news) reports on murder and press conference, and shows mourning of the 'Friends of Theo' illustrated with interview excerpts from the Friends.
	19.30: Lawaaimanifestatie—at Dam Square, with speeches by Mayor Cohen and Minister of Integration Verdonk, thousands of people attending.
	22.00: *NOS Journaal*—national television news reports on the murder, press conference, and Lawaaimanifestatie.
	22.30: *Nova*—two 'Friends of Theo' are main guests on *NOVA*, a 'BBC *Newsnight*'-type information programme.
3 Nov.	**Speech in Al-Kabir mosque**—Alderman Aboutaleb delivers a speech in Al-Kabir mosque and argues that 'Moroccans should choose to live here and integrate or go back'. In a subsequent **street interview** shown on AT5, local television, Aboutaleb argues that Moroccans who do not want to integrate should 'pack up' and go ('koffers pakken').
	Address to the City Council—Mayor Cohen addresses the City Council and emphasizes that there is no alternative to 'keeping things together'.
	18.00: *Twee Vandaag*—Aboutaleb is main guest on the news programme *Twee Vandaag*.
5 Nov.	**22.30: Talk show *Barend & Van Dorp***—Theodor Holman ('Friends of Theo') guests on this top-rated talk show, reads an 'open letter' to Mohammed Bouyeri from the Friends of Theo.
8 Nov.	**22.30: Talk show *Barend & Van Dorp***—Aboutaleb guests on the talk-show, which starts with 'Friend of Theo' Jan Mulder reporting on the party/memorial service in honour of Van Gogh.
9 Nov.	**17.00: Cremation**—Theo van Gogh's cremation is broadcast live on Dutch television.
	22.30: *Nova*—Friends of Theo (Holman, Van de Westelaken) appear on the main news programme *NOVA*.
11 Nov.	**22.30: Talk show *Barend & Van Dorp***—Mayor Cohen guests on this talk show to respond to various allegations in newspapers.

At the press conference the mayor emphasized the aspects of collective security and (in his own words) that of being 'the father of the city'.[3] He expressed anger, disgust, and shock that this could happen in Amsterdam and announced a 'Lawaaimanifestatie' or 'manifestation of noise' (a term that was literally invented just moments before the press conference) at Dam Square to protest against the murder and in support of freedom of speech. In response to the question of a journalist, Cohen stated he would be among the speakers. Chief Prosecutor Leo de Wit revealed the

---

[3] Anonymous (n.d.), 'Job Cohen, Burgemeester van Amsterdam; De boel bij elkaar houden!' Available from: *http://www.burgemeesters.nl/node/694*.

background of the suspect and explained the judicial procedure. Chief of Police Bernard Welten described the events of the morning, emphasizing that the suspected murderer had been caught after 'an unprecedented exchange of fire' and after one of his officers had shot the murderer in his leg. When speaking about the assassination, Welten—for whom this was only the second day in office—seemed to address his own police organization rather than the general public; using the press conference primarily as a an external message path (Graber 2003).

Although the division of roles for the press conference had been carefully planned beforehand, it resembled in no way the tightly orchestrated ceremonies of routine symbolic politics (like an inaugural speech). It was improvised, unwittingly underlining the uniqueness of the situation and the fact that everybody was taken by surprise. Chief Prosecutor Leo de Wit argued later that: 'In times of stress the Triangle is the most trust generating symbol that the city can show' (Schulte 2005*b*),[4] but the inability to provide journalists with information fed their distrust, for instance when the administrators refused to answer the question whether the letter that was stabbed onto Van Gogh's body had been written in Dutch or Arabic. When looking back on the performance, Cohen was nevertheless content with the attained effect: 'We had to say quite often that we did not yet know. Moreover, there was information in the press conference that we had to correct later. That is always very complicated. But given the difficult situation, the press conferences contributed to a feeling of trust that we were on the case and that we showed leadership after this shocking incident. It determined in large part the success of our approach.'[5]

However, this was just the first episode in an unfolding symbolic struggle. What is more, the press conference also revealed a cleavage between local and national politics. When journalists confronted the Amsterdam Triangle with the fact that Mohammed Bouyeri had been known by the AIVD (the organization responsible for national security), it turned out that none of the local actors had been informed about this, causing journalists to conclude that: 'The state knows more than the municipality.' It was clear to all that politics was conducted at multiple sites and that these different sites of policy-making did not operate in a fully coordinated way, perhaps even disagreed on strategies. Their struggle would remain a

---

[4] 'De driehoek is in tijden van stress het maximaal vertrouwenwekkende symbool dat de stad uit de kast kan halen.'

[5] Anonymous (n.d.), 'Job Cohen, Burgemeester van Amsterdam; De boel bij elkaar houden!' Available from: *http://www.burgemeesters.nl/node/694*.

constant factor during 'the crisis after the crisis', and would emerge again the very same day around the 'manifestation of noise'.

Setting 2: The manifestation of noise

On the evening of the murder more than 20,000 people came to Dam Square, bringing banners, whistles, pans, rattles, and sirens to an almost exorcist-like ritual organized by the city government to 'canalize emotions' (Aboutaleb, as quoted in Schulte 2005a). When we consider the manifestation of noise through a lens of indexicality, the chosen setting is significant. Dam Square is a central square in Amsterdam, and is the location of the national war memorial. It is used for the annual commemoration, broadcast nationwide, of those who died in World War II. Location, timing, and the request for two minutes of silence connected the manifestation of noise to this well-known event, thus giving a spatial expression to the concern about freedom and democracy as it was felt after the assassination of Van Gogh; on this evening World War II and the murder of Van Gogh were indexically linked as attacks on the freedom of speech.

Centre-stage of the manifestation was a podium, erected earlier that day, at which first Mayor Job Cohen and then Minister of Integration Rita Verdonk spoke before a bass-drummer led the collective making of noise.[6] Cohen spoke sternly and firmly, and emphasized the crucial commitment to freedom of speech, arguing that he often disagreed strongly with Van Gogh but 'that this is allowed in this country' ('En dat mág in dit land!'). Citing Voltaire, he underlined that he would always fight for the right of opponents to speak out freely. Minister Verdonk, nicknamed 'Iron Rita' and one of the most important proponents of an uncompromising policy towards immigrants, expressed grief but also suggested that Van Gogh was a supporter of her hard-line policies: 'I knew Theo. And I came to know him better and better. Theo was the one who on the one hand said: "Rita, keep that back straight!" But Theo was also the one that said: "But think about yourself... and think about the people." '

And although her main message was that the country needed to resolve the tensions in unity, she also made utterances that led to insecurity, most notably among the Moroccan-Dutch community and ethnic minorities in general: 'We cannot understand everything yet and do not know all the facts. What is clear is that this is an awful deed and that a Moroccan-Dutch

---

[6] Speeches can be livestreamed via *www.omroep.nl*.

suspect was arrested...', which linked the murderer to a larger (predominantly peaceful) ethnic community, and: 'Do we say: we don't want this; this is not the society we have in mind. A large number of minority organizations have made this choice today. They condemned this deed. And that is a bit of light (*lichtpunt*) on this day that is so utterly dark', which suggests that these organizations (most of which had been in constructive contact with the government for decades) might not have been inclined to condemn the murder.

With their contradictory performances Verdonk and Cohen, unwittingly, illustrated how the murder could be accommodated in diverging discourses. We see the process of indexicality at work when we consider the way in which both politicians highlighted some elements of the situation, while deliberately ignoring other aspects, thus urging the audience to regard the murder as 'such-and-such an event'. Cohen avoided any ethnical or religious stance and conceptualized the murder as an attack on the shared core values of the country and the capital ('Today, an *Amsterdammer* has been killed'). On the other hand, Minister Verdonk spoke on behalf of the government, but framed the event in a much more personal, but also a particular political, narrative: it was part of an attack against those who supported an uncompromising attitude towards immigrants in general and Muslims in particular ('a *Moroccan-Dutch suspect*'). Their speeches were obviously not only directed to those people present at Dam Square, but also to the various publics watching the manifestation on television. Given the contradictory statements, these audiences would find serious difficulty in reading the meaning of this manifestation.

The double interpretation was not orchestrated. In fact the manifestation of noise was very much a collusion of two different scripts. Immediately after the assassination the 'Friends of Theo' were planning a gathering to express their outrage over the murder. For them, it was out of the question to organize a 'silent march', since this would convey the impression that the murder silenced Van Gogh's voice. At the press conference Mayor Cohen had already announced that he would speak at the public ceremony. He felt he needed to do this, referring to his administrative role, 'being the mayor' in times of crisis. For obvious reasons he could not claim to share the same outrage as Van Gogh's friends (cf. Wagner-Pacifici 1986). The 'Friends of Theo', on the other hand, wanted to communicate to the public that they were not just grieved but also outraged and determined to continue Van Gogh's crusade against political correctness (with Cohen as figurehead). As Cohen had already announced he would speak, they counter-scripted the public gathering not only as a moment to express grief but also as a public accusation against all those who bowed before the intimidation of Islamic extremists. At the very last minute Cohen heard that the 'Friends of Theo' had decided that Verdonk would replace Van Gogh's long-time personal friend Theodor Holman as second speaker. So, behind the scenes, representatives of the two opposing camps negotiated a format that accommodated both the possibility for expressing anger and the possibility of re-fusing the outrage into a conciliatory discourse (cf. Alexander 2004*b*).

Setting 3: The speech in the Al-Kabir mosque ('great mosque')

While Job Cohen, as mayor in charge of security policy, was beleaguered with security and intelligence issues, alderman Aboutaleb—locally in charge of integration and welfare policies—had more opportunities to speak in public. What is more, many people looked towards Aboutaleb with interest and curiosity as he was the city's first alderman of Moroccan descent. In an emotional address at the Al-Kabir mosque he argued that 'the Muslim community would be wise to not have their religion hijacked by radical extremists' (Breed 2007):

> I am a strong supporter of a powerful, diverse city in which there is a place for everyone. Yet a diverse city can only prosper when we have an agreement over the core values that we should all adhere to. For people that do not share these collective core values, there is no place in an open society like the Dutch. The freedom of religion, the freedom of speech and the principle of anti-discrimination are the most important parts thereof. Whoever does not share those values, should be so wise to draw his con-clusions and go.... Claiming tolerance is only acceptable if people behave tolerantly. It is reciprocal.

Aboutaleb claimed that many people must have observed the radicaliza-tion process of Mohammed Bouyeri, and hammered his fist on the table when he said that 'I should have known that! People should have told me! They should have reported this to me!' He also underlined that Moroccan parents had the duty to teach 'four, five year-olds' that 'the word is the only weapon to fight with others, not the fists or a weapon' (ibid.): 'I want to say that the Moroccan community is burdened with the extraordinarily weighty task of cooperating in restoring quiet and to work on the produc-tion of a "counter toxin" against intolerance.'

The situation possessed all the characteristics of a pseudo-event, includ-ing its ambiguity. While the setting of the mosque suggested that the prime audience was the local Islamic community, Aboutaleb clearly realized he was also communicating with a different, much larger audience. The context (staging) added to the news value of the speech and a series of television stations registered the event of the 'Moroccan alderman speaking to the Moroccan community'. Significantly, what was highlighted in the many media reports was Aboutaleb's statement that Moroccans that do not want to comply to the rule of law should 'pack up and go; there are planes leaving for Morocco every day...'—a storyline summarizing his speech which he first invented and used in a quick television interview directly after leaving the mosque.

Aboutaleb's performance thus effectively reconfigured the discourse of 'keeping things together'. While this was argued to be 'soft' by the critics of Cohen, the tough language and stern performance of Aboutaleb gave it a new meaning. Both the Al-Kabir speech and the subsequent street interview ('pack up and go...') were widely reported in the local and national media. Yet to insiders the chosen setting was curious, as the mosque in question was well known as comparatively liberal and a long-time partner of the municipality. Indeed, many of those present felt publicly reprimanded and expressed themselves as being flabbergasted by the performance of Aboutaleb.[7] But while staging a stern, decisive attitude to the outside world, the city intensively collaborated with a network of key players in the migrant communities and policemen from the neighbourhoods (*buurtregisseurs*) in which Moroccan migrants were highly represented. Apparently, collaboration was a story that simply could not be persuasively told in this context.

Setting 4: The mayor's address to the City Council

On the same day Mayor Cohen delivered a speech to the City Council, in which he sought to give meaning to the situation using the same 'freedom of speech' frame as at the manifestation of noise at Dam Square (Breed 2005): 'Dear council members, yesterday morning Theo van Gogh was murdered. A cowardly deed that arouses anger, horror, and dismay. A deed that impacted on the freedom of speech in this country, in our city.' He went on to explicitly defend his credo: 'I can tell you what I will do and what I am doing. Yes, keeping things together. Everybody knows. One can be cynical about this, I don't mind...' Yet if we examine the definition of 'keeping things together' we see that this had acquired an entirely new meaning: it was first of all about 'tough action', with the dia-

---

[7] Interviews by the authors.

logue with the city coming in second place: 'Keeping things together by tough intervention, yes. But not only that. Keeping things together is, in second place, the dialogue with the city.' Keeping things together is now first and foremost about toughness, not about softness and understanding as the antagonists would claim. And although it was a speech related to the murder of Van Gogh, here Cohen broadens the agenda and links it to the need for a tougher stand against youth causing trouble in neighbourhoods, drop-outs from schools, and so on.

- In the 'Tough Approach to Youth' (Harde aanpak jeugd), which is implemented in several neighbourhoods and by which hundreds of youths have followed a trajectory in Den Engh or Glenn Mills [youth detention centers, MH/JU]
- In the use of the Van Traa Team, as was done for instance in the case of the Kooistra Imperium [the Van Traa Team was developed to destroy the legal infrastructure of criminals, MH/JU]
- In the involvement of and cooperation between all aldermen of the central city and the boroughs in the implementation of the integral security policy. This means identifying hot spots, defining groups of offenders, improve security in public transport, etc.

Cohen's speech remained almost unnoticed in the outside world, but had a marked effect on civil servants. Interviews show that the speech impressed officials, lifted morale, and provided them with guideposts as to how to move on at a time when criticisms threatened to undermine support among civil servants and others responsible for promoting and implementing Amsterdam's official ideology of 'keeping things together'. Internally the speech served to perform authority, but it was not picked up in the media (although a short version of it was published in the Amsterdam newspaper *Het Parool*). The broader public, including the antagonists, remained largely unaware of this shift.

Setting 5: The talk show Barend & Van Dorp[8]

In the ten days following the murder both protagonists and several antagonists were guests in the late-night talk show *Barend & Van Dorp*. It was aired at 22.30 on an RTL commercial channel. At that time it had the highest ratings of all programmes addressing political issues in the Netherlands, and it was recognized to be a crucial non-official political stage. This can

---

[8] All excerpts are taken from the original DVDs of the programmes provided by RTL.

be illustrated by the fact that statements at *Barend & Van Dorp* frequently led to debates in parliament, as politicians consciously chose *Barend & Van Dorp* as the stage on which to announce their plans or visions, which then subsequently led to parliamentary (and further media) attention.

The programme was a typical example of the 'infotainment' genre (see e.g. Schutz 1997; Ilie 2001) combining information and entertainment, and was structured and scripted to stage guests as emotional subjects in a creative process of improvisation. Apart from the two presenters who lend their name to the show, Frits Barend and Henk van Dorp, the programme features a third actor, cast especially for this purpose: Jan Mulder, a former soccer star who is also a writer and columnist for *De Volkskrant* (a *Guardian*-type newspaper), invariably expresses strong emotions, ranging from moral outrage (very frequent) to strong praise (less frequent).

On 5 November 'Friend of Theo' Theodor Holman used the stage to read an open letter to Mohammed Bouyeri:[9]

> Dear Mohammed and friends, what a pity that it all came to this. We really had no idea that it was this sensitive. We have learned our lesson. How is your leg? Let's try to keep things a bit together but with a little mutual respect this should work... Could you give us a few guidelines about what we can say in the future? That this has to happen during Ramadan!...We hope that this letter does not contain anything that could hurt you and your fellow-believers. Please forgive us, we are also a little confused...

The letter was subsequently discussed with the other guests, two of whom were Muslim and one of whom was clearly uncomfortable with the tone and style of the open letter. Holman here connects the terrorist Mohammed Bouyeri with the general group of Islamic believers, thus using the murder to impose a discursive cleavage between Muslims and non-Muslims.

Both Aboutaleb and Cohen came to the show with the exact opposite goal in mind, aiming to defend their policy principle of tolerance and 'keeping things together'. However, their respective performances were markedly different in style and effectiveness (measured in speaking time and in terms of framing the subsequent discussion). Aboutaleb was guest on Monday, 8 November. He was immediately confronted with the 'Friends of Theo'. At the start of the programme sidekick Jan Mulder reported on a memorial party for Theo van Gogh. While Mulder described the presence of a flock of goats at that party with a sign saying 'for those

---

[9] Excerpts taken from video. Text also available via *www.sargasso.nl/index.php?p=57*.

who feel the urge', the camera showed a close-up of Aboutaleb's face.[10] The extraordinary interest in the emotions of Aboutaleb also came out in the way he was introduced: 'He came to the Netherlands when he was fifteen and is the first Moroccan, well, Dutch but with a Moroccan background, Ahmed Aboutaleb. He is also protected, cannot see his daughter. How is it to be alderman of Amsterdam?' The interviewers subsequently pitted the approach of 'keeping things together' against that of Deputy Prime Minister Gerrit Zalm, who had argued that we were 'at war'. When asked whether Cohen had been too soft, Aboutaleb passionately appealed to condensing symbols that are vague yet have a universal appeal in countering this critique from anti-multiculturalists:

> **Barend**: Cohen says for example: we have got to keep it all together. Well the journalists and columnists of certain papers are struggling to be the first to call Job Cohen a weakling, or something like that...uh...uh...an asshole (*klootzak*), if you know what I mean.
>
> **Aboutaleb** (*tries to answer*): there is, there is...
>
> **Barend**: So Zalm may feel a little worked up, feeling the heat from Geert Wilders [an MP and fervent critic of Islam, MH/JU], who just last week started his new party, 18 seats already according to Maurice de Hond [a mediagenic pollster running a Gallup type firm]...
>
> **Aboutaleb**: Yes.
>
> **Barend**: So if Zalm would have said that we should keep it all together, let's not get all worked up... We would have said [suggesting outrage] 'That is our deputy prime minister!'
>
> **Aboutaleb**: Yes, no it is indeed sort of drawn into those political cleavages.
>
> **Barend**: So haven't they got you worked up?
>
> **Aboutaleb** (*angry*): There is, let me restate this to this platform, no alternative to the line of Cohen, we have got to keep...
>
> **Barend**: No...?
>
> **Aboutaleb**: ...it together, it is a constitutional duty of the mayor to keep it all together.
>
> **Barend**: But you also read how people react to him.
>
> **Aboutaleb** (*determined*): It is complete nonsense to assume that there is any alternative. This is what you need for a world city like Amsterdam. A multitude of measures: and, and, and, and...The big picture is keeping that large group of the well-meaning people together in order to isolate and make visible the ill-meaning and to control them. But the majority must be kept together by the mayor, it is his constitutional duty, assisted by us as his aldermen. There is no alternative, so I would say let's stop moaning about 'keeping things together' because this really is the only way.

---

[10] Van Gogh had referred to Muslims as 'goat-fuckers'.

Aboutaleb here naturalizes what is, in fact, a highly controversial and contested approach. He is very stern, even aggressive ('there is no alternative', 'it is complete nonsense'). For Aboutaleb, 'keeping things together' has nothing to do with sloppiness or naivety: he invokes the constitution to back up their policy orientation. At one point he speaks in terms of various procedures ('a multitude of measures'). We will see below how Cohen employed the same repertoire without any success in this infotainment setting. But Aboutaleb does not tell us any details about the 'multitude of measures', and instead immediately links the policy to a broader issue: the distinction between well-meaning and ill-meaning groups.

Here he employs the repertoire of what we call 'bridging and wedging'. He provides an alternative for the dualism 'Muslim versus Dutch' by driving a wedge between the 'large group of well-meaning' and the 'small group' that needs to be isolated and removed. Keeping things together is reinterpreted for the general public: it is no longer soft. Aboutaleb is now authoritatively setting the terms of the discourse, and hitches onto another frame when he refers to the constitution and argues for action against ill-meaning groups. Usually these rhetorical strategies—to appeal to the rule of law and to argue for tough action against deviants—are reserved for his antagonists. But Aboutaleb succeeded in using the same signifiers for entirely different purposes: to defend the position of Cohen.

Cohen himself appeared on *Barend & Van Dorp* on 12 November, but only after his communication advisors had urged him to do so. *De Telegraaf*, the most popular newspaper of the Netherlands, had suggested that morning that Cohen had been weak in his handling of the aftermath of the Van Gogh murder,[11] and his goal was to set things straight. He seemed to be given that opportunity when the issue came up of whether the Amsterdam government had been 'too tolerant of intolerance' and the hosts suggested that if a mosque preaches intolerance or a discotheque discriminates against Moroccans they should be closed immediately: 'You administrators are not used to this. Take decisions…I mean it!' Cohen was put on the spot and responded:

> **Cohen**: Well it iiiisss, this point of intolerance, this was exactly what we discussed Tuesday in the local Cabinet, this point also came up there. I do agree with you. I agree that we did a number of things but if I look back on it now we should have been tougher.
> **Mulder** (*the former soccer star, exploding in anger, trying to find words*): But…there that…that is…that point is *crucial!* That is…

[11] Anonymous, 2004, 'Cohen wilde boycot Verdonk.' *De Telegraaf*, 12 Nov.

(*Several people talking*)

Van Dorp: Can I ask something?

Cohen:....which does not mean that we did not do anything...

Mulder: But this is *dramatic!!*

Cohen: But...But...yes one must not pretend as if, I mean, that would close the place down. That wouldn't be a way out.

Mulder: Yes it would! Yes it would!

While others gesticulate and raise their voice when they interrupt, Cohen remains calm and passive: he waits and thus only gets speaking time when someone gives it to him. When he starts speaking, he does so in a pedagogical tone: he explains. Two references to the government are prominent: he starts by saying that he and his colleagues talked about 'exactly this issue', and then emphasizes that it is not so easy to do something. Both tactics do not seem to work in this setting: Cohen does not get time to argue his case.

Analysis

The analysis of the media resonances of the various performances illuminates that alderman Aboutaleb profited significantly from what Herbst called media-derived authority, an authority acquired not by his formal status as alderman but by the type and amount of media attention he received (Herbst 2003). On *Barend & Van Dorp*, Aboutaleb effectively reframes the issue by drawing on the script he elaborated over the previous days, a script in which the speech in the Al-Kabir mosque played a central role. In an interaction with the media this speech had quickly been remodelled into a single storyline: 'if you don't like it here, leave!', or even more crisp as *koffers pakken!* (literally: 'pack your suitcases!').

On 4 November, the day after Aboutaleb's speech, the alderman featured prominently on the front pages of two national newspapers (*Het Parool* and *De Volkskrant*). They emphasized the clarity of his message (*koffers pakken!*), and featured him on photographs that showed him surrounded by bodyguards (Figure 3.1). The security was, in fact, not the result of his firm statements; Aboutaleb had been found on a death list of the 'Hofstad Group', the ring of extremists to which Mohammed Bouyeri belonged. Yet it reinforced the image of a bold political leader, speaking out and standing firm under siege, and it was this image on which the talk-show hosts drew while introducing him. In the following week two other leading newspapers (*NRC* and *De Telegraaf*) published page-long feature articles

Figure 3.1. Alderman Aboutaleb surrounded by bodyguards (reprinted with permission from ANP Photo).

in which he was celebrated for his unusual clarity and boldness. His performance was sometimes explicitly compared to that of Cohen, as when the newspaper *Parool* stated that: 'the toughness of Aboutaleb is just a little tougher, and his softness is just a little softer' than that of Job Cohen (Wiegman 2004). The content analysis of six national newspapers reveals that Aboutaleb was more successful than Cohen in performing authority in the period after the murder.[12]

An analysis of the discourse employed at the five stages described above reveals that Cohen and Aboutaleb in fact substantially reframed their discourse. Whereas critics ridiculed their urge to 'keep things together', they rebutted such criticism by reaffirming their commitment but simultaneously giving it a substantially different meaning. Suddenly 'keeping things together' was primarily about tough action, not understanding or dialogue. Furthermore, as the mayor's speech to the City Council reveals, he employed a discursive figure that linked the issue of terrorist violence to the widely reported obnoxious behaviour of youth groups in Amsterdam

---

[12] In the months November and December 2004 criticism of Aboutaleb was expressed 18 times while he received praise on 26 occasions. Cohen received criticisms 32 times and praise only 15 times.

neighbourhoods. Here he followed a controversial figure of speech that was employed by anti-immigration politicians who were constantly connecting 'terrorism' to 'street terrorism'. Cohen also accepted *post hoc* the critique of Van Gogh himself that had suggested that the mayor's approach to street gangs showed that his whole take on integration was utterly inadequate.

The public performances further reveal three distinct means to enact authority on the side of the protagonists. The first is what we call 'procedural assurance' and aims at showing that the event has not impacted on the routine-based functioning of existing institutions. Cohen consistently employed this repertoire, performing as mayor, staying calm, and emphasizing that established parliamentary institutions were adequate to deal with the present situation and that policies were appropriate. The prime stage for this performance was the City Council but, under pressure of his communication department, he later took to the stage in the *Barend & Van Dorp* talk show, in which setting this approach was less successful.

The second means we call 'emotive rerouting'. It was employed primarily by Aboutaleb. Here authority is established by a combination of (quasi-)spontaneous and strong expression of emotions and the subsequent linkage to strong, unifying symbols, a transformation for which we use the term 'rerouting'. In this repertoire the emotions of the debate are not avoided but come to be expressed by the political leadership, or as Aboutaleb puts it 'people want to see that you are moved by what has happened'.[13] Yet, crucially these emotions are subsequently channelled and transformed by tactically referring to unifying symbols, public policy commitments, and governmental institutions. It was employed in a range of non-parliamentary settings, of which Aboutaleb's speech at the Al-Kabir mosque is probably the most important. The organization of an event like the 'manifestation of noise' also fits within this repertoire.

The third instrument is 'bridging and wedging' and was employed by both politicians and by the antagonist 'Friends of Theo'. It is a political ordering as it attempts to 'wedge' (cf. Lakoff 2004) by showing precisely where the differentiation is between 'friend' and 'enemy', between the 'bad' elements and the 'good' elements. The politics of meaning in crisis situations is often about who is 'in' and who is 'out', and this makes bridging and wedging a sensitive task. It allows, in principle, for a redefinition of categories to facilitate the inclusion of some groups, and can serve

---

[13] Interview broadcasted by Radio 1, 21 Dec. 2004. Available from *http://www.vpro.nl/programma/marathoninterview/afleveringen/?programs=18160988*.

to build a bridge between two categories that were previously considered to be mutually exclusive (i.e. the Dutch and the Muslims; the Dutch and the foreigners; we the people of Amsterdam versus 'those politicians in The Hague'; etc.). But while reassuring one audience one might alienate another, as statements to migrant communities are also listened to by critics, or a broader audience is addressed via a suggested performance to a particular public. The Al-Kabir speech is a case in point.

The antagonist 'Friends of Theo' primarily employed the discursive tool of satirical cynicism which ridiculed the efforts of the political leadership as utterly inadequate. It was often effective in exposing weakness in the governmental rhetoric. Moreover, it invoked discursive categorizations that created markedly different divisions between friends and foes, 'us' and 'them'. This not only concerned the differentiation between the Friends of Theo and the others, but was particularly effective in linking the murderer Mohammed Bouyeri to Islam in general, framing Islam as a violent or backward religion. Being very rich in images and metaphors, their language was able to give a noticeably different idea of the meaning of the murder in the changing socio-political context.

In terms of dramaturgy, the performance of authority was markedly influenced by the mass media. The performance perspective leads to an appreciation of the many different stages on which crisis is enacted. It confirms the findings of Wagner-Pacifici in her description of the Moro kidnapping, where she concluded that 'there was no *one* ritual center in the Moro social drama...the picture was one of (albeit unequal) competition among several centers of symbolic discourse' (Wagner-Pacifici 1986: 275). In the ten days after the murder the media conformed to the well-known media format of using protagonists and antagonists, basically creating the Friends of Theo as the antagonist to pit against any statement by the authorities. So when, on the day of the murder, prime-time news covered the events, it brought news facts, including Cohen's statement at the press conference, into a mix with interviews of members of the cultural scene around Theo van Gogh. Here Heleen van Royen, a writer of best-selling women's novels and wannabe celebrity, not only displayed her grief, she was also quoted as saying: 'I do not hear anger from Cohen, I want to hear anger!' The point here is not that Van Royen is by herself an authoritative source; the point is that she is given the stage by a media format that functions according to the protagonist–antagonist logic (cf. Boomgaarden and De Vreese 2007 for the media coverage of the murder).

Interestingly, the most obvious means for an administrator to restore authority, procedural assurance, was ignored by the media (Cohen's speech to City Council) or rendered ineffective (in the talk show). The emotive rerouting and bridging and wedging as employed by Aboutaleb fitted much better into the ruling media-format, not least because it expressed that something out of ordinary was happening. As Wagner-Pacifici (1986) also found, at times of moral shock authority does not come from merely following the rules, it is also about the management of emotions. The media are not interested in statements made in settings where politics is routinely performed, so a disorderly press conference could be better than a routinely smooth-running one, a formal speech could be less effective than one with recognizable shock but that managed to reroute the emotions to governmental action.

In this case, emotive rerouting seemed to be a central means to take the heat out of the debate on such topics as radicalization, terrorism, and religion-based violence and restore the public authority. Performing authority was here based on acknowledging the dislocation, reinforcing the authority of the state, and creating a large 'in-group'. The curious combination of emotionality and governmental discourse was complemented by identifying 'out-groups' that threatened the cherished universals (the constitution, the state, society). In his speech at the Al-Kabir mosque, Aboutaleb employed the discursive tools of 'emotive rerouting' and 'bridging and wedging': he spoke with a lot of emotion and anger, but also provided cues as to what was expected of those who saw their future here. Emotive rerouting effectively linked his own emotions of outrage ('I should have known! People should have told me!' or 'it is nonsense') to symbols that are vague yet have universal appeal (the idea of the alderman as fully in control, i.e. as one who could control all information on radicalization of individual youth; or, in the talk show, the appeal to 'the constitution'), and was thus used to express testimonies of commitment to the public cause. Ultimately, Aboutaleb created a means by which the 'very large majority' of the people were provided with a way to move on.

The feel for the game

Performing authority depends on more than the rhetorical skills or rational calculation of political leaders. Politicians act out of a feel for the game that they have accumulated over time and in environments inside and outside of politics, what is described as a 'performative habitus' (see Chapter 1). Administrators, in this sense, are similar to the boxers in the ghetto analysed by Loïc Wacquant (2004): they develop certain discourses and dispositions over the course of many years that help or hinder them to respond tactically when they need to act in highly contingent, emotionally loaded and stressful situations. Thus, we argue that a large part of the behaviour of administrators in the initial phases of crises can be understood as responses that derive from *embodied dispositions* shaped over many years of symbolic labour. Embodied dispositions allow administrators a level of agency and tactical intelligence in particular settings but restrict at the same time the range of behaviours that can be performed.

The notion of 'performative habitus' (cf. Chapter 2) can help to transcend the dualism between the model of the politician as a rational actor in pursuit of predefined goals and the models of the politician's actions as being determined by a pre-given 'personality' or by the context in which he performs. We argue that the authority of a politician is *a co-production of his performative habitus and the setting in which he operates*. Aboutaleb was hailed for the authoritative voice he found in his Al-Kabir speech. But this capacity to use the occasion had been cultivated over the years in which he continuously had to keep an eye out for the concerns of the general (native) Dutch public in his daily interactions with religious and ethnic minorities. In other words, it was his performative habitus that allowed him to quickly switch repertoires and to authoritatively perform a role that was in great demand during the days after the murder. Cohen, on the other hand, could not take up the role of an outraged yet bold and determined administrator. 'There is just no way that Job will ever lose his temper,' sighed one of his associates in our interview. They consciously did not script Cohen in this role because he would not have been able to perform an unconventional role even if he wanted to. Due to his long career as an administrator (Cohen was a university vice-chancellor and junior minister in the Dutch cabinet before he came to Amsterdam), he embodied the disposition to always be reasonable and calm. The following newspaper comment is illustrative:

> Will Cohen ever succeed in getting rid of the image that was created not least by Van Gogh himself? Cohen, the man 'who confines himself to having tea with fundamentalist imams'. The 'preaching scoutmaster' of the multicultural society. This man can say: this is the final threshold. But will we believe that? Cohen tries. He tentatively defends himself. But still his message does not seem to come through: tough repression of criminality should be paired with dialogue. (Wiegman, 2004)

Although Cohen's communications staff was clearly aware of this image, the governmental script and role division also emerged in a more gradual way than just by consciously taken decisions. For instance, after the speech in the Al-Kabir mosque and some other performances, including *Barend & Van Dorp*, Aboutaleb received many positive comments in the press and directly from citizens. He says that this 'strengthened' him; he became 'confident'.[14] He now had a script and a role; as a Moroccan and practising Muslim, Aboutaleb was the only one with 'the ticket' to say the things he said to the Moroccan community without running the risk of being accused of racism.

Crucial in their role division is the employment of 'referential', respectively 'condensing' symbols. In the literature on moral shocks, it is argued that those who discuss an event in public are expected to, and will feel the need to, channel feelings of outrage and despair by appealing to 'condensing symbols'. Rather than 'referential symbols' with a relatively straightforward meaning, a 'condensing symbol' 'strikes deeper and deeper roots in the unconscious and diffuses its emotional quality to types of behaviour or situations apparently far removed from the original meaning of the symbol' (Sapir 1935, cited in Jasper 1997: 160). An appeal to such symbols can provide a compensation for the loss of senses of belonging, attachment, and familiarity that typically occur during dislocations (see also Dixon and Durrheim 2004). Whereas Aboutaleb frequently employs condensing symbols, Cohen mainly confines himself to referential symbols. That is an effective strategy in the daily business of government (the meeting between the mayor and aldermen in the local cabinet) or when explaining the practical difficulties encountered in executing policy ('how can we do this?'). However, judging the contextual responses, it failed to perform authority in the setting of an infotainment programme, whereas Aboutaleb's emotional, condensing symbols did help him to get speaking-time and argue his case.

The role division between Aboutaleb and Cohen was not only picked up, but also partly generated by the media. For instance, we saw how the hosts of the talk show addressed Cohen as part of a collective of bureaucrats: 'You administrators are not used to this. Take decisions...I mean it!' Thus, it was not only that Cohen mainly employed the administrative language of procedural assurance himself, but also that the media cast him in the role of the typical administrator. On the other hand, Aboutaleb was not framed as an administrator but as an outsider, an individual, a player, someone with whom you could disagree but who deserved to be admired for his biography and personal courage—an admiration that he

---

[14] Personal communication.

95

in turn used to direct people back to 'the system' ('there's no alternative'). Given the media's tendency to tell stories in simple formats of heroes and villains, it seems likely that the two roles were complementary and that the one could not have existed without the other.

Both Aboutaleb and Cohen were important for the performance of authority, each in his own right: Aboutaleb could do what Cohen could not do at that time. As soon as both politicians noticed how they had 'grown into' their respective roles, they agreed to stick to this division of labour and their staff arranged the performances of both politicians accordingly.

Ironically, it is the Muslim and Moroccan alderman who voices the concerns of large parts of the native Dutch population when he grows into his role as a fierce critic of the passivity of Muslims with respect to tendencies towards radicalism and extremism. Aboutaleb crucially performs much more on non-parliamentary stages like talk shows, discussions in various places throughout the city, and in radio interviews.

Yet while Aboutaleb resonated with those who thought a firmer stance was required, Cohen's performance resonated with those who felt Islamophobia was a bigger problem than Muslim extremism. As one of our Islamic informants put it: 'I only know one person in my environment who likes Aboutaleb. Nobody likes him, really.' At bit later he added, with an enthusiastic smile 'Cohen is cool—a cool Jew!' Building on their experience, the Amsterdam leadership had found a way to perform authority in an age of multiplicities.

4

Contested Authority in Rebuilding Ground Zero

Introduction

On 11 September 2001 a terrorist attack hit and destroyed the New York World Trade Center and its surroundings. The horrific facts are well known: the two towers collapsed, leaving more than 2,700 people dead and many more injured and traumatized. As the initial shock slowly faded and the rubble was being cleared, the crucial question became what to do with the site of the World Trade Center. What should one do with a site that was so full of symbolic meaning? What is more, how should one, in light of this shattering event, come to a decision? What sort of planning process could possibly account for the traumatic experience, the moral shock that the attack had been for society?

Theoretically, we could of course approach the rebuilding of Ground Zero as 'just another' siting issue. Surely there were many different interests that were played out in the policy process, and probably those who were most powerful in the end more or less got what they wanted: mobilizing relations, imposing their ideas, ignoring demands from others. Moreover, it never was to be a fully open process, as many restrictions came from the many rules and regulations that needed to be respected for a project of this size and magnitude. And those rules and regulations could, of course, themselves be mobilized to exert authority, to block decisions, or to twist the development in a particular direction.

If the history of the site could tell us anything, it was not reassuring. The WTC had always been more than simply two tall skyscrapers (Glanz and Lipton 2003). The project was surrounded with controversy from the start, as the building of the complex required the demolition of 164 buildings and the closing of five streets. Local community groups depicted the scale of the complex as alien and inappropriate to Lower Manhattan, whereas architectural critics scorned the Yamasaki design. But when built, the WTC came to be seen as a landmark, and quickly became part of the psyche of the city and its inhabitants (Fernandez 2002; cf. Nasr 2003). It figured as an icon for the United States in numerous popular movies, and it had, partly because of its symbolic appeal, already fallen victim to terrorist bombing once before 9/11, in 1993, when an extremely powerful bomb damaged several floors and killed six people.

Yet one does not necessarily have to be aware of the peculiar history of the World Trade Center to appreciate the semiotic importance of the WTC site after the terrorist attack of 2001. Before 9/11 the WTC represented one of the key symbols of American capitalism, with other markers such as 'Wall Street' and the 'Dow Jones'. It was the unrivalled centre of the global economy (Alexander 2004b)—even though only a year before 9/11 the Port Authority of New York and New Jersey had wanted to demolish the expensive and uncomfortable building and only abstained from this because the costs of removing asbestos were too high. This alone implies already that, with the towers gone, what would be done with the site was to be an intricate semiotic act. The rebuilding of 'Ground Zero' would, potentially, be judged in terms of the way in which 'America' or even 'the Western world' responded to the challenge of Islamist terrorism. Let us retrieve and reconstruct the politics of meaning that took place following the impact.

Starting from scratch: 'Ground Zero'

The symbolic inscription of the WTC site starts immediately as it is redefined into 'Ground Zero'. It expresses the broadly shared feelings of many whose lives have been shattered. Yet 'Ground Zero' is also a confusing term.[1] It suggests a need to start from scratch; an annihilation of history. But while the buildings might have been destroyed, the site is not empty; quite the contrary, it is full of competing meanings. What these meanings are, how these meanings relate to one another, and what significance they have for the process of rebuilding are, initially, open and ambivalent issues.

---

[1] The term 'Ground Zero', now generally used to refer to sites destroyed by bombs, originally was a reference to the Trinity Site, the place where the first nuclear bombs had been detonated in 1945.

In terms of power relations the situation was relatively straightforward, at least if we confine ourselves to the rebuilding of the complex itself. The Port Authority of New York and New Jersey owned the land, and property developer Larry Silverstein and his partner Westfield America, an international shopping-centre operator, had signed a ninety-nine-year lease on the 10 million-square-foot WTC just weeks before the event. According to the lease, Silverstein and Westfield had the right to rebuild what was there before 9/11—but for deviations from the design approval of the Port Authority was needed (Goldberger 2002*a*; Gittrich and Herman 2001). Given the fact that Westfield and Silverstein Properties had to pay on the lease, their concern was to rebuild as much office and retail space on the site as quickly as possible. The Port Authority and Larry Silverstein (and, to a lesser extent, Westfield America) constituted two very strong actors with a big commercial interest in rebuilding. Indeed, if we only take the legal rights and the ownership of the land into account, the rebuilding could be expected to be decided between these two parties. Yet given the symbolism of the WTC and 9/11 this planning process was unlikely to simply be about rights, building volumes, square feet, building layout, and 'programs'.

The politicians in charge, Governor Pataki of New York and to a lesser extent Mayor Rudy Giuliani, appreciated that 'planning business as usual' was not a credible option. In November 2001 they set up a special public organization to oversee and control the process of rebuilding the site: the Lower Manhattan Development Corporation (LMDC).[2] The LMDC also got the important responsibility to distribute the state and federal funds destined for rebuilding Lower Manhattan. Its task was complex: how to deal with strong parties with equally strong legal rights and economic incentives to rebuild; with a societal need to come up with a symbolically adequate answer to the attack on one of America's prime symbols of success; and with a political need to devise a process that would satisfy an array of politically highly sensitive claims to the area. The LMDC committed itself to making the redevelopment of Ground Zero into 'an open and participatory' process and promised to organize the planning in such a way that the many sensitivities would be taken into account.

What this means exactly was initially unclear; even the exact legal relationship between the LMDC and the Port Authority remained undefined,

---

[2] Allegedly, the creation of the LMDC was also a safeguard to make sure that Democratic candidate Mark Green, the then assumed successor to Rudy Giuliani as mayor of New York, could not get control over the rebuilding process. It is perhaps significant that when Green lost to Michael Bloomberg, the LMDC Board was expanded with four members, to be appointed by the mayor and an extra one by the governor.

and their respective jurisdictions would not be clearly demarcated for a long time. Given the stakes, this is a remarkable omission that can partly be explained by the awareness of the mutual entanglements and interdependency. The insecurity about how one can arrive at a workable decision in an ultra-sensitive case like rebuilding Ground Zero was felt at the time, or as LMDC president Lou Thomson put it (*Gotham Gazette* 2002):

> The exact legal relationship of our corporation to the Port Authority has never been precisely defined. One reason we entered into the collaboration agreement with the Port Authority is to avoid questions concerning whether the Port or LMDC has ultimate decision power but roughly, I believe, the Port has ultimate legal authority over the site. And we, in conjunction with the city, have the power off the site.

The political sensitivity enhanced the depth of the institutional void. Who was in charge, if anyone? Could the established rules be applied? Or was the political meaning of the event such that it called for a unique, tailor-made institutional process? Public pressure groups asked for both more involvement in the process and for a 'visionary leader', stating that democracy and leadership go together and urging 'one governmental body to develop a transparent, long-term process for the rebuilding and to be solely accountable for that process' (Kuo 2003)—the *New York Times* even called for a 'sensitive Moses' (Purnick 2002)—referring to Robert Moses, the controversial master-builder who left his imprint on New York in the mid-twentieth century. With the installation of the LMDC, Pataki and Bloomberg essentially and deliberately *created* ambivalence about which rules should apply, and hence they opened an arena for contestation in which all sorts of actors could claim the right to have a say. How did this process evolve?

On being authoritative at Ground Zero

In situations where one is not entirely sure if one's own definition of the situation is generally accepted, political actors have two options to exert their authority. They can either simply try to impose their own definition of the situation on others and make claims to authority ('I am the owner', 'I have the experience', 'I am the expert'), or they can try to circle round the question, feeling out the variety of ways in which others relate to the situation. In the former case one claims that everything is 'just normal', and one can see actors addressing the issue of 'what should be done' head-on, using the vocabulary that confirms their claim to authority ('legal contracts', 'track record', 'acclaimed authority'). In the latter case people tend to tell stories: stories of experience, stories of memories, stories of expertise, and stories of governance. Whereas the power of the direct mode lies in its clarity, the second mode thrives on ambivalence. Narratives can be 'read' and understood by different audiences; they can help to convey meaning across the boundaries of particular institutional backgrounds. Examining the stories of Ground Zero, we can make out four different discourses.

Discourse I: The Program

The Program is a discourse that suggests 'business as usual'. Uttered primarily by powerful players, it is the prime discourse that seeks to suggest that, despite the tragedy, in the end the approach to rebuilding is pretty straightforward. Everything is 'just normal', and hence this is a way of reasoning about rebuilding that privileges financial, judicial, and commercial arguments. On 5 October 2001 the *New York Times* quotes Silverstein as saying (Stanley 2001): 'I am obligated by my lease to pay rent for 99 years, I am obligated to rebuild, and I have the money to rebuild...It seems to me I am going to end up rebuilding; the only question is how best to accomplish that.' Mayor Bloomberg argues in July 2002 (Hirschkom 2002): 'Nobody knows what any building would look like.... You have to see who wants to rent or buy and when the economy really needs them.' It is a discourse prioritizing feasibility and an assessment of returns, as indicated in the argument made by Silverstein in September 2001 (Wax 2001): 'It's more economically feasible to do 50-storey buildings...Constructing four towers at heights similar to the rest of the Manhattan skyline would avoid creating a new set of terrorist targets as well as erase fears businesses might have of renting space 100 storeys up.'

In the political arena this discourse will, by itself, not be able to generate the widespread legitimacy that most of those involved deem necessary. On the other hand, it has the obvious advantage of being very well supported by legal rights and financial power and developing interests.[3] This line of reasoning is partly supported by the Port Authority of New York and New Jersey, not least because of financial reasons (McGeveran 2002): ' "However that property [the WTC] is ultimately planned, the important

---

[3] Leaseholders Silverstein and Westfield America have a legal right to rebuild the rentable space that was lost when the towers were destroyed, and Westfield even has the right to expand the retail space by 30% (Goldberger 2002*a*).

thing from the P.A.'s point of view is that we address the need to have a comparable revenue stream," said Mr. Martini. "I think we'll depend on a lot of input from a lot of people, so long as everybody understands that somehow the Port Authority has to receive revenues." ' These revenues are necessary to finance public transportation infrastructure, for which the Port Authority bears regional responsibility. But as a public agency, the Port Authority also has to take into account the view of the citizens of New York and New Jersey—on whose list of priorities revenues, retail space, and legal rights do not figure high.

Discourse II: Memorial discourse

Early on, memorializing becomes the predominant way to address the central issue of rebuilding Ground Zero. While in office Mayor Giuliani focuses on relatives of the victims rather than on rebuilding, and he seconds their plea to designate the entire 16-acre area as a memorial. His successor Bloomberg takes a different stance, recognizing the importance of rebuilding for restoring the city's economic vitality. This leads to conflicts with groups like the Coalition of 9/11 Families, Give Your Voice, and September's Mission, who point to the fact that Ground Zero is the final resting-place of their loved ones. For them, even the use of casual building terms like 'street grid' or 'property value' is painful and disrespectful. This claim has direct consequences for what should be done (Coalition of 9/11 Families 2002: 3): 'Treatment of the site must respect the personal grief of all families of victims of 9/11, and the collective pain and shock experienced by the city, state, nation and entire world....Structural development at the site should serve the purpose of memorializing the many facets of the events of September 11th for future generations.' John Whitehead, newly appointed as head of the LMDC suggests that (Gittrich and Herman 2001): 'We need a very important memorial of some sort, be it a park, a chapel, who knows what it should be. But land must be set aside.' When Larry Silverstein points out that he feels obliged to rebuild and has the money to rebuild, he adds that 'a memorial' at the site to the victims of the attack 'is necessary and totally appropriate' (Wax 2001). Memorial discourse captures the need to move very carefully, acknowledging that many other actors have a 'right' to speak on what should happen at the site. But how to accommodate that right with The Program? Stephen Push of the Families of September 11 argues that building commercial buildings in the exact spot where the towers stood will be 'sacrilegious' (Gittrich and Herman 2001); many families of victims emphasize that the site is a 'sacred, hallowed space' for them. The discourse of 'memorial' resonates widely, but while some suggest this is about 'a memorial', others see it as a way to conceive of the whole site. What is a good memorial? Leaving the land free? A tower? A chapel? A park? The Coalition of 9/11 Families (2002: 3) has strong views: 'The site must be treated with all of the reverence due to a hallowed burial ground.' Yet others link the idea of memorial, quite remarkably and directly, to the ideas of The Program, suggesting that the memorial will give the site new potential: 'The site can have a positive impact on the economy of the City through its contribution to tourism and to the cultural and spiritual life of New Yorkers' (ibid.). The need for appropriate commemoration of the dead is combined with the positive economic effects this could have for the area. The outgoing mayor, Rudy Giuliani, emphasizes in his farewell address that (Cardwell 2001): 'I really believe we shouldn't think about this site out there, right behind us, right here, as a site for economic development. We should think about a soaring, monumental, beautiful memorial that just draws millions of people here that just want to see it.'

Designating the whole area as a memorial is seen as economically and socially infeasible, and memorial discourse at some point gets its focal point in the idea that the 'footprints' of the two towers of the WTC should fulfil a special role. At the first LMDC public hearing, on 23 May 2002, Edith Lutnick, executive director of the Cantor Fitzgerald Relief Fund, argues: 'We polled our families, to see what it was that they wanted, and what they said was they wanted the memorial to be where the people that we loved and lost lived. They would like the memorial to be the footprints of the two buildings and the mall area directly in front of it.'[4] The metaphor of the 'footprints' sticks in the imagination and solidifies when Governor Pataki, up for re-election, embraces the idea that nothing should be built on the 'footsteps' of the Twin Towers. So respecting the footprints becomes the way to pay respect to the families of victims of the event.

Memorialism structures the discussion of the initial phases of the rebuilding process. At a minimum, 'memorial' comes to be a compulsory prefix. The six initial plans presented by the Port Authority the LDMC in July 2002 are called Memorial Plaza, Memorial Square, Memorial Park, Memorial Promenade, Memorial Triangle, and Memorial Garden. Memorial Plaza and Memorial Square do not build on the footprints of

---

[4] See for transcripts: *http://www.gothamgazette.com/rebuilding_nyc/features/public_hearing_one/victims_families/lutnick.shtml*.

the Twin Towers, whereas Memorial Triangle leaves the footprint of the south tower free and includes a public pavilion on the footprint of the north tower (Lower Manhattan Development Corporation 2002a). The architects had merely worked according to the parameters given to them by the Port Authority and Silverstein Properties, that combined the need to rebuild all rental space with the fear that companies would be unwilling to host their employees in high buildings—a 'magic number' of fifty storeys had appeared virtually overnight (Nasr 2003: 202). The resulting six designs are as difficult to distinguish from each other as their names already suggest. None of them comes near the symbolic sign of strength New Yorkers long for: 'They all look basically the same', or worse still: 'They look like Albany' (Berkey-Gerard and Pearson 2002) are common reactions, and the *New York Times* describes the designs in an editorial with the ominous title 'The Down Town we don't want'). Given the worldwide high media profile of the meetings, the devastating criticisms are virtually impossible to ignore, causing the PA and the LMDC to start the process all over again.

Discourse III: Phoenix

Memorial discourse has found its focal point in the footprints. But is that to be it? The discussion shows a growing sense that something more is needed, calling for a symbolic statement that will reflect the capacity to grow stronger, to 'soar'. Cleverly, outgoing Mayor Giuliani refers to it in his farewell address (Cardwell 2001):

> We have to be able to create something here that enshrines this forever and that allows people to build on it and grow from it. And it's not going to happen if we just think about it in a very narrow way....This place has to become a place in which when anybody comes here immediately they're going to feel the great power and strength and emotion of what it means to be an American.

Initially this 'Phoenix discourse' is expressed in the call to rebuild the Twin Towers (Ed Koch allegedly said 'Rebuild them exactly as they were', and several polls found a considerable percentage of respondents in favour of rebuilding). Calls like these led to a growing worry, especially on the part of experts such as architects, that the newly emerging consensus would lead to too direct a 'translation' of the deeply felt and widely shared wish to commemorate into cityscapes that fall short of the design possibilities: what is required are 'monuments as imaginative as the immensity of the tragedy' (Stark and Girard 2006: 2). But this urge on the part of designers is quickly followed by the worry of a rival group of experts, urban planners, that a wrong programme would lead to 'proposals in which design leads the program instead of the program leading the design' (ibid.), thus reiterating a familiar line of quarrelling in the professional debate among architects and planners.

Later on 'Phoenix discourse' is rephrased and gains in subtlety. One of its most outspoken protagonists is Paul Goldberger, architecture critic for the *New Yorker*; like other designers he seeks to guide the process away from a mere rebuilding of the office space ('Albany'), into a more daring, more innovative direction (Goldberger 2001):[5] 'The thing to do, I am more and more convinced, is to build a great tower—not an office building or an apartment tower, but just a tower, like the Canadian Broadcasting tower in Toronto, or the Eiffel Tower—that can be an observation tower and a television tower and, most of all, a symbol.' The public similarly calls for a restored confidence and pride in a renewed skyline: 'Please do not diminish the memory of all of these good people [the victims] by building 50-, 60-, or 70-storey mediocre buildings on the site. Please, if you are going to put buildings on that site, build one of the seven modern wonders of the world. And please, give us a skyline that will once again cause our spirits to soar.'[6]

Discourse IV: Revitalization

Once memoralization seems to resolve the sensitive issue of paying respect to the victims and their families in rebuilding Ground Zero, local groups start to call attention to their particular stake. These groups, most notably R.Dot ('Redevelop Downtown Our Town'), argue against a 'Necropolis' and make it clear they 'don't want to live next to a cemetery'. Residents feel that they are not being heard in the process, and fear that grand construction efforts will continue to disrupt their lives for several years (resident of Battery Park City, quoted in Low 2004: 336.): 'Remember that there is a community here that needs to continue with their lives. I have faith that in the end it will be wonderful. I was at "Listening to the City". But we have lives, we need emergency services, shopping. We have daily lives. Don't forget our needs during the

---

[5] Cf. also Goldberger's (2002*b*) keynote address at the Regional Planning Association, available from *http://www.rpa.org/pdf/ra2002-goldberger.pdf*.

[6] Transcript from public hearing, available from *http://www.gothamgazette.com/rebuilding _nyc/features/public_hearing_one/build_high/excerpts.shtml*.

rebuilding. We are willing to help, want to help, but allow us to go on living in the meanwhile.'

Moreover, they challenge the claim that the task of redeveloping Ground Zero is to be confined to the 16-acre site. It should be a broader effort to rejuvenate Lower Manhattan, to undo some of the mistakes that had been made when the WTC was constructed and produce an accessible and vibrant environment. Rebuilding should help to correct the failures of the past, particularly by revitalizing the commercial environment and by restoring the old street pattern that had been wiped out when the Twin Towers were built. It is a new claim that takes issue with an emerging combination of a maximum capacity office programme-cum-memorial. For instance, the Civic Alliance to Rebuild Downtown New York, a coalition of more than eighty-five business, community, and environmental groups, in partnership with the New School University, New York University, the Pratt Institute, and the Regional Plan Association, argues in February 2002 that (Anonymous 2002): 'the best monument honoring those who died at the trade center would be the reconstruction of the area as a beautiful and liveable new district of the city and a revitalized center of the regional economy.'

Organizing the policy process

So initially the public corrects The Program, and designers help them to do so (Memorial, Phoenix). In the meantime, planners tend to see the redevelopment process as a chance to correct what has gone wrong on the ground or even below the surface (Revitalization). The focus comes to lie with the definition of a positive statement, a confident proclamation of the strength of the city. Jonathan Rose of the Congress for the New Urbanism thinks it (Anonymous 2002): 'an opportunity to rethink our cities... Rarely have we had a large site, where people accept density, that has world recognition, at the center of so much transit. It's almost like we have a chance to look at what we did wrong with urban renewal in the 1960s and do it right this time.' Alex Garvin, head planner at the LMDC, suggests (Berkey-Gerard 2002): 'It is important to think about lower Manhattan as a way to change the entire city of New York... It's not just another project.' With four discourses suggesting different orientations for development and a political commitment to an open process at hand, the question is how to arrive at a widely shared plan for rebuilding.

The policy process on the rebuilding of Ground Zero is not merely complicated by the fact that there are so many different ideas and visions on the table; the whole process brings out the features of the politics of multiplicities. It is clear that the authority of the old politico-administrative routines is contested. Even if there had been a business consensus on what to do, just 'imposing' this on the political process will not work. Rebuilding Ground Zero is 'the world's most visible urban redevelopment project' (Sagalyn 2005), and takes place in a fully 'mediated' environment (cf. Bennett and Entman 2001). Politics is to be conducted across a range of stages where different actors can reach out to various key audiences, using a myriad of ways to influence the decision-making process. As the initial reluctance to make bold statements withers away, lots of competing ideas start to float around, some with political heavyweights backing them up. Legitimacy has to be derived from the process, not from a reference to having been appointed to do something, or simply having the legal rights. In such a situation of institutional void one must think about the various ways in which the acts of policy-making themselves convey meaning, give people a sense of who is in charge, of what is at stake, and how this is received by the variety of audiences that are at least very interested and in some cases nothing less than genuinely concerned and deeply suspicious. The policy process becomes a sequence of staged performances in which not one but two things have to be settled: (1) what to build at Ground Zero; and (2) how to decide. As the LMDC is to coordinate the process, we will follow them in their efforts.

Initially, the LMDC has to draft a plan for the process. Alexander Garvin, head of planning at the LMDC, argues that the events of September 11 underline the importance of involving citizens in public policy decisions. 'This was an attack on democracy, and we need to demonstrate to the world how a democracy functions...There's no choice here' (Rosegrant 2003). This is an example of a *positional statement*: a claim that, if not rebutted, creates a particular discursive reality (cf. Chapter 2). As nobody dares to speak against Garvin, it creates the storyline that remains central in the whole rebuilding process: we must rebuild like a democracy. At first this storyline supports the creativity in finding practices with which to give meaning to the storyline; later on it serves as an unintended reference to the 'scam' that the whole process had become. By invoking the idea of an 'attack on democracy', Garvin puts his LMDC forward as the appropriate organization that could deliver on the responsibility to secure a broadly supported plan.

If Ground Zero is a case *sui generis*, the LMDC is to be the unique institutional vehicle to deal with it.

By allowing the public in, the relative freedom of powerful stakeholders such as the Port Authority and leaseholder Silverstein is confined. September 11 had left the Port Authority as a traumatized organization. It lost seventy-five of its members, including its director, plus its former headquarter in the WTC—approximately 2,000 of its employees narrowly escaped death. That might explain why the LMDC could initially expand its power base without directly confronting the PA. However, when the LMDC issues a request for design proposals (RFP) in March 2002, protests of the PA force the corporation to withdraw it. A second RFP is issued on 23 April by the Port Authority, 'in cooperation with the Lower Manhattan Development Corporation'.[7] After this, the LMDC and the PA negotiate a Memorandum of Understanding that finally formalizes their relationship. Although the agreement, according the press release, 'affirms the close partnership that the two agencies have developed', public demarcation statements further underline how tense relations are.[8] For instance, PA director Seymour is quoted in the *New York Observer*, saying that (McGeveran 2002): 'It's no secret the Governor wants the LMDC out there to manage the public process and get public input, and the Port will be doing the planning', and that: 'We can't lose sight of the fact that it's the Port Authority's property, and the Port Authority's responsibility for what is eventually re-created on the site.'

As the powers of the LDMC are legally vague, it depends heavily on public support for its legitimacy. But as the LMDC is a new institution, the trust of the public is by no means self-evident. This implies that it has to be very conscious about its actions, as the various audiences will read any statement in an effort to understand what sort of institution the LMDC is trying to be. Having been criticized almost immediately after its inauguration in November 2001 for its 'business, white, and male' bias, the LMDC initiates nine advisory boards, with representatives of various stakeholders, in January 2002. It needs to constantly perform to the script of the rebuilding as being an open participatory process and, acting outside the reach of the safety-nets of representational democratic organs, to stage the policy process in such a way that the legitimacy of its decisions

[7] Press Release, 23 Apr. 2002. 'Governor Pataki, Mayor Bloomberg set target for LMDC plan; Port Authority issues RFP's for integrated urban design, transportation study.' *http://www.empire.state.ny.us/press/press_display.asp?id=115.*
[8] Ibid.

will be enhanced and entry to many different groups will be allowed. Hence it has to take account of the fact that all these different constituencies are actively monitoring its actions and are ready to attack it as soon as it seems to not pay attention to their special concerns. It has to position itself vis-à-vis various new associations that have become active, such as the aforementioned Civic Alliance to Rebuild Downtown New York and New York/New Visions, a coalition of twenty-one architecture, planning, and design organizations that aim to improve the quality of the planning process, and the variety of aforementioned stakeholder groups. To channel all these contributions it sets up a range of events that are to result in the sequence of staged performances that is, eventually, supposed to produce a legitimate decision.

Here two important practices can be made out: (1) 'Listening to the City', a major public meeting, held in the Jacob Javits Center on Saturday, 20 July 2002 to 'shape the future of Lower Manhattan', the outcomes of which contribute to the brief for the 'design study'; and (2) the 'design study', out of which the choice of the architects emerges and in the context of which designer-experts can present their contributions to the process of rebuilding (August–December 2002) with the public announcement of the result of the design study in February 2003.

Table 4.1. Rebuilding Ground Zero: chronology of events

November 2001	Mayor Giuliani and Governor Pataki found the Lower Manhattan Development Corporation (LMDC).
January 2002	Nine advisory councils are added to the LMDC, representing, among others, residents of the WTC area and the families of the victims.
February 2002	'Listening to the City'.
May 2002	LMDC hosts its first large public hearing.
July 2002	PA and LMDC unveil six designs for the WTC area; start of the campaign for citizen participation. 'Listening to the City II': citizens react very negatively to the presented designs.
August 2002	LMDC starts the 'design study'.
December 2002	The nine winning designs are presented.
January 2003	LMDC organizes public hearings on the designs.
February 2003	The Libeskind design is chosen.
July 2004	Cornerstone for Freedom Tower is laid.
May 2005	Freedom Tower to be significantly redesigned to satisfy new security concerns.
March 2006	Construction on Freedom Tower site commences after Governor Pataki publicly says: 'start building [FT] or move out of the way.'
April 2006	Silverstein surrenders control of the $2 billion Freedom Tower, along with more than one-third of the Ground Zero site, to the Port Authority of New York and New Jersey. Silverstein retains the right to build three office towers on the most valuable parcels.
September 2006	The federal and New York State governments agree to become anchor tenants in FT.

Reaching out

In February 2002 the Civic Alliance organizes a meeting called 'Listening to the City', to develop a broader sense of what vision people have for redeveloping Lower Manhattan. The meeting is facilitated by AmericaSpeaks, a non-profit organization specialized in '21st century town meetings'. According to the president and founder of AmericaSpeaks, Carolyn Lukensmeyer (Rosegrant 2003: 12): 'Democracy is not just participation...It needs to be informed participation. If you don't have the informed side of it, you don't have the core of democracy.' This approach—facilitated by modern communication technology—is welcomed and adopted by LMDC and PA officials. On 24 April the LMDC and the Civic Alliance announce the intention to organize a 'major forum' to discuss the future of the trade center site. The format of the forum will be based on Listening to the City I; it is to be a fully scripted and staged event in public participation.

Listening to the City II

'Listening to the City II' is held in the giant Jacob Javits Center on 20 July 2002, and is followed by an exhibition of the six initial plans for the rebuilding of Ground Zero at the sacrosanct Federal Hall just off Wall Street (Fig. 4.1). It is organized by the Civic Alliance in cooperation with and subsidized by the LMDC and the Port Authority. As the organizations have a different focus, planning the agenda of the day proves to be extremely difficult (Rosegrant 2003: 7–8):

> 'I've never gone through a design process that was so politicized and where there were so many battles over things like sequence of activities,' says Daniel Stone [of *AmericaSpeaks*]. Of particular concern was the question of who would begin. LMDC was determined to present the site plans in the morning when attendance was likely to be highest, and before reporters left to file their stories after lunch. The Civic Alliance, however, insisted that site decisions couldn't be made outside of the context of the larger goals of redevelopment, and that those macro issues had to go first.

At the Javits Center some 5,000 participants from New York and the tri-state area seek to have their say—an astounding number compared to the first version of Listening to the City, in which only about 600 persons participated. The organizers decide on this large number of participants partly to ensure that the meeting will be able to attract sufficient media attention: 'The New York media market is very competitive,' says project

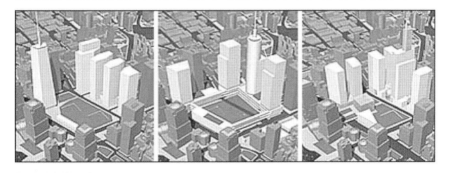

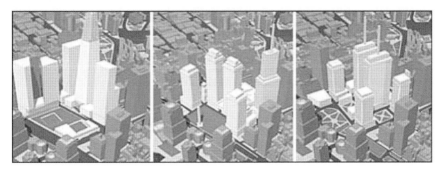

Figure 4.1. Ground Zero: the six designs as presented to the public in July 2002 (reprinted with permission from Lower Manhatten Development Corporation).

manager Ashley Boyd, 'and a 1,000-person meeting doesn't make headline news' (Rosegrant 2003: 7).

The focus of discussion is the six plans that have just been released by the LMDC. Using high-tech information equipment, opinions of the people are collected on key issues. These are then classified and generated into different development options, and on some issues people can vote. Governor Pataki argues that (LMDC 2002*a*):

> The six plans provide a framework within which the various options for the World Trade Center site can be examined. Now it's up to the public to use these plans to generate their own ideas for the site and to play an active role in the redevelopment effort.... The LMDC and the Port Authority have done an excellent job developing this first round of plans and finding innovative ways to involve as many people as possible.

Excellent or not, the public is not immediately convinced that they are acting in the heart of an open process. Indeed, most participants did not believe that they had a pipeline to power or that their recommendations would be followed by decision-makers, but participated nevertheless because they wanted to be part of the dialogue (Polletta and Wood 2003: 15). Roland Betts, a member of the LMDC board, tries to reassure the participants, saying: 'Everyone seems to fear that the real meeting is going on in some other room. Let me tell you something—this is the real meeting' (Civic Alliance 2002: 5).[9] Whether this is true or not, the staging of this meeting with 5,000 people under the heading of a New York style 'town meeting' creates a media event which conveys the idea that the LMDC clearly is in the centre of the process. The second part of the 'Listening to the City' outreach is an exhibition at Federal Hall. LMDC president and executive director Louis R. Tomson mobilizes this setting to show the commitment to the resurrection and democracy:

> I can think of no better place to contemplate our nation's future than the site where the Bill of Rights was adopted and where George Washington pledged to uphold it as the first president. The exhibit continues this tradition by embodying our nation's most important guiding principle: democracy. By expressing their opinions and suggestions at the exhibit, the public will play an integral role in the rebuilding and redevelopment process. (LMDC 2002b)

Port Authority executive director Joseph J. Seymour takes up the reference and adds:

> Before it became the first home of the continental Congress, Federal Hall was the site of New York City's first city hall. New York and the United States really started here. How fitting that Federal Hall should once again be the site where New Yorkers and people from all over the region, can come to let their voices be heard, as we try to build a consensus on the plans for Lower Manhattan's rebirth. (ibid.)

In terms of staging an open and transparent participatory process, 'Listening to the City' should, despite all possible criticisms, be regarded a success (cf. Moynihan 2004; Polletta and Wood 2003; Rosegrant 2003).[10] Mediating a meeting with more than 5,000 people in the giant Javits Center is the sort of dramatic performance that was needed to show the commitment to involving the public. What is more, it has a real political effect. On 14 August 2002 the LMDC announces that, having examined

---

[9] This feeling was not limited to the citizen participants, but apparently also applied to the politicians. Sagalyn (2005: 40) quotes a respondent (who wants to remain anonymous) that: 'Everyone thinks they are missing something going on in another room, even the governor.'

[10] For a critical assessment, cf. Sorkin 2003.

the public response, the six designs are rejected and new designs are to be developed. This suggests that the public is indeed listened to. A comment from the former LMDC vice-president for design and planning suggests that this is not least because the organizers of the event had been able to generate intelligent information:

> It wasn't just that there was some overwhelming reaction of 'this is not good enough.'...There were other things that came out that had a big influence: 'we liked that promenade on West Street. We want our skyline back. We want a street grid. We want a variety of different sized open spaces, and we want you to treat the footprints with respect. (Garvin, as quoted in Polletta and Wood 2003: 26)

The 'design study'

The practice that the LMDC subsequently introduces is what it calls the 'design study'. This is not a standard phrase. A 'design competition' is standard practice in planning. It is a competition leading to the choice of one particular design that then gets built. In the case of Ground Zero the 'design study' is a new, ambiguous term introduced to generate ideas that could then be 'input' in a further process involving other actors (cf. Nobel 2003). The design study is to allow up to five selected architects to develop 'new flexible program alternatives shaped by public input'. But it remains unclear what the role of these alternatives will be. No Port Authority officials are present at the announcement of the new study, and Tomson, president of the LMDC, declares that the two agencies 'have different points of view on how to proceed' (Wyatt 2002). The press release of 14 August 2002 states the provision that (LMDC 2002c): 'LMDC/Port Authority planning staff and consultants, including Beyer Blinder Belle and Peterson Littenberg, *will continue to explore* varied approaches to the World Trade Center site based on the new program alternatives' (emphasis added). Indeed, the plan itself warns in bold script that '**This is NOT a design competition and will not result in the selection of a final plan**' (LMDC 2002d). If the LMDC wants to make this an open and participative process, this provision is a serious threat to live up to (self-imposed) expectations.

The 'design study' connects the LMDC to another key stakeholder, New York/New Visions, a coalition of twenty-one architecture, planning, and design firms that is brought in to help draw up the criteria and select the winner of the design study. Initially, Garvin asks NYNV to manage the competition, but the group is unsure about the motivations for this request and refuses the offer.[11] On 26 September 2002 nine designs are selected out of a pool of more than 400 contributions. In December 2002 the designs are presented.

At this point the LMDC starts to visibly lose control over the process. Key participants begin to doubt the strength of the 'official' process and other stages emerge. The Civic Alliance holds its own workshops for planners to come up with good plans, and Imagine New York stages alternative community workshops. These stakeholders are no longer sure about their own appropriate role in the process and the best way to exert influence. Should they confine themselves to the facilitation of deliberative meetings; should they actively advocate the plans that had resulted from those earlier deliberations; should they just remain monitoring insiders (cf. Polletta and Wood 2003)? As an indicator that the script no longer holds, on 12 December 2002, just days before the announcement of the winning design from the design study, Mayor Bloomberg of New York takes up a role as alternative director, setting the stage in his own terms:

> Next week, the LMDC will make public seven proposals for the future of the World Trade Center site—this is the product of months of work by some of the best design teams in the world. What you will see will be very different from the six site plans that were presented last summer. Some of these new designs make eloquent statements about what happened on 9/11; they truly are capable of instructing and inspiring future generations. Some speak of hope—and renewal—more powerfully than any words can. Some boldly restore the skyline—in ways that say, in no uncertain terms, this is New York—and the terrorists didn't win. Some do all three.... But no matter how magnificent the best designs for the 16 acres of the World Trade Center site prove to be, it must be complemented by an equally bold vision for all of Lower Manhattan—a New Beginning for Lower Manhattan—that meets the needs of all of New Yorkers...and of the entire region....We have underinvested in Lower Manhattan for decades....The time has come—to put an end to that, to restore Lower Manhattan to its rightful place as a global center of innovation—and make it a 'Downtown for the 21st Century'.[12]

---

[11] Sagalyn (2005: 42): 'Marcie Kesner ... was not sure why NYNV was being asked to manage it. Like other "on-call advisers", she was concerned that the LMDC might just want them to provide cover. The extent to which Garvin relied on the group was "flattering" but always caused NYNV committee members to ask, "What is our role?" '

[12] http://www.lowermanhattan.info/news/read_mayor_bloomberg_s_80515.aspx.

Bloomberg's speech seems to indicate that he inadvertently had fallen victim to the previous administration's decision to create an independent LMDC at arm's length from the established City Council. Realizing the bureaucratic power of the Port Authority, Bloomberg here tries to enlist and confirm the public as a key player to influence decision-making in his own city by talking to the press.[13]

On 18 December 2002 the results of the design study are presented. The stage is dominated by Daniel Libeskind, who, more than most other architects, masters the art of using narrative to capture the imagination. While the business coalition has just continued with the preparations for The Program, and has in the meantime forced Skidmore, Owings, & Merrill (SOM) into the design study, this is the moment at which any alternative has to present itself if it is to stand any chance. SOM presents itself discursively as if this is just a straightforward job they are ready to take on:

> Our proposal is to reconnect the city by creating a dense grid of vertical structures that support multiple strata of public and cultural spaces. Our vision is one that moves beyond the historical drive to build high only in order to maximize the limited resource of land, it is one that builds to multiply that very resource for the greater public. Our proposal covers 16 acres, and in turn, returns those 16 acres twice, by providing within its various horizontal strata, 16 acres of sky gardens and an additional 16 acres of cultural space. We believe that the future of the global city must provide substantive solutions for increasingly densified space; space for public, space for culture and the vitality of commerce that will support those resources and needs.... Our proposal reaches beyond the historical exchange of equal commerce for equal land. It doubles the return in our quest for quality of environment. And in turn gives Lower Manhattan a larger expanse of square footage dedicated to cultural activity than the sum of all the city's existing cultural spaces. It does this with the greatest efficiency, economically and environmentally. It provides for more than adequate retail and commercial space and does so by creating betterment for the public good.[14]

Although frequently referring to the public good, these architects relate primarily to Silverstein, the leaseholder, and frame their contribution as

---

[13] The speech also was a statement of *planning* in which the 'true' challenge was defined to be the redevelopment of Lower Manhattan and the key 'variables' were new high quality transport links. The costs of his plans added up to an estimated $10.6 billion, $8.8 billion of which would go into the infrastructure.

[14] *http://www.renewnyc.com/plan_des_dev/wtc_site/new_design_plans/firm_c/default.asp.*

an almost default 'client–architect' exchange ('a dense grid', 'the vitality of commerce', 'doubles the return', 'the greatest efficiency', 'adequate retail and commercial space'). United Architects frequently uses the memorial discourse, but primarily to describe the tourist qualities of its design:

> The entire site is a monument to the tragedy of 9/11 consisting of an interconnected series of five buildings that creates a cathedral-like enclosure across the entire 16 acre site. A vast public plaza and park is formed around the connected footprints by a protective ring of towers. A living memorial will develop over time becoming both a monument to the past and a vision for the future. Preserving the footprints of the World Trade Center, the memorial visitor descends seventy-five feet below ground along a spiral walkway to then look up through the footprints to the sky. Rather than looking down, the memorial directs visitors to look upward in remembrance. A Sky Memorial atop the first tower will allow visitors to complete the memorial pilgrimage by looking down over the hallowed ground where so many heroes lost their lives.

Peterson & Littenberg, who also participated in the first competition, take more or less the same approach, starting the presentation with: 'This plan creates a whole new city district with many different places and experiences.'[15]

Interestingly, the other architects interpret the event according to a different script. The consortium THINK, Foster, Libeskind, and to a lesser extent Richard Meier all basically present their plan to the public. What is more, they exploit the institutional void and arguably *create* the broader public as client and put forward their plans as offering solutions to public problems.[16] Here they pick up on a range of sensibilities that had emerged out of the public outreach meetings staged by the LMDC in the months before. This is THINK:

> The moral obligation in rebuilding Ground Zero is not just how best to remember those who perished in this tragedy, but how to make their memory the inspiration for a better future. The issues at stake in planning

---

[15] *http://www.renewnyc.com/plan_des_dev/wtc_site/new_design_plans/firm_b/default.asp.*

[16] The following quote is illustrative: ' "If you start with office buildings, all the money will get sucked up into the towers," argues landscape architect William Morrish, a member of the Think team. "So you have to start with streets and parcels, the public realm, to show that it is as important as the private world of the towers. When was the last time that a city created a public space that really was a public space? It's the great opportunity." ' Quote from Dillon 2003.

the site have a local dimension as well as global repercussions; therefore the design should address the specific conditions of our city from a perspective that could also transcend its limits. Ground Zero should emerge from this tragedy as the first truly Global Center, a place where people can gather to celebrate cultural diversity in peaceful and productive coexistence. Finding the proper balance between the two main objectives of the project—Remembrance and Redevelopment—depends on the way in which investment in the public infrastructure contributes to the Renewal of Lower Manhattan. An inspired plan will rededicate our City to the ideals of diversity, democracy, and optimism that have made New York the World's Center for the exchange not only of goods and services, but also of creativity and culture.[17]

Or Foster Associates:

The Rebuilding of the World Trade Center site is the most important urban planning and architectural challenge of our time. It is about healing, repair and rebirth. We have a duty to commemorate the dead in the form of a solemn and respectful memorial. We have a duty to repair and regenerate the city fabric. Above all, we have a duty to symbolize the rebirth of New York on the skyline, to demonstrate to the world the resilience, the resolve, the strength and faith in the future of all those who are dedicated to liberty and freedom....The renewal of the World Trade Center site can be the catalyst for the regeneration of the whole of Lower Manhattan. We can repair and rebuild the neighborhood street pattern that was eradicated in the 1960s. Fulton Street and Greenwich Street will be extended and revived. We can reinvent Liberty Street as a vibrant street market. Instead of a barren plaza, there will be streets on a human scale lined with shops, restaurants, cinemas and bars to ensure that the area has a life around the clock.[18]

Daniel Libeskind takes this one step further, very explicitly putting his design in the context of the popular imagination of the site (see Fig. 4.2):

I arrived by ship to New York as a teenager, an immigrant, and like millions of others before me, my first sight was the Statue of Liberty and the amazing skyline of Manhattan. I have never forgotten that sight or what it stands for. This is what this project is all about. When I first began this project, New Yorkers were divided as to whether to keep the site of the World Trade Center empty or to fill the site completely and build upon

---

[17] *http://www.renewnyc.com/plan_des_dev/wtc_site/new_design_plans/firm_e/default.asp.*
[18] Ibid.

Figure 4.2. 'Life Victorious': the Libeskind entry of the 'design study' (© Studio Daniel Libeskind)

it. I meditated many days on this seemingly impossible dichotomy. To acknowledge the terrible deaths which occurred on this site, while looking to the future with hope, seemed like two moments which could not be joined. I sought to find a solution which would bring these seemingly contradictory viewpoints into an unexpected unity. So, I went to look at the site, to stand within it, to see people walking around it, to feel its power and to listen to its voices. And this is what I heard, felt and saw.... The exciting architecture of the new Lower Manhattan rail station with a concourse linking the PATH trains, the subways connected, hotels, a performing arts center, office towers, underground malls, street level shops, restaurants, cafes; create a dense and exhilarating affirmation of New York. The sky will be home again to a towering spire of 1776 feet high, the 'Gardens of the World'. Why gardens? Because gardens are a constant affirmation of life. A skyscraper rises above its predecessors, reasserting the pre-eminence of freedom and beauty, restoring the spiritual peak to the city, creating an icon that speaks of our vitality in the face of danger and our optimism in the aftermath of tragedy. Life victorious.[19]

[19] Ibid.

Libeskind's performance is markedly different from the usual presentation of an entry in an architectural competition. He chooses a different key audience, a different language, and very different supporting acts. Unlike the other firms, Libeskind communicates with a personalized ('I arrived', 'I went back to the site'), emotional (amazement, death, hope, vitality, 'life victorious') narrative.[20] What is more, both Libeskind and THINK seek to develop an exchange with a range of public groups during the actual design study (Iovine 2003). Libeskind, quite obviously, shows himself well aware that this is a mediated event, and that the media are a component in the decision-making process in their own right. Himself staged by his PR-consultant, he appears live on *the Oprah Winfrey Show*, is interviewed in the *New York Times* in his cowboy boots and his glasses and in *Rolling Stone* to discuss his five 'coolest' things in the critical months of discourse formation and decision-making.[21] Libeskind turns into a public figure and wins himself a central role at the cost of such first-class designers as Norman Foster, who literally has no answer to the multi-stage performance.

Deciding on the design

At this stage of the planning process two distinct coalitions emerge, one centring essentially on building The Program, with Silverstein, the Port Authority, and SOM; another aiming at developing a broader public design with components from the discourses of Phoenix and Rebuilding, with a clear role for Civic Alliance, New York/New Visions, the planners from the LMDC, and in which both THINK and Libeskind located their designs. Whereas the first discourse coalition is well grounded in legal and economical practices and can operate outside the public eye, the second discourse coalition typically depends on public performances and outreach both for its legitimacy and influence.

Still it is unclear how to move on. Slowly the commitment to make the rebuilding of Ground Zero into a truly open process becomes compromised. In January the LMDC organizes 'public hearings'. Whereas the ambiguous and obviously heavily staged 'Listening to the City' created possibilities for participation, the traditional format of a 'hearing' predictably only arouses

---

[20] For full presentations of all plans, cf. *http://www.renewnyc.com/plan_des_dev/wtc_site /new_design_plans/*.

[21] For an analysis cf. Gillmore 2004.

irritation and disappointment—this exercise does not even figure high on Arnstein's (1969) age-old ladder of participation, where it would qualify as 'consultation' (but cf. Corona 2007).

However, the ambiguous commitment to openness is not the result of a 'decision' to decide elsewhere, although the costs of public participation were higher for the involved agencies in this phase of the process (cf. Moynihan 2004). There is evidence that no one knows exactly which stage(s) are relevant for the ultimate decision-making. Hence actors who allegedly are in control speak out in public in ways that suggest that they are attempting to *gain* or *keep* control: apart from Mayor Bloomberg in his address on 12 December, there are public statements from Betts (LMDC) on 10 December, Tomson (LMDC) on 18 December, and, probably most significantly, Silverstein on 31 January 2003. He sends a long open letter to John Whitehead as head of the LMDC, with offprints to all rebuilding officials of importance, underlining the need to be realistic and to rebuild as much space as possible. Arguably most insightful are his closing remarks quoted here:

> we certainly do not maintain that our group has the unfettered right to build whatever we desire...But we must find a way to make sure that all responsible parties come to agreement on a plan that will be architecturally spectacular, will meet the demands of the tenants that we must bring back to lower Manhattan and, most importantly, will assure the safety of the occupants of the buildings and assure them a fast, safe and efficient egress in the event of an emergency.[22]

His letter indicates that the LMDC tries to impose on Silverstein the claim that Libeskind should be given a powerful role as master-planner. Silverstein, who had until then put his cards on Beyer, Blinder & Belle as chosen builders and on SOM (David Childs) as architects, thinks it necessary to publicly reiterate that there is a clear difference between a master-plan and a built project. (When Silverstein was asked, after 'Listening to the City II', whether he had seen anything he would like to build, he answered: 'That wasn't the purpose of the thing'.)[23]

The vague commitments to 'openness' and participation that initially accompany the LMDC's declarations vis-à-vis the decision-making process and the emphasis on this being a collaborative effort, in the end generate unease among all parties, with what we might call the 'demarcation statements' of top players (Bloomberg in December, Silverstein in January)

---

[22] 31 Jan. 2003; the full transcript can be found at *http://reconstructionreport.org/article. pl?sid=03/02/03/2052224*; also cf. *http://www.nydailynews.com/news/story/56367p-52778c.html.*
[23] 10 Dec. 2002, *http://www.nydailynews.com/news/local/story/42241p-39866c.html.*

as the result. On 4 February 2003 the LMDC announces Libeskind and THINK as finalists. By then the lack of a clear and well-organized decision-making process makes several actors nervous (McGeveran 2003):

'The rebuilding process has become so convoluted that it's difficult to know what to make of the selection of the two design teams,' said Robert Yaro, president of the Regional Plan Association and chairman of the Civic Alliance to Rebuild Downtown. 'Both teams clearly represent some of the world's most talented architects, but it's not apparent what they'll be asked to do or what impact they'll have on the final master plan.' 'What we need is a clear decision-making process that incorporates public input every step of the way,' he continued. 'Now, it's impos-sible to tell who is making the decisions or what the process is for the next six days, not to mention the next six weeks or years.'

Yaro points out the problem that arose out of the failed design of the policy process: new publics emerged out of the discussions about the design study, only to be disregarded later on. In a politics of multiplicity a one-off design will almost never hold; the discursive dynamics is hard to anticipate and hence the commitments in the decision-making process should be reconfirmed and reiterated. Where necessary the procedures should be readjusted to be able to deal with situations that arise unexpectedly. Obviously there will be moments in which decisions are made, but it is also clear that the process needs space to handle the dynamics of a politics of multiplicity—particularly if the designs that emerge as winners depend on the support of a particular public.

On 27 February 2003 the LMDC chooses the design by Daniel Libeskind for the site of Ground Zero. The decision is reported worldwide as a victory for Libeskind, but the small print suggests otherwise. Days later the invention of a differentiation between 'master planner' and 'project architect' is reinforced, with David Childs being announced as suggested architect of (Silverstein's) Freedom Tower, while Libeskind should be seen as responsible for the urban layout.

After this the politics that was to be open and public disappears into the backstage of behind-closed-doors bargaining, with the odd breakout into the media for mudslinging and the attribution of blame. Every now and then actors seek to control the public unease by reassuring performances, the most remarkable probably being the laying of the cornerstone on 4 July (sic!) 2004. Larry Silverstein comments that 'the Freedom Tower will forever stand as a testament to our resilience, our resolve and our glorious rebirth. . . . Now, we build' (LMDC 2004). Alas, since then politics has gone back to the wrestling-mat. Unfortunately for those involved, the initial storyline is still in the public imagination. The commitment to 'rebuild like a democracy' remains the measuring-stick for all those monitoring the events in and around Ground Zero, with as an obvious result the sense that politics fails to live up to expectations, expectations which it itself has done so much to create.

Conclusion

Getting to an agreement about the rebuilding of Ground Zero was never going to be simple. It started reluctantly, then generated lots of enthusiasm, ideas, and attention, but afterwards turned sour. What began under the banner of 'we must rebuild as a democracy' and rose to be an interesting attempt at finding the appropriate dramaturgy of dealing with the many intricacies and widely differing interests, ended up being a hallmark case of 'old politics' dominated by clashing business interests, hard financial bargaining, a mayor fighting for re-election, leaseholder and owners suing insurance companies, and a politics of deal-making taking place behind closed doors. In this sense, nothing new. Indeed, it is very much a continuation of the story of the building of the original World Trade Center, a saga which is so wonderfully put into words in Glanz and Liptons' *City in the Sky*. Our interests here are with the dynamics of opening up, the moments at which the discussion on the future of Ground Zero was first forced open, then achieved its expression at the many stages at which the debate took place. Even if in the end the rebuilding of Ground Zero returned to old politics, with a media involvement that first and foremost prolonged the actors' internal contests, it teaches us something about how a politics of multiplicities works and might have worked differently.

The Ground Zero case is analytically interesting as it illuminates how discourse matters in policy processes. The discourse analysis shows that stories fulfil a central role in cases in which planning is to take place following moral shock. Planning was not based on facts-as-information but on facts-as-experience presented in accounts, through metaphors and with all the ambiguities and amplifications that come with storytelling. Some metaphors stuck, like the 'footprints' that catered for being respectful in redesigning the site. Some stories performed politics; some soothed, while others created tensions, disappointment, and anger. The remarkable way in which Daniel Libeskind—who had never designed, let alone built, a skyscraper in his entire career—exploited the possibilities of the politics of multiplicity to the full shows how actors can mobilize unanticipated power resources to influence the policy process. Libeskind made the process into a broad, multi-stage affair. Yet once the decision was taken, he lost his public power base and quickly also lost his central role in the overall design of the site.

The Ground Zero process also showed very clearly how power is a result of a *dramaturgical* interplay. From the deliberate 'anti-drama' of the protagonists of The Program to the heavily staged presentations and meetings at Federal Hall and at the Javits Center ('this is the real meeting!'), we can see how locations and stagings were mobilized in an effort to persuade people, either to underline the recognition of the symbolic importance of the policy process or of the intention to reach out to the public. Most people would have no difficulty in employing the term 'performance' to describe the way in which Libeskind went about trying to win the competition.

In a situation as symbolically laden as rebuilding Ground Zero there was bound to be a multitude of actors searching for ways to get a handle on the process. An interesting finding was that all actors—even those whom we would normally regard as being 'in charge', such as the leaseholder Silverstein and the all-powerful Port Authority—were at points uncertain about the significance of particular practices in the decision-making process. Their authority was challenged and the order of political decision-making appeared more open than some would suggest. Yet ultimately the case is that of a failed attempt to find a format for being authoritative through reasoned elaboration and to 'rebuild like a democracy'. New techniques were employed, many publics were allowed into the policy conversation, and while this created new possibilities for design that might have generated more legitimacy, the scripts for the policy process did not allow for this to be enacted as a hallmark for the revitalization of democracy.

The high economic stakes, the moral obligation to respect the families of victims, as well as the need to find a symbolic reply to the terrorist attack of 9/11 made it difficult to find a consensus on a new plan from the outset. In the event, the Lower Manhattan Development Corporation was created to oversee the process. After an initially bad start, they sought to win public confidence by committing themselves to an open, participatory process. In many regards, this became an 'unhappy' performative, as the LMDC was unable to extend this deliberative process beyond the successful initial outreach. Surely, the 'Listening to the City' meetings were an achievement in themselves. Yet they could never have been more than a starting-point of a deliberative design. The 'design study' was an improvised follow-up that lacked the conscious process architecture that proved so valuable in the 'Listening to the City' spectacle. Yet as a follow-up it was interesting where (some of the) experts cooperated with various citizen groups and other stakeholders. One quality of a deliberative design surely must be that (design) professionals collaborate over a period of time with stakeholders, thus allowing the design to be strengthened by public input. In this case there was no creative follow-up, allowing the public to advise, for instance, on the various designs, or to assess what qualities the different designs had for the site. The public hearings of January 2003 misperformed: they did not allow for an assessment in terms of the discourses that had been built up over the course of the planning process.

Despite the elaborate techniques involved in 'Listening to the City' and despite the creativity of the design study, the process ultimately failed to dramaturgically deliver on its promise to be a democratic answer to the terrorist attack. Both 'Listening to the City' and the resulting design study had the potential to become transitional rituals that could have transformed the negative emotion of 9/11 into the positive emotion of the idea of a resurrection, a phoenix. But the policy process and main political actors lacked the dramaturgical loyalty (Goffman 1959) to maintain the storyline of 'rebuilding as a democracy': after the choice of the Libeskind design, the process stumbled from one incident to the next, while the boldness of the designs was ground in the mill of various extra demands (office space, relocation, security). The fact that key protagonists initially constantly invoked the terms of democracy and participatory process of course contributed to the unhappy performative. It suggested that participation and democracy were at best conceived of in terms of exchanging ideas but not as public deliberation, decision-making, and public accountability. The lack of a follow-up, and the failure to somehow keep the public dramaturgically involved in the meandering process, ultimately meant that the process did not deliver on the commitments that the political leadership initially presented. Rebuilding Ground Zero should have become an outstanding case of democratic policy-making. In the end it was not to be.

5

Authority Through Deliberative Governance: The British Food Standards Agency in Action

Maarten A. Hajer with David Laws and Wytske Versteeg

On 20 March 1996 the *Daily Mirror* opens its front page with the headline 'MAD COW CAN KILL YOU'. The paper reports that British health secretary Stephen Dorrell is to announce that there might be a risk of humans contacting a form of 'mad-cow disease' (bovine spongiform encephalopathy or BSE) from infected meat. Until then the government had insisted that there was no evidence that the cow disease could be transmitted to humans. Hence there was no risk for beef consumers of being contaminated with Creutzfeldt-Jakob Disease (CJD).[1]

Over the next few days BSE and CJD turn into a media hype as newspapers and television media jump on the issue: 'COULD IT BE WORSE THAN AIDS?' (*Daily Mail*, 22 March 1996) or 'WE'VE ALREADY EATEN 1,000,000 MAD COWS' (*Daily Mirror*, 20 March 1996) (cf. Brookes 1999). The hyperbolic frames are not without consequences. Consumption of beef drops 37 per cent in the first week and there is a transnational spill-over effect: the British BSE crisis fuels an international 'food scare'. The European Commission seizes the chance to show its value for European consumers, picks up a role as supranational protector, and closes the borders for UK beef. While beef consumption climbs back to normal over two years, the BSE crisis leaves a lasting institutional scar in the United Kingdom. To this very day 'BSE' is shorthand for a government that prioritized production

---

[1] In scientific circles the link between BSE and CJD was assumed as early as in 1988, cf. Dressel 2002 and Loeber and Paul 2005.

interests over those of the consumer. In that sense BSE was a fundamental dislocation of the classical-modernist genre of a non-transparent, secretive regulatory system; it lost its authority and aroused suspicion instead. The UK government faced the task of having to completely reinvent its food-safety strategy.

Ironically, in that same month, March 1996, Mark Warren publishes an article on deliberative democracy and authority in the *American Political Science Review* (Warren 1996). Explicitly referring to the very issue of food safety, he argues: 'We trust airline controllers, food inspectors, and the judicial system, and we do not feel any particular compulsion to substitute our judgement for theirs simply because those who guide planes, inspect food, or handle criminals and conflicts do so according to appropriate standards of expertise and appropriate procedures' (1996: 49). When things go wrong, Warren continues, we feel that our trust in these systems was misplaced. Warren observes that in complex societies authority must often be based on trust. Yet he strongly disputes the suggestion that authority should imply the surrender of judgement. Being one of the few theorists who do not see authority and deliberation as fundamentally opposed concepts, Warren argues that it is a neo-conservative bias that suggests that authority is always damaged by questioning and opening up for participation: 'it cannot be said that expert authority requires a surrender of judgement. Authority requires precisely the opposite; only because authorities are scrutinized critically do they come to possess authority' (ibid. 56). Interestingly, in Warren's radical democratic theory, food safety is not subjected to deliberative governance: 'democratic participation will be especially important at margins of trust. Few object to this; we want safe airplanes and food, not the chance to participate in meat inspection and airline safety' (ibid. 49). In actual fact, however, the introduction of deliberative practices in food-safety regulation was exactly what was about to happen in Great Britain.

The BSE crisis and its aftermath have been very well researched.[2] Yet so far hardly any attention has been paid to the newly created British Food Standards Agency (FSA) as an empirical example of deliberative practice (but cf. Hajer and Laws 2003; Rothstein 2004, 2005; Hellebø 2004). That is, however, what makes the FSA remarkable. As a case in authoritative governance it goes beyond the control of the definition of the situation

---

[2] See e.g. Dressel 2002; Forbes 2004; Millstone and Van Zwanenberg 2000, 2001; Oosterveer 2002.

(the case of the aftermath of the Van Gogh murder) or attempts to put the powers-that-be off their stride and create openings for a more inclusive and deliberative policy process (as in the Ground Zero case). In the FSA case we can study how the attempt is made to generate authority through deliberative governance in considerable detail.

In Warren's account, a truly democratic authority 'comes from a set of institutionalized protections and securities within which the generative force of discursive challenge is possible. More specifically, authority operates when the possibility of discursive justification exists and is occasionally exercised, but is not brought to bear on every authoritative decision, precisely because the critical background of attentive publics renews the authoritative status of the decision maker' (1996: 57). Key here is that individuals trust authorities because the authorities will always bear the possibility of an open discursive challenge in mind. In my words: a democratic authority does not require a continuous debate, but should always institutionally allow for a discursive interpellation.

We know for a fact that the first directors of the FSA were familiar with the work of Ulrich Beck on risk society. They had his theories about dealing with uncertainty in mind when designing the operational rules of the FSA.[3] In Beck's evolutionary model of social change BSE is regarded as the type of crisis that marks the failure of his 'first modernity', and which calls for a new, deliberative, second modernity. My alternative take is to examine the ways in which the situation is politically enacted. Depending on the particular way in which this is done, a particular genre of regulation will prevail. This chapter focuses on the FSA as an experiment with deliberative governance. It highlights the creativity in responding to the new 'networked' and 'mediatized' realities of governance and illuminates the intricacies of establishing an authoritative governance on a deliberative template in today's world of multiplicity.

From BSE to FSA

BSE is a perfect phenomenon for the era of mediatized politics: it is a direct threat to the public, it comes with strong symbols (cows with wobbly legs) and high numbers (of casualties, or of infected livestock), or a combination of both (images of piles of burning carcasses of cows in the British

---

[3] Suzi Leather, first deputy director of the FSA, in personal communication.

countryside). No surprise therefore that newspapers quickly picked up on the case. Moreover, BSE was also grist to the mill of the Labour Party, that was still in opposition in 1996. BSE became the emblem of 'old, secretive' politics; it presented a showcase of a failing Conservative government and created the chance to show what Labour meant with its commitment to a 'new governance' (cf. Newman 2001).

BSE is a history written in two parts: before and after March 1996. One image epitomizes the first, pre-1996, part of its political history. It is the widely published photograph of the then minister for agriculture, John Gummer, sharing a hamburger with his daughter at a staged photo-op on a sunny Wednesday morning in 1990.

The message the government wanted to convey with this pseudo-event was clear: all was under control, eating beef was safe. Yet introducing strong symbols is politically risky. In the second part of the history of BSE, which commences in March 1996, 'Gummer with daughter' got its second life, and became iconic for the secrecy of the government, its immorality even

Figure 5.1. Old style staging of governmental authority. Minister John Gummer trying to convey beef is safe (reprinted with permission from PAP Photos).

(cf. Harris and O'Shaughnessy 1997). Once it turned out the government had been misleading the public for almost a decade, the BSE issue caused what Jasanoff called a *civic dislocation*: the inability of public institutions to provide the public with credible reassurance, here expressed in a mismatch between what institutions were supposed to do for the public and what they did in reality, a discrepancy resulting in a loss of trust (Jasanoff 1997: 223).

Robbed of the comfort of being able to rely on the government for their food safety, people initially turned to non-governmental, alternative institutions—media, supermarkets, farmers, 'green' butchers, and restaurants—for advice and to restore their confidence in food.[4] The government, clearly unable to recognize the crucial political impact of its discursive repertoire, initially uttered reassurances that 'any BSE-related risk from eating beef or beef products is likely to be extremely small'. These official statements only fuelled public distrust, something which was aggravated by the fact that the government of prime minister John Major failed to speak in a concerted way.[5]

Food safety, never a front-stage political theme, becomes what the Germans nicely refer to as *Chef's Sache*: leading politicians of opposition parties jump on the issue and turn BSE into a call for institutional change. Until 1996 responsibility for food safety rested with the Ministry of Agriculture, Fisheries, and Food (MAFF), that was also responsible for defending the interests of the agricultural sector and the food-production industry at large. Consumer organizations had long argued that MAFF was too much under the influence of the farming lobby (cf. Lang 1999; Loeber and Paul 2005; Millstone and van Zwanenberg 2000: 66–7), and after Dorrell's announcement this criticism receives ample media coverage once again. Paddy Ashdown, leader of the Liberal Democrats, argues that the MAFF cannot balance the interests of farmers and consumers, and pleads for a new agency modelled upon the US Food and Drug Administration (Rentoul 1996). Labour announces that, if elected, it will establish a Food Standards Agency with 'enormous powers' to protect

---

[4] A well-timed survey among meat consumers showed that whereas before 20 March 1996 respondents were willing to trust family and friends *as much as* expert witnesses on the topic of food safety, after Dorrell's announcement respondents were *more* willing to trust family and friends than scientists (Smith, Young, and Gibson 1999).

[5] Minister of Agriculture Douglas Hogg declares himself willing to incinerate millions of cattle only to 'restore confidence', but is painfully corrected as his colleagues cannot justify the slaughter of healthy animals at a cost of billions to the taxpayer and do not see how this would improve the reputation of British beef. The next day it is the powerful National Farmer's Union that asks for precisely this oblation. When the European Union bans all British beef export one week after Dorrell's announcement, it seems clear

129

the public's health. Tony Blair, leader of the opposition, invites Professor James, director of the Rowett Research Institute in Aberdeen, to write a report containing recommendations concerning the structure and functions of a Food Standards Agency.

The James report comes out in April 1997 and identifies three issues that a new agency is to resolve. The double responsibility of the MAFF is seen as one of the key failures within the system. A second problem is the fragmentation and lack of coordinated food policy and monitoring of food safety among many bodies; the third weakness is the uneven enforcement of food law throughout the United Kingdom. The section concludes that (James 1997: part 1, sec. 6):

> Social science research reveals a widespread distrust of government, science and business and of any regulatory authority seen to be close to vested interests. Furthermore, surveys reveal that providing consumers with a more detailed understanding of, for example, biotechnology issues tends to amplify rather than allay anxieties. Thus, public information and education in themselves are an inadequate means of coping with the public's crisis of confidence. *The public needs to have faith in the systems that are intended to protect them and confidence in the decision-making process in these complex issues.* International experience demonstrates that there is a need for instituting substantial structural and cultural change in Government before public opinion begins to shift. The introduction of a high quality authority which manifestly takes public health and consumer protection as its first priority and has investigative and executive powers to rectify problems is a fundamental component of the series of developments needed to build public confidence. (Emphasis added.)

This 'high quality authority' should separate 'the role of protecting public health and safety from that of promoting business. An Agency must operate openly so that decision-making becomes more transparent and the true balance of interests is subject to public scrutiny.'[6] The new agency is thus conceptualized on the very definition of demo-

---

that—in the words of the *Financial Times*—the government has turned a drama into a crisis (Anonymous 1996). The definition of the BSE episode as a crisis or policy disaster remains a question for discussion (see BSE Inquiry on *www.bseinquiry.gov.uk*; Forbes 2004).

[6] Ibid. This commitment would become a central recommendation in the report of the official governmental inquiry into BSE, led by Lord Phillips. Here rebuilding public trust was seen to be depending on the commitments to openness and transparency especially in relation to the communication of risk and scientific uncertainty: 'To establish credibility it is necessary to generate trust; trust can only be generated by openness; openness requires recognition of uncertainty, where it exists' (BSE Inquiry: vol. 1, sec. 14. on *www.bseinquiry.gov.uk*).

cratic authority as promoted by Warren: on the one hand the public should be able to 'trust' the authorities to handle food safety well, on the other hand a new authority should be achieved by creating the possibility of discursive challenge of those in charge. As we would call it, authority through deliberative governance. James specified details: public interest groups should nominate the majority of board members of the agency; public health and consumer protection must be paramount—although the interests of the agricultural and food industries also have to be properly represented in the political and legislative process. The James Report acknowledges that the agency will have a rather difficult position, as it must be perceived to be removed from the government, but at the same time stay close enough to be able to exert real influence (ibid., part 2, sec. 1): 'An agency is needed which puts the public interest first and is seen to be removed from political pressure and interference from vested interests. Yet it must not be divorced from, and thereby potentially side-lined by, governmental processes.'

On 14 January 1998, with Labour in power, the UK government presents the White Paper *The Food Standards Agency: A Force for Change* to the House of Commons, announcing the intention to erect an independent Food Standards Agency. The paper supports the main conclusions of the James Report and shares its emphasis on the importance of independence and consumer confidence. Still, the documents diverge on some points; most important in this respect is that the government downplays James's appeal for significant consumer involvement, although it still emphasizes that the independence of the board members will be crucial (Hellebø 2004: 18). In the preface of this White Paper the prime minister again stresses the government's commitment to openness and transparency in relation to the rebuilding of public confidence (MAFF 1998): 'The Government is determined to do away with the old climate of secrecy and suspicion and replace it with modern, open arrangements which will deliver real improvements in standards. This fresh approach will help to command the confidence of consumers, industry and our partners in the EU and beyond.'

The inception of the FSA is not without its problems, however. When the bill to establish the new agency—a top priority of Labour's manifesto commitment—is severely delayed, media and opposition are quick to accuse Labour of being swayed by its increasing closeness to the food industry. Minister of Agriculture Jeff Rooker has to defend himself in the House of Lords against the claim that the food industry has caused him to shelve the plans for the FSA.[7] The Food Standards Act finally receives Royal Assent on 11 November 1999, creating the legal basis for a new, legally independent agency.

The enactment of independence

In January 2000 MAFF and the Department of Health jointly announce the appointment of Sir John Krebs as the chairman of the FSA. Krebs is an Oxford scientist, son of a Nobel laureate, fellow of the Royal Society, and primarily known for his study into whether badgers are responsible for transmitting bovine tuberculosis. Suzie Leather, a former consumer campaigner, is to be his deputy; Geoffrey Podger, former head of the FSA forerunner the JFSSG, is appointed as the FSA chief executive.

The authority of the newly established FSA is first tested via a quick scan of the CV of its incoming chairman. The Department of Health argues that Krebs's lack of contact with food-safety issues is an advantage, as it will give him a neutral outlook. Some commentators underline that his strong scientific reputation will be helpful in relating to the academic community and in gaining the trust of some stakeholders, who are sceptical about the technical knowledge of the FSA board. However, consumer organizations show themselves disappointed with the appointment of Krebs, as they had hoped for a 'strong, credible FSA chairman', familiar with the regulatory field. Newspapers quote food-policy experts as say-

[7] Lord Sainsbury, the former chairman of the supermarket chain, is an important donor to the Labour Party and trade minister in Blair's cabinet. Other Labour sponsors include the Somerfield supermarket chain and Lord Haskins, chairman of the food producer Northern Food, and by Blair ennobled and made chairman of the government's Better Regulation Task Force.

Cf. Select Committee on European Communities (1998, q. 613): 'So far as the Food Standards Agency is concerned, I want to make it absolutely clear that in due course the Agency will in fact become the UK competent authority for assessing the novel food applications under the Novel Foods Regulations. In other words, the Advisory Committee on Novel Foods and the Food Advisory Committee will report to the Agency, not to MAFF, and let us make that absolutely clear. This is a serious organisation that is contemplated and, contrary to some of the fabrications in the weekend press, it remains a Government commitment. Nevertheless, in preparation for the Agency, we have made considerable changes within MAFF and in fact in June of last year, 1997, by setting up the Joint Food Standards and Safety Group which is a joint operation of approximately 300 staff, with 250 from MAFF and 50 from the Department of Health, and they are headquarters civil servants dealing with all these issues relating to food safety in its widest sense. They actually answer to one civil servant who happens to be coincidentally a DH civil servant who had been on secondment to MAFF for some time, but a very senior civil servant, and he reports both to myself and to our colleague, Tessa Jowell, the Minister for Public Health, so the embryonic functions of the Agency and the staff are actually in place in many ways.'

Table 5.1. BSE to FSA: chronology of events

1985	First signs of BSE in UK: cause of death 'Cow 133' recognized as a novel progressive spongiform encephalopathy.
1986	Official recognition of BSE.
1987	UK ministers are informed about the disease, and of meat-and-bone meal as the likely cause of it.
1988	Scientists assume a link between BSE and CJD.
1989	The Southwood Committee reports that BSE is unlikely to pose a threat to humans.
1990	The Food Safety Act approved to end 'cosiness' between regulators and vested interests.
May 1990	Photo-op with Minister of Agriculture John Gummer.
May 1990	A cat, 'Max', is reported to have BSE-like symptoms; the species barrier is now broken in the real world.
20 March 1996	The expert committee SEAC announces a probable link between BSE and CJD; British Health Secretary Stephen Dorrell declares that there might be a risk of humans contacting a form of mad-cow disease from infected meat.
25 March 1996	Call for institutional change to MAFF.
March–May 1996	Consumption of beef drops 37%.
April 1997	Professor James publishes recommendations for a 'Food Standards Agency', as commissioned by Tony Blair.
December 1997	Establishment of the BSE Inquiry.
14 January 1998	The Labour government presents the White Paper *The Food Standards Agency: A Force for Change*.
11 November 1999	The Food Standards Act receives Royal Assent.
January 2000	Sir John Krebs and Suzy Leather are appointed as directors of FSA.
October 2000	Results of the BSE Inquiry are released.

ing that the FSA should not be neutral but have a strong, public outlook (Wrong 2000; Smith and Meade 2000; Walker 2000), and that 'Sir John's lack of experience in food leaves him open to manipulation by civil servants and the food industry' (Blythman 2000).

Complying with Rosenau's model of 'spheres of authority', the appointment of Suzi Leather as deputy-chair extends the credibility of the new agency. Via Leather, who has a background as consumer consultant, the FSA covers an alternative public of interest groups campaigning for the integration of consumer interests in the regulation of food.

Learning from the lack of links to the environment of stakeholders of the previous food-safety authorities, and following the recommendations of the Nolan Commission, the FSA actively brings in the policy network (cf. Newman 2003). Following a widely advertised call for applications to become board members, it chooses individual board members for their relationships to different parts of the food industry and food-safety sector. The first board represents a broad range of segments of society, ranging from farmers to cooks and from businessmen to academics. There is no common level of experience to start from; whereas one member is involved in no fewer than fifty company boards, other members have never attended a single board meeting in their life. This means that the board has no shared behavioural repertoire to draw upon and has to invent a new logic of what is appropriate to do and what is not (March and Olsen 1989).

After the appointment of its leadership and board, the character of the organization is clarified further in the discussions of what should be regarded as the core values of the FSA. Krebs, Leather, and the senior staff find agreement in a discourse of openness and transparency: the core principles of the FSA will be to 'put the public first', 'be open', and 'be independent'. This discourse seemingly leaves much space open, but it nevertheless precludes a guiding role for other potential organizational principles. Pleas to make 'sustainable development' and 'social justice' key principles are not welcomed by the senior staff.

Meanwhile the outside image of the FSA threatens to be drawn in another way than its leadership will have imagined, as various publics are eagerly scanning the first concrete acts of the new leadership for meaning. Distrust of consumer organizations is fuelled when in February 2000, only one month after the establishment of the FSA, Sir John Krebs chairs an OECD-sponsored conference on genetically modified (GM) food. His bold statement in September of the same year that organic food is not healthier than 'normal' food echoes through the media and complicates his task to put himself forward as independent chairman of the strong and autonomous FSA. Perhaps it is Krebs's lack of experience with the mediatized realities of governance, but various newspapers portray him as starting with a pro-GM agenda (Edwards 2000; Jones 2000). Following a logic of multiplicity, these initial performative statements turn out to have a long-term influence on the image of the agency. Indeed, years later some stakeholders will still regard these moments as a defining factor for their relationship with the FSA (Dean of Thornton-le-Fylde 2005: 40).

The commotion serves to make painfully clear how delivering on a discourse of openness and transparency isn't going to be easy. Here other rules apply, and the authority of the agency is to be established in a virtual house of glass. The FSA will have to prove its 'true' character in the handling of particular instances and incidents, which might then start to function as 'evidence' for its character as a new, open, and independent approach to food-safety regulation. It is not rules and procedures *per se* that are to determine its success, but public perception and the public awareness of its new procedures. Hence the FSA does not only have a crucial task in mediating between the general public, experts, and policy-makers; it also has to invent practices that could help perform authority to less well-defined publics that were nevertheless also key to its success.

Mediatized regulatory strategies: the 'spin of anti-spin'

No more than a week after the appointment of Krebs, the FSA leadership recruits a senior director of communications and an eight-person strong PR team. These professionals have to fulfil a rather complex task. The previous attempts of the government to deliver a paternalistic message of expert-based certainty have eroded public confidence and led to general distrust. What is more, the first years of the Blair government have, in a different way, raised the suspicion of governmental spin. The agency has, therefore, every reason to communicate its independence. But this also carries a risk: it also has to make clear that it is not an 'independent but toothless' watchdog, but is a legally embedded government agency, able and prepared to intervene if necessary.

It may seem an obvious choice to strongly promote consumer interests to enact this image. Yet for its regulatory task the FSA also has to cooperate closely with producers, scientists, and local authorities; overemphasizing consumer interests will cause doubt about the expertise and credibility of the new agency among these actors. So the FSA faces its own politics of multiplicity: it cannot come up with a 'generic' account of what it stands for to persuade all publics. Moreover, it realizes it cannot seek to win the trust of each public individually at the costs of other key publics: a mediatized politics means that all signs are likely to be picked up by those others. In that sense the FSA has to find a communication strategy acceptable for very different audiences with often contradictory interests.

Given the crucial importance of this task, it is decided that PR professionals are needed to perform it effectively. The PR unit set itself the task of 'spinning a politics of anti-spin'.[8] In order to construct an image of honesty, the FSA communication team uses a range of discursive techniques. It actively produces stories about the agency and its activities. In sharp contrast with usual government strategies, it reaches out to the media and engages in the politics of multiplicity instead of taking a defensive and reactive attitude. Several new stages are identified for this communication

---

[8] Suzy Leather, interview.

strategy. Jeremy Paxman's *Newsnight* is seen as a key stage for branding the FSA as an agency 'committed to openness and transparency'.[9] In 2001 the FSA models its 'Talk Food Conference' on the format of BBC's *Newsnight* and asks Paxman to chair it, thus using the authority that is infested in the Paxman formula for its own purposes.

From the start, the FSA regards the World Wide Web as another important stage for communication. In 2003 its website (*www.food.gov.uk*, cf. *www. eatwell.gov.uk*, *www.salt.gov.uk*, *www.talkfood.org.uk*) receives an average of 180,000 visitors each month (as compared to a yearly total of 16,000 callers to its central call-centre) (NAO 2003: 51). It contains a variety of information: minutes, responses to formal consultations, enforcement data and live streamed board meetings, extensive data about BSE, GM, and novel foods, target-group oriented nutrition advice, food surveys, food and allergy alerts by SMS and e-mail, consultations from a nutrition expert ('Ask Sam'), and (starting in 2006) a weblog of the agency's chief scientist. Openness is also conveyed in another form: the websites contain catchy phrases, interactive features, cartoon figures, lots of photos, and are written in a language that is easily understandable (indeed, the site offers publications not only in the English language, but also in Welsh, Bengali, Chinese, Greek, Gujurati, Hindi, Punjabi, Turkish, and Urdu). According to the National Audit Office, the website gains widespread approval from stakeholders for its different 'look' and its easy access.[10]

However, the FSA's dependence on a website as the first vehicle of communication also receives criticism. A website is used by those with an active interest, as opposed to the general public—and these stakeholders find the language used on the website apt for consumers but inappropriate for professionals like themselves, describing it as 'semi-scientific and not detailed enough' (Bailey 2007: 17). Those without internet access will not be able to gather the information from the website, and this applies particularly to FSA target groups like low-income families (Dean of Thornton-le-Fylde 2005: 11). And even for those who have internet access, it is hard to find the information they're looking for, precisely because of the huge amount of published data: 'Specialists know where to find things, but

---

[9] Paxman is famous in Britain and in those countries able to receive BBC television for his almost savage approach in political interviews. His iconic status can be exemplified by a question asked in the House of Commons: 'It has been a disaster, has it not? Why do you not say it, before Jeremy Paxman asks you?' (House of Commons 2004).

[10] Whether this strategy is effective remains to be seen. The National Audit Office reports that in 2002 only 3% of the public claims to have used the FSA as a source of information, compared to 3% for the consumer groups and 2% for the food manufacturers (NAO 2003: 53).

some of the most interesting things are not always flagged up and the information you need is buried in the minutes of a meeting.'[11] This raises the profound question of whether being open (providing all the information that might be relevant for the public) equals being transparent (providing the information in a way that is understandable and easily accessible). It obviously does not.

Being authoritative in the mediatized age

Performing authority also requires making sure you are a recognizable entity. At the FSA casting is seen as another essential part of its public presentation. The roles of the communication team, and that of John Krebs and Suzi Leather, have to be carefully managed. It is decided that, depending on the issue and the target audience, the FSA should literally show a particular face to a particular type of FSA story. The messenger should always be someone with whom the specific public can identify, for example, a female spokesperson will do the communication about problems with baby food. As the message conveyed depends not only on what is said but also on who is saying it, important messages should have a different face from topics that are less important. For instance, Krebs speaking about a certain issue implies that the topic is important, regardless of what he says—so other persons are needed for the communication about less crucial issues.[12]

Then there is the determination to avoid any isolated expert views from FSA scientists and to make sure that any opinion given in the media is the opinion of the FSA as a whole. The framing of scientific evidence is crucial, as different pressure groups use science to suit their case. As John Krebs puts this (Randerson 2006):

> If you look you can always find some experts who are prepared to take a contrarian view that goes against the mainstream. I think that's very common and it's not just the industry that might selectively quote information, but also the pressure groups....It's always tempting when you are an expert and you are asked for advice to come up with an answer. Sometimes actually what you should come up with is 'We simply don't know.' That, of course, is unpopular.

[11] Quote from Bailey 2007: 17.

[12] The communication manager did not necessarily share this with those involved. It led to an interesting, slightly cynical comment in one of our interviews: 'Mmm, I suppose I am the face of the unimportant news.'

In order to 'keep people on message', all the chairs of scientific committees and nominated other members receive an aggressive media training. After this, only selected members are allowed to act as a spokesman.

Considering the agency's well-developed strategies to convey an image of honesty, the difference between the FSA and its predecessor the MAFF is not that one of them uses dramaturgical methods whereas the other does not. The FSA tries to keep a high media profile partly as a result of its commitment to openness, but this also means that it has to tightly control who is allowed to say what, how, and where—both to save the image of the organization and to keep its message clear and understandable. A crucial difference between the FSA and MAFF is, however, that it is now no longer certainty but, on the contrary, honesty about *uncertainty* that has to be staged. From its inception, the FSA combines its commitment to basing decisions on scientific facts with the policy to 'be honest about uncertainty': understanding the facts where there are facts to be understood and being open about uncertainties where there aren't (FSA 2002*a*). As one respondent puts this:

> John [Krebs] and Susie [Suzan Leather] who are our two principal spokespersons for the media, are both terrific at saying, 'I don't know', in a way which is frank and upfront but it doesn't sound ignorant. You NEVER get a politician who says to any question, they will never say, 'I don't know the answer'. And it would be fantastically good for their personal profiles if some of them did learn to say 'I don't know.' But we've got it down to an art form now...[13]

The concept of staging might invoke the notion of performance as deceit, as a strategic effort to control a situation (see e.g. Futrell 1999). But just as regarding 'science' and 'performance' as opposite ends of a dichotomy does no justice to reality, so it would also be too easy to assume that the agency only pretends to be open without being really committed to it.

Honest about uncertainty: open board meetings and consultations

Centrepiece of the enactment of deliberative governance is undoubtedly the FSA open board meetings. This practice has now become common among other organizations as well, but was rather revolutionary when

---

[13] Interview FSA Je_02_#4, respondent Richard Ayre.

The FSA in practice—Sudan 1: the incident that became a scandal

An incident that is definitely no success in terms of public relations, is the way in which the agency handles the commotion surrounding Sudan 1—an incident causing the largest recall in UK history. Sudan 1 is a banned red dye with the potential to cause cancer found in a batch of chili powder that is used in a Worcester sauce, which in turn is used in more than 400 own-label and top-brand products. The FSA is informed about the presence of Sudan 1 in the Worcester sauce on 7 February 2005, but waits ten days before raising a public alarm, in order to identify all products that contain the sauce. This delay, combined with the fact that illegal presence of Sudan 1 was already reported in May 2003, causes an outcry in the media; the papers draw parallels between Sudan 1 and the BSE crisis. Although the risk associated with consuming low levels of Sudan 1 is negligible, the media frenzy exacerbates it to a major cancer scare. Here the limits of being open about uncertainty become painfully clear. For instance, the *Sunday Times* calls it 'embarrassing' that the FSA cannot provide its European counterparts with a comprehensive list of blighted products. The newspaper writes about 'history repeating itself', and states that the most important difference that the establishment of the FSA has made is that now no one can be held accountable (Ungoed-Thomas and Leake 2005). Both in the media and in the House of Commons, questions are asked about the functioning and the remit of the agency.[14] The FSA is criticized for its delayed reaction and its faulty communication with small shops (who allegedly heard the news from the press), although other reactions point to the sheer complexity of the food chain as the most worrying factor. On the other hand, the agency also receives criticism for 'hyping up' the story. It is perhaps not that surprising that *The Grocer*, a weekly magazine for the grocery chains, comments that 'the agency's zeal and excessively precautionary warnings represent a PR move to convince consumers that their government food watchdog agency is indeed doing its job' (Whelan 2005). However, the Better Regulation Commission also quotes the FSA response to Sudan 1 in its report *Risk, Responsibility and Regulation: Whose Risk is it Anyway?* The Commission wonders whether—if the substance were not banned—the risks would have been low enough to allow products to stay on shelves, and whether consumers were given balanced and accurate regulation. This last question stems from the fact that different countries approached the issue in very different ways, as can be seen by comparing the statements of the FSA with its New Zealand counterpart. The latter issued a statement that 'the risk, if any, for anyone who has consumed food made with chilli powder as an ingredient is so small as to be immeasurable and consumers are advised not to be concerned' (quoted in Better Regulation Commission 2006: 6), whereas the UK FSA states that 'Sudan 1 could contribute to an increased risk of cancer and it is not possible to identify a safe level or to quantify the risk' (FSA 2005*a*). The agency advises that 'Sudan 1 could contribute to an increased risk of cancer. However, at the levels present the risk is likely to be very small but it

---

[14] Illustrative is the following comment by Chris Grayling, health spokesperson of the Conservatives: 'I am genuinely quite worried that the FSA seems to have acted very slowly. It was set up as a food safety body but has been trying to reinvent itself as a much more broad-ranging public health education creature…I would ask: has this organisation become too big, too bureaucratic, too ill-focused to do its job?' (Quoted in Winnett and Ungoed-Thomas 2005).

is sensible to avoid eating any more...we will continue to take action to remove these [affected products] and minimise the risk to consumers' (quoted in Better Regulation Commission 2006: 6). The nuance of the FSA message is understandable in the light of its communication policy of telling the truth and treating the people like adults, inspired by the BSE crisis. Or, as Krebs formulates this: 'We've had to tread a very fine line and acknowledge that the risk [with Sudan 1] is actually very small, but nevertheless it is an illegal substance' (Revill and Townsend 2005). The assessment of the agency and the decision to order a total withdrawal of affected products is not primarily based upon the physical risk of Sudan 1, but on the necessity not to damage the trust of the public: 'the key point is that it is illegal, and I think that from a regulatory point of view I would turn it round the other way: how would consumers feel if we turned a blind eye to the food industry using an illegal dye that is used as an industrial boot polish, present in their food? I do not think consumers wanted that and that was our assessment.'[15]

However, this strategy causes a panic—if not among the public, then at least in the media, and leads to criticism from stakeholders suffering major economic damage. Kevin Hawkins, director-general of the British Retail Consortium, accuses the FSA of sending out mixed messages (McLaughlin 2005):

> There was a contradiction, in that the FSA was saying the risk of contamination was very, very small, but then in the same statement telling people to stop eating certain foods...They just can't sit piously back and let the media make of it what they will. The FSA has a communications team, and it's up to them to ensure that the consumer, whom they are supposed to represent, gets a balanced and realistic message in terms of the level of risk.

One of the lessons of the Sudan 1 incident is that, notwithstanding its communication strategies, the agency is also caught in existing media logic. Media logic comes with conspiracies, heroes, and villains, and as a governmental agency the FSA is seldom cast as the hero. In the words of John Krebs (Anderson 2005):

> I think there were occasions when we were actually the hero but ended up cast as the villain because we were part of government. For example, we found that chicken condemned as pet food had been recycled illicitly back into the food chain: people were essentially taking pet food and turning it into chicken nuggets. We were part of the enforcement operation that uncovered this. But the media then portrayed it as our fault for allowing it to happen in the first place.

started by the FSA. As such, it gave meaning to the commitment to transparency and openness more than anything else: it is in these open board meetings that the confidence in the procedures of determining food standards must be restored.

> Good morning board members and good morning members of the audience. I would like to kick off by saying a few words to those of you who are

---

[15] Quote from Andrew Wadge, FSA Director of Food Safety Policy and Acting Chief Scientist. House of Commons (2006: qu. 658).

here as observers. As you know, the Board of the Agency always decides and discusses its policies in public, in a forum like this. And your presence and your participation as an audience is a very key part of our commitment to openness and transparency. So thank you very much for coming to attend.

We also make a point of travelling around the United Kingdom to different parts so that not only those in London and the major capitols can see us at work and take part, but also those in other parts of the country. And we are particularly pleased to be here in Armagh City.

Once we start the Board meeting, we will carry on as though the audience didn't exist. But when we get to the end, at around quarter to one, I will hand over to Suzi Leather, the Deputy Chair, who will chair a question and answer session. At which point you as members of the audience will have an opportunity to make comments, ask questions, either on the issues we've discussed today, and we have a very full agenda, or on other items that may occur to you.

This is the way Sir John Krebs opens the open board meeting held in Armagh City on 13 June 2002—a routine way of opening the board meeting, wherever it is held. The scene is a large hall with an oval table standing at one side of the room, and behind the table a large backdrop featuring two versions of a logo with the initials 'FSA'. On the other side of the room tables covered with white cloths are set up in long rows. Both the front table and the rows of tables host groups of men and women dressed in suits and talking informally with one another. This is quite literally a staged board meeting. There is a stage-set (the green-and-white FSA backdrop with a build-in video screen), and it is also quite directly staged as an open board meeting as there actually is an audience that can observe the deliberations of the board. All open board meetings can be livestreamed via the website of the FSA.

The decision to meet in public is taken as this seems the only way to overcome the moral shock and dislocation that the British system of food-safety regulation has suffered in the BSE crisis. Among FSA board members there is a strong awareness that the FSA has to be a real break from the past. Even when it is not mentioned, BSE is always there and provides the example that will play in people's heads when judging if a particular line of action is appropriate, and it provides the markers within which the

---

[16] Consider for instance the following comment by board member Michael Gibson during the Armagh meeting on 13 June 2002: 'Could I say that I think that as an industry if we get one case of BSE proven in sheep it will be an absolute disaster. *We have got to make absolutely sure that we are mindful of Phillips and what happened with BSE in cattle and we don't go into denial.* We must be very, very careful about how we tackle this.' (Emphasis added.)

agency develops its decision rules.[16] As the 'foundation food scare', it is constitutive for the practices of the Board: never again will British food safety be compromised because of a secretive culture of regulation. Now, deliberation and decision-making are to be livestreamed so as to show the FSA, in the words of Offe (1997: 84), to be 'fact-regarding, other-regarding, and future-regarding'. Every meeting becomes an attempt to define by experience what the abstract idea of being 'a trustworthy agency' means in practice.

This implies that, while recognizing that everybody might have something meaningful to contribute to the deliberations, interests of people should be taken into account. At the FSA it leads to the introduction of a practice that board members are asked to declare interests, in order to determine whether they should be allowed to participate in the discussion about a contentious agenda item (cf. FSA 2007).

The open board meeting is an institutional practice that dramaturgically creates a climax in its decision making process in front of the public: there

---

The FSA in practice—Micro-practices in deliberative governance: the declaration of interest

From the FSA Board Meeting at Armagh City, 13 June 2002:

> JK—Sorry. Just before that I should ask Board members to declare interests before discussion and whether or not they intend to contribute to the discussion.

What follows is an example of the enactment of deliberative governance, making onlookers a witness of the negotiated and openly deliberated character of the internal standards of the FSA:

> BOARD MEMBER—Mr. Chairman. I have to declare an interest as a farmer, although not a sheep producer. I also use natural gut casings in my business, but it is not a material item. And therefore with your permission I would feel able to remain within the discussion.

The Chair renders his decision quickly and the second case comes up for review:

> CHAIR—Fine. Thank you. Other? Carol?
> CAROL—Yes, Chair. I also have to declare an interest both as a sheep farmer and a sausage producer using natural casings. Again not a major material interest, but I would like, with your permission, to carry on in the debate.

Carol's declaration demands more scrutiny. In the interaction the Chair's authority is affirmed as is the possibility that someone could be excluded from discussion.

> CHAIR—Is it actually a material interest to you Carol, because you...?
> CAROL—I use the casings, but I wouldn't say it is a major material part of the business. No. [Yeah] It's up to you entirely.

To assist, Carol volunteers information about the anticipated character of the interaction.

CAROL—I don't have major questions. I just have a question to ask.

With this the matter is resolved. Carol can participate and the discussion moves on.

CHAIR—OK Fine. Thanks. In that case over to you Geoffrey.

And Geoffrey Podger introduces the content of the issue that is to be discussed.

is an interaction between players to determine an approach to collective issues, enacted in front of a public witness. It thus employs essentially the same principles as Heurtin described for the early French revolutionary parliaments; it is the enactment of its procedure that lends authority and legitimacy to the decision taken. The decision to have open board meetings itself is a once-and-for-all decision and of course impossible to reverse, as it is crucial for the identity of the organization. As one of the board members puts this:

John and Suzi proposed that all of our decision making should be held in public. And as you would expect, across the board as a whole there was a real spectrum of views, from fully supportive of John and Suzi to aghast, terrified, scared shitless at the thought of doing all our business in public. I had an absolute intellectual commitment to the John-and-Suzi position, but like everybody else, I thought 'Jesus, I know nothing about food and I know nothing about BSE. In two months time am I really going to sit in public and television cameras may be there, and feel confident to be part of a decision-making process?'[17]

Once the open board meeting has been introduced, the participants have to interactively find out what it means. While discussing the institutional design of the FSA, a principal question that comes up is whether open meetings will allow the board members to take proper decisions in a considered fashion. There are concerns that openness will lead to grandstanding and cause people to polarize the discussion. Some board members therefore suggest rehearsing the arguments beforehand:

Not rehearse the outcome, no one *ever* was as cynical as to suggest that we should rehearse the outcome. But in the early months, a lot of board colleagues felt that we should rehearse the argument—partly so we didn't look stupid, but that sort of belittles the seriousness of their concern. It

[17] Interview: FSA_Je_02_#6, respondent Richard Ayre.

> was that we should be capable of handling the arguments in public and under the spotlight of media scrutiny....I and significant other numbers of Board members felt that we should either decide to go public or we should decide not yet to go public with the long-term aim of going public, but that it was completely unacceptable to say we were going public but then to have private meetings where in effect whatever we said to ourselves we would in effect rehearse the decision....Then it would have been a bit of play-acting.[18]

The proposal is discarded on the ground that rehearsing will unavoidably convey a sense that the discussion is being staged—we would say staged in an inappropriate way—and that will be at odds with commitments to openness and transparency and will undercut, rather than secure, public confidence. Experiencing the struggle to find the best answer is seen as the proper way of food regulation in the era of high uncertainty and low trust.

However, looking foolish or uninformed may undercut the board's authority, and it requires courage to ask for clarification in public. Board members commit themselves to a procedure that they know has a high risk of making them look foolish, either in the eyes of the public or in the eyes of the experts involved. As one board member comments, talking about striking the balance between the quest for openness on the one hand and being able to profit from the excellent expert knowledge the FSA can rely upon on the other hand:

> You have to be assiduous—and this is where the briefing sessions are so important—you have to be assiduous at asking 'dumb' questions if you don't understand what the paperwork says. And as you can imagine, in the early months that was really difficult because we're all learning the business, no one likes to look stupid and you tend to assume in life that the guy sitting next to you knows more about the business than you do and you don't want to reveal the fact that it's—it's the emperor's new clothes.[19]

Hence, in order to avoid looking foolish when difficult issues are on the agenda, the board decides to meet privately and review the technical and factual aspects beforehand if necessary. These meetings also enable the board to consider commercially sensitive information that could not be discussed during open meetings. To ensure the transparency of the process, key stakeholders are invited to attend the closed meeting and present

---

[18] Interview: FAS Je_02_#6, respondent Richard Ayre.   [19] Ibid.

their view on the subject. Still, the decision to have closed board meetings in advance of the open sessions remains at odds with the endeavour to convey an image of openness and independence (Bailey 2007: 20): 'If they really want trust more spontaneity is required. Having private sessions before Board meetings always leads to the suspicion that minds are made up and that members are being rehearsed.'

Board members are strongly aware of this 'this is not the real meeting' sentiment, but keep having difficulties disciplining themselves not to start rehearsing for a long time after the start of the public meetings:

> For the first at least year, even year-and-a-half...colleagues started at these private meetings to indulge in argument, not just elucidation but argument. And to expound their own personal position, or to try to tease out the position of other Board members. And John was usually on the ball, saying 'Stop! That's taking us into a policy discussion, we're not here to talk about policy, we're here to understand the science and to understand the argument.' But sometimes, either because even John makes mistakes from time to time, or because his antennae were not always finely tuned on this one issue, it fell to me as the open-government guy to hit my fist on the table and say 'Stop! John, you've got to stop this because we're getting into discussion.'[20]

In its board meetings—as in its contacts with the media—the FSA tries to stage transparency, even if this means being seen as not having the answer or asking dumb questions. And just like its contacts with the media, the result remains somewhat paradoxical. Of course, the possibility to attend the meetings either live or livestreamed via the internet can be called revolutionary. The very fact that the board meetings are open to the public, the frequent stakeholder consultations, and the amount of information on the website alter the debate in a fundamental way, as these practices remove the basis for the previously dominant criticism that everything in food politics is decided behind closed doors. But then—why does the board stick to a meeting format that pretends that the stage-set and the web technology are not there? Why does the board proceed 'as if the audience does not exist'? This format might enhance openness, but whether it really contributes to transparency is doubtful. An open meeting shows the process, whereas a transparent meeting provides the opportunity for clarification and enhanced understanding, giving the audience the possibility to deliberate, ask questions, or call to account.

---

[20] Ibid.

Enacting rules through 'critical moments'

It is significant that an incident that various respondents refer to as 'constitutive', occurs when the public is *not* ignored, during the BSE stakeholder reviews right after the inception of the FSA. During a discussion about the relationships between the existing practices of risk assessments and the failure to act on the evidence for the possible transfer of BSE to human beings, members of the audience take the floor and narrate what they have been going through while nursing members of their family who are dying from CJD. In the words of Suzi Leather:

> And they had the courage to talk about that in front of people whose connection with the issue is a purely professional, non-emotional one. They run an abattoir, or they work for a government department in Wales with responsibility for meat production, or they're a vet—whatever. But when they heard those conversations, even those people who had nothing to do with it emotionally, I think they felt engaged with it in a way they didn't before.

Here, the carefully staged meeting makes way for a politics impromptu. The discursive interpellation forces the FSA leadership to act instantaneously on the incident and thus creates a 'critical moment' (Leary 2004) in the institutional development of the FSA: what do its rules and guiding principles about openness really mean in practice? Emotions are often seen as hindering proper deliberation, but this misses the social-psychological significance of such incidents in the institutionalization of norms and routines. In this case the shared experience of having seen people express intense emotions leads to a definitive move away from old routines, brings about a change in discourse, and enacts new institutional commitments. It facilitates reflection on what the proper way of discussing food standards is and becomes the key marker of the new FSA convention of deliberative regulation. The testimonies by the family members of the CJD victims allow Board members, stakeholders, and staff to experience that they are 'talking about lives here'. Afterwards, the reference to this incident serves as a symbolic trope, a marker that constantly reminds those involved of the institutional need to define their own practice of deliberation. This foundational myth makes tangible the abstract understanding that the FSA cannot rely on the old, secretive procedures and is crucial for the willingness to engage in new, unknown, and often threatening procedures (cf. Collins 2004).

Whereas the BSE-victims incident is strongly related to the past, another defining element is much more future-oriented. Part of the organizational

identity of the FSA seems to stem from the perception that the organization leads the way forward to a new mode of governance for complex
policy issues, echoing Dewey's statement when he argued that: 'By its
very nature, a state is ever something to be scrutinized, investigated, and
searched for. Almost as soon as its form is stabilized, it needs to be re-made'
(Dewey 1927; cf. Gomart and Hajer 2003). Both staff and board members
show a strong awareness of the experimental character of the FSA, of the
need to keep innovating and searching for new forms. This awareness also
surfaces during the Armagh meeting:

> CHAIRMAN—If we are just trying to highlight some of these recommenda-
> tions. I thought under stakeholder groups, Eileen had done a very good
> job in identifying how they play a part in our openness operation. And
> since there are now so central, not just stakeholder groups, but open pub-
> lic meetings, focus groups, the whole way in which we take evidence and
> build that into the development of, for instance, the matter we were dis-
> cussing in the previous agenda item is vital. Perhaps we should become
> more expert in the process by which stakeholder groups would work
> optimally. In other words, developing a kind of research into that, which
> I would like to extend to our openness and communication strategy.
> Because, just as we've been discussing a moment ago, the communication
> of what we've said is vital. So composition of stakeholder groups, how do
> we operate, how do we use the information, how do we cascade it. I think
> you've identified an important area for us to work on.[21]

Dealing with the politics of multiplicity

The practices of deliberative regulation that the FSA develops and employs
prove to be remarkably effective in terms of dealing with the politics of
multiplicity. The open practices of the FSA differ so much from the usual
procedures that these tend to depoliticize the issues that the agency deals
with. The media simply do not believe that important topics are to be discussed in public, and only show up when BSE or GM food is on the agenda.
Even when they are present, the format does not provide much room for
interaction with the media (Bailey 2007: 18): ' "They" (the board) do allow
questions at the end, but these are more designed for stakeholders and
interest groups than journalists.' Paradoxically, the FSA commitment to
openness thus grants the organization room for policy manoeuvre in an
era of multiplicity and media-derived escalations.

[21] Quote from the previously mentioned Armagh meeting.

The FSA also has considerable freedom in framing the basis of its consultation and is not obliged to follow the results of consultation exercises (Wooding *et al.* 2004: 92). Probably as a result of this, the circle of
consulted stakeholders remains relatively small; genuine consultation (as
opposed to consumer research) is limited to 'the usual suspects'.[22] This
leads to a problem for the smaller stakeholders in particular; there are so
many opportunities to participate in and to contribute to the debate that
they feel overwhelmed, as they cannot attend all the meetings that they
are invited to.[23] Wales (2004: 45) even quotes a NGO actor referring to this
'burden of openness' as a shield for the agency; when stakeholders have
had all formal opportunities to participate, it is hard to criticize decisions
afterwards.

Stakeholders also worry that the format of the open meeting inhibits
in-depth discussions. Food-safety decisions are so complex that it is sometimes hard to discuss them in the limited time available for the open
board meetings. A dilemma is caused by the government's simultaneous
emphasis on the sometimes contradictory objectives of 'evidence-based
policy' on the one hand and 'openness and transparency' on the other
hand. Whereas the first objective requires a strong reliance on experts and
expertise, the latter goal presupposes public participation. Hence open
board meetings may increase transparency, but can be counter-productive
to the objective of reaching balanced decisions (cf. Stilgoe and Wilsdon
2006: 7): 'Opportunities for policy officials to engage with Board members
other than at open Board meetings would benefit overall policy making'
(Bailey 2007: 18).

Despite these concerns, stakeholders do not doubt that the open board
meetings must continue (Dean of Thornton-le-Fylde 2005). Indeed, the
board's decision to meet in public generates a continuous pressure for
the other elements of the organization to meet in public as well. The FSA
has no fewer than eighteen independent scientific committees and work-

---

[22] Simultaneously, the number of received responses to consultation exercises is often low
in relation to the number of documents sent out. Bailey (2007: 38) states that for consultations in 2005 and 2006 the average number of received responses is 27 whereas usually
hundreds of documents have been sent out. In the most extreme case the FSA received only
11 replies to a consultation of 845 actors. Numbers like these would ask for a closer consideration of costs of openness and consultation procedures in comparison to the benefits.

[23] As Richard Ayre puts this (interview FSA Je_02_#6): '[stakeholders] say, "You keep invit-
ing, you do so much open stuff, and you keep asking us to contribute to so many policy
debates. We're a small organization, we can't possibly come to all of these meetings."...So we
somehow have to find a way that they are comfortable with, of limiting their opportunities
to participate but making sure that those opportunities are the REAL opportunities to influence
the argument.'

ing parties providing advice to the government about themes like micro-biological safety, carcinogenicity, nutrition, and—not least—spongiform encephalopathies like BSE, CJD, and scrapie. If the board meets in public, why wouldn't the scientific advisory committees meet in public as well?

Scientific evidence: translating something very technical into something meaningful

The board is newly established; the principle of openness is adopted in the beginning and—after a difficult start—becomes a part of its identity. Some of these committees, like the Scientific Advisory Committee on Nutrition (SACN), have been established following the setting up of the Food Standards Agency. For most of the scientific committees the situation is quite different: they were already installed under MAFF and some of them have a history dating back to the 1970s. Important here is the fact that the FSA inherits nearly all its staff from the old institutions, and that the existing scientific committees already share a history and a particular logic of appropriateness. The continuity of the staff may provide expertise but could easily be used by critics to point out that the FSA is 'basically' the same old shop but with a new front.

Scientific advice always struggles with a built-in clash of scripts and role conceptions. Dressel (2002) describes this as the 'double-bind identity' of scientific advisers: politicians tend to see, or at least present, their actions as nothing more than the recommendations of scientists, reformulated for the sake of public policy purposes. However, the expert members of the scientific committees themselves do not regard themselves as in charge of making decisions, nor do they want to be seen as such. Although providing advice frequently means to be asked for a judgement (often under political pressure), the committee members are perfectly aware that judging policy questions is different from what they are trained for. They prefer to see their task as the purely rational, systematic evaluation of scientific facts—but political pressure often forces them to step outside this preferred role.

This problem is exacerbated by the difficulty of staging uncertain scientific knowledge in the political sphere in a meaningful way. Scientific reports describe in detail the available evidence and the arguments that would support or undermine specific conclusions, but politicians are usually neither able nor willing to read more than a few pages of a report (Dressel 2002). As political decisions are often presented as nothing more than logical conclusions from 'sound science', the scientific committees run the risk that their findings will be used in an entirely different manner than the committee had originally intended (cf. Hajer 1995), as was indeed the case in the BSE crisis.

Given the fact that the treatment of scientific knowledge played such a major part in the BSE debacle, one would expect a major restructuring of the advisory committees.[24] The FSA strongly emphasizes the value of direct expertise and implements measures to remove any barriers, not only to develop in-house scientific knowledge, but also to fund external research and to participate in virtual networks of scientists, stakeholders, and legislators. Combined with the open recruitment procedure as required by the Nolan standards, this is a clear break from the past, at least in principle. The FSA pays substantial attention to the translation of scientific advice into policy, and to the connection between its scientific committees and other parts of its organization, and indeed the public domain. The committees have to provide clarity about what is and what is not known about the risk they are considering, and about the way that they will carry out the risk assessment (May, Donaldson, and Krebs 2000: 7). Moreover, since May 2005, when the FSA Board considers proposals that rest on scientific evidence the Chair of the relevant scientific advisory committee is invited to the open board meetings, in order to provide an independent view on how the proposal reflects the advice of his committee (FSA 2006: 3). As it was formulated in the Report on the Review of Scientific Committees (FSA 2002b):

> Chairs of advisory committees have a number of responsibilities, and these include ensuring that every member of the committee is heard and that no view is ignored or overlooked, and also ensuring that unorthodox and contrary scientific views are taken into account. The Chair is also responsible for ensuring that the proceedings of the committee are

---

[24] The BSE inquiry identified a long list of lessons to be learned concerning the setting up of the committee, the role of the committee in relation to policy and the form, communication, and review of the advice. (BSE Inquiry, vol. 11; vol. 1, sec. 14, see *www.bseinquiry.gov.uk*).

The James Report (James 1997) states the need for revision as follows:

There is a need to revise the way that advisory committees operate. The principle of openness which will underpin the Agency's work will have to apply equally to the advisory committees. There should be declaration of current and former interests, formal appointment procedures, and publication of minutes and reports. Meetings should as a rule be held in public, but matters of commercial confidentiality can be heard in closed session before the public meeting. There needs to be agreement on the nature of commercial confidentiality so that it is not used to convert an open committee structure into a closed system of scrutiny.

Also available from *http://archive.food.gov.uk/maff/archive/food/james/part2a.htm#(j)*.

properly documented so that there is a clear audit trail showing how the committee reached its decision.

Note the potential friction between the responsibility to take unortho-dox views into account and the earlier-mentioned determination to keep people 'on message'. Here again, communication turns out to be a crucial component of a deliberative governance, both with policy-makers and with the public. The close cooperation between the committee Chairs and the communication team of the FSA should make scientific findings more accessible to stakeholders and the general public:

> And what they [the scientific committees] tend to do is produce very con-sidered reports on sometimes significant issues, so we [the communica-tion branch] then have to work with them in terms of communicating that.... Usually in risk assessment it's pretty scientific, it's often very, very technical. And the big issue is how you translate that into something meaningful that's still accurate.[25]

Another attempt to make the input of scientific evidence more trans-parent to the public is the decision of several scientific committees to organize open meetings themselves. The 2001 review group recommends that 'all committees should move as quickly as possible to a position where they conduct as much of their business as possible in open ses-sions, allowing the audience to interact at the end' (FSA 2002*b*: 17). Following this recommendation and the precedent of the open board meeting, some of the committees decide to have all their meetings in public, though reserving the possibility of treating confidential issues in closed sessions. Others see more difficulties in taking this step. Committee members utter concerns about the possible disruption of the meetings by animal-rights activists, the attribution of comments to individual mem-bers and the safety risks involved in this, and the discussion of commercial in-confidence items. They also fear that the presence of observers will inhibit the discussion.

Given these worries, it is no wonder that the committees pay consid-erable attention to the format of the open meetings. The seating of the observers is a case in point (FSA 2002*b*: 24):

> Where there are good reasons for a number of observers being present, the Secretariat should arrange the seating in such a way that their presence does not inhibit the committee's discussions. Recent experience with the COT [Committee on Toxicity of Chemicals in Food, Consumer Products

[25] Interview FSA Je_02_#7, respondent Neil Martinson.

and the Environment] has shown that this can lead to improvements in group dynamics during committee meetings.[26]

The lunch is another point of concern. Some of the committees opt for separate lunches for observers and committee members, others allow mixing during lunchtime, because (COT 2003: 2): 'The Secretariats felt that although there was a possibility of members being lobbied over lunch, mixing tended to decrease any "them and us" nature of the meetings.' Concerns like these might seem trivial at first sight. However, they reveal the anxiousness of the committees and their secretariats in trying to accommodate an entirely new element in their working routines: outside observers.

Still another way in which the FSA hopes to translate technical risk assessments into something meaningful is by incorporating into each scientific committee at least two *consumer representatives* or non-specialist members. This practice is not entirely new or unique. MAFF had already started to create some places for non-expert members representing the interests of consumers, but these members were almost always chosen from government-funded consumer bodies and their influence was relatively limited (Lang 1999; Millstone and Van Zwanenberg 2002).

Some of the scientific committees had not had consumer representatives as part of their membership before, and most of them start with only one instead of two consumer representatives. It is not hard to conceive how difficult the role of these non-specialist members is. Although they can use the FSA library and get some FSA support in their quest for information, this is hardly comparable to the resources that their expert colleagues can request from their universities. They do not speak the scientific language and their own task seems hard to define—in contrast to the roles of the specialist members. In order to be successful they have to disrupt the common practice of the scientific committee, by demanding attention for the perspective of 'ordinary people'. Again, critical moments in establishing new institutional routines.

---

[26] COT has also asked the other committees about their experiences with having open meetings. In its 'Proposal to hold COT meetings in open session', the Secretariat of the committee notes that (COT 2002a: 6): 'The ACR arranges the room such that the Committee and Secretariat occupy three sides of a square with observers seated away from the fourth side...' In the minutes on the discussion about this proposal (COT 2002b: 10) can be read that: 'Members sought clarification of the anticipated size of the meetings. Resource implications mean that regular large open meetings are not feasible, and therefore the aim would be to allow a few places for observers within the Agency's meeting rooms (analogous to public seating in law courts). This was considered to be appropriate to the expected interest and resources...'

The FSA hopes that non-specialist members will challenge assumptions of the experts and ensure that the considerations of the committee meet the needs of, and are expressed in terms that can be understood by, consumers generally. The task of the non-specialist members is to ensure that the experts answer the real questions and not the ones that were just scientifically interesting, to try to pin the experts down to what their assumptions would mean in real life, instead of on a hypothetical level. Their presence should be a reflexive element within the advisory committees, or as one respondent put this: the consumer representatives make a risk assessment on the advisory committees:

> And there would be this high-level discussion, highly technical quite often, about what the risks might be. And she [the consumer representative] would sit there, and in the end she couldn't contain herself any longer and she would say 'I want to know whether it's safe for me to give lamb to my children.' And she would bring them down—this is really what we need to know. We don't need to know whether a prion is in a particular way in this part of the body or that part of the body. And although there may not be an answer to the question, 'Is it safe to give lamb to my children?', it was forever bringing them back to what they were really there for, where they might sometimes just get very excited about highly technical issues which may or may not be relevant to you or me.[27]

This endeavour is of course not always welcomed, and it is no wonder that the consumer representatives often feel isolated in this environment. Some of the committees, having a long history without any involvement of consumer representatives, are rather suspicious of these new members with their habit of disrupting interesting technical discussions, and even tend to regard consumer representatives as a nuisance.[28] The FSA tries to alleviate this isolation by assembling the representatives from the different committees once or twice a year. These meetings provide the opportunity for exchanging experiences and strategies to handle difficult situations,

---

[27] FSA Je_02_#1, Barbara Richardson.

[28] As Barbara Richardson, responsible for the coaching of the consumer representatives, comments (ibid.): 'One of the roles, if you like, is to say: "OK, this technical issue you're talking about is all very interesting from a scientific point of view, but you need to actually put what you're saying into plain language so that the general public can understand it." And they can bring to that sort of debate the concerns of the ordinary person, if you like, as opposed to the concerns of a manufacturer or a scientist, not just the technical issues. But in doing that, they sometimes feel quite isolated within that particular environment. And I think some of them—because some of the committees were in existence for some time before they had these people—sometimes they were viewed with rather a lot of suspicion by the scientists who were on them, thinking "Why do we need these people coming along to disrupt our interesting technical discussions?" [laughs].'

for letting off steam and for further training of the representatives. An adapted training package from the National Consumer Council (*Stronger Voice*) is used to boost the confidence of the non-specialist members in their quality as 'expert consumers'.[29]

In terms of trying to introduce and define a new genre of deliberative governance, it is a 'meaningful friction' that will help define a deliberate break in an established routine. Gradually, the scientific committees seem to become better adjusted to the idea of non-specialist members. Chairmen in particular start to accept the value of the consumer representative, not least because advice of the committees is more likely to be accepted if it includes the viewpoint of 'the' general public.

Yet, notwithstanding all these policies, the above-mentioned problems concerning scripts and role conceptions of scientific committees will continue to apply to the FSA. Staff members state that there should be more openness about the political context within which decisions are made (Bailey 2007: 20). Stakeholders identify 'explaining the reasons for decisions and policies' as the second most important characteristic for an open organization, but according to reviews published in 2005 and 2007 they find it often difficult to see how and why the agency comes to certain conclusions. The evidence on which decisions are based is not always clear to them, as 'there is inadequate explanation of changes in thinking that occur in the lead up to decisions being taken' (Bailey 2007: 15; Dean of Thornton-le-Fylde 2005: 13; cf. Jensen 2004). Given the policy goals as outlined above, this is of course a painful criticism.

The FSA in practice—Traffic lights

An example of the (political) difficulties of translating 'something technical into something meaningful' can be found in the struggles about nutritional evaluation schemes. Nutrient profiling models are developed to classify and signpost foods as either healthy or unhealthy, and form the basis for deciding which foods can be advertised to children. Again the FSA struggles with the trade-off between providing understandable and transparent information on the one hand, or more in-depth and balanced information on the other hand. Whereas many industry actors prefer to label foods using the Guideline Daily Amount (GDA) system, the FSA opts for a

---

[29] Barbara Richardson (FSA Je_02_#1.): 'it helps them to represent their constituency in a group of people who might not be aware of what the people they're representing feel about things. It tends, really, to give them more confidence because they're there, they are experts in their own right, but they are a different type of experts than the scientists that they are dealing with. But they're "expert consumers", if you like, to a certain extent, and they have a valid argument to put each time. And it helps them to show how they can do that and how they can interact with these people.'

simpler system of on-pack signposting. Based on its research among consumers, the agency wants to introduce either a simple traffic-light system of red, amber, and green to indicate how often food should be eaten, or a multiple traffic-light system that indicates high, medium, or low levels of the key nutrients. Introduction of a system of this kind is unprecedented and rather controversial. As John Harwood, the current chief executive of the FSA puts it in the context of the nutrient profiling model for advertising: 'That's a really difficult decision process to undergo, because you're trying to reduce quite widely different foods to a binary—yes or no—it can be advertised, it can't be advertised.'[30]

The nutrient profiling model becomes the subject of bitter argument. The 'label war' is described as the biggest challenge to the authority of the FSA since its establishment. As front-of-pack labelling is voluntary, the FSA has no legal means by which to force actors into adopting the traffic-light system, but receives support in the media from NGOs like the National Heart Forum, *Which?*, and Children's Food Campaign. Whereas the FSA's traffic-light scheme is backed by Sainsbury's, Waitrose, Co-op, Marks & Spencer, and Asda, the supporters of the GDA-system are at least as powerful and include Cadbury Schweppes, Coca-Cola, Nestle, Danone, Masterfoods, PepsiCo, Unilever, Tesco, Somerfield, and Morrisons. The GDA supporters start a £4 million publicity campaign, 'Know What's Going On Inside You', to promote their own labelling scheme, including a website (*www.whatsinsideguide.com*). *The Grocer* (a national grocery-chain magazine) starts a campaign directed against the FSA's traffic-light system under the slogan 'Weigh it up!', and is backed by the Tories. They call the nutrient profiling model ludicrous and the traffic-light system crude. Both parties attack the preferred system of the other as being 'non-scientific', and the industry ridicules the traffic-light system for being in conflict with common sense. The nutrient profiling model would ban adverts for proclaimed healthy products like cheese and whole fat-milk during TV-shows, and both Coca Cola and apple juice would receive a red label for sugar. The conflict threatens to cause enduring damage to the relationship between the FSA and its industry stakeholders (Bailey 2007: 22):

> There are some areas of the Agency's work where the trust of the food and drink industry in the consultative process has been eroded. For example, FSA decided to continue with developing its Nutrient Profiling Model, despite the robust criticism received in response to its consultation. This model, which in our opinion is scientifically flawed, is now to be adopted for the purpose of restricting the television advertising of food to children. This experience stands out as a watershed in industry's relationship with FSA.

Interestingly, a partial solution for the struggle is provided by casting the conflict in terms of a scientific experiment. On 9 March 2006 the FSA board decides that, whereas the FSA shall keep working with stakeholders to promote its recommended scheme, it will also issue an independent evaluation to assess the impact of the various signpost labelling schemes. As Dame Deirdre Hutton, FSA chairwoman, comments (Miles and Rumbelow 2007): 'What we've done is engage 55 million UK consumers in the biggest piece of behavioural research that's ever been done anywhere in the world . . . We will get the sales data that comes out of the supermarkets, so effectively you get everybody. I think it's terribly exciting and nobody else in the world has done anything like this.'

---

[30] Quote from Taylor 2007.

Putting the consumer first: the problem of the phantom public

In a way the FSA's motto, 'putting the consumer first', suggests a homogeneous public with uniform interests. In actual fact this hides the much more complex reality of our politics of multiplicity. Even an individual consumer often has competing interests (e.g. between a cheap diet and eating healthily), let alone the variety of needs and wishes of a whole nation of consumers. What is more, it is difficult to assess when a risk is 'socially acceptable', as the norms for acceptable risks differ among various groups (Soderstrom *et al.* 1984; Schofield and Shaoul 2000). The FSA seems to avoid this difficulty by defining its task as enabling the consumer to make his own, informed decisions—but the agency still has to make choices, for instance between protecting the consumer and respecting his or her freedom of choice, between the needs of (often better-informed) higher- and lower-income classes (who tend to consider food safety as one of the less urgent problems), and between the needs of minorities and those of the majority (Rothstein 2005). This means that the FSA continuously has to ask itself: where is 'the general public', what does it want, and how can we reach it? Again, there is the division between a more classical attempt to incorporate the consumer via representatives on the one hand, and a 'media aware' attempt to reach the consumer directly through the media. The FSA employs both and both come with their own dilemmas.

The very design in and of media campaigns comes with a range of political choices on what putting the consumer first really requires. Reading the Agency's (2002c) *Criteria for the Use of Fresh, Pure, Natural, etc in Food Labelling* raises the question of how far the FSA should go in protecting the interests of consumers. It contains the FSA criteria for the use of the words 'fresh', 'pure', 'natural', 'traditional', 'original', 'authentic', 'home made', 'farm-house', but also recommends that (FSA 2002c: 5):

> Pictorial representations should be subject to the same scrutiny and control as the words used to portray similar images and concepts....Country scenes may lead a consumer to believe that animal products have been obtained from extensively reared, free-range animals; kitchen scenes may lead a consumer to believe a product is hand-made or at least produced in a small-scale operation.

Some stakeholders regard this as over-regulation. Designer Sharon Brundt, cited in Murphy (2004): 'Visual communication is more open to interpretation (than words). I can't help feeling uneasy at the thought of civil servants passing judgement on whether or not a picture of a country scene is misleading a consumer to believe the animal product has been obtained from extensively reared, free-range animals.'

A more classical response to the idea of putting the consumers first is the idea of including the consumers in the organizational operation of FSA. The FSA organizes regular stakeholder meetings, yet it also tries to get into contact with the 'ordinary consumer' by methods like its interactive website, opinion polls, focus groups, scenario workshops with low-income consumers, regional seminars, forums, and the establishment of a 'Consumer Committee' early in 2002 to signal the FSA response to emerging public concerns. The committee is part of the Corporate Resources and Strategy Group—a central part of the FSA.[31] Its task is, among other things, to alert the FSA to key issues of consumer concern, to provide the FSA with feedback on the effectiveness of its policies in responding to consumer concerns, and to advise on consultation methodologies, including ways of contacting vulnerable and hard-to-reach groups. It also has the responsibility of reviewing the work of consumer representatives on advisory committees (Webster 2002).

The Consumer Committee meets four times a year and consists of twelve members, six of whom are from consumer organizations. The other six are selected on the basis of their reactions to advertisements in the national press. In order to give the Consumer Committee as many links into different groups of consumers as possible, one of the criteria in the selection of members is to ensure a spread in age, colour, sex, and places of origin. Moreover, members are explicitly questioned about their connections in different communities:

> We considered what they could bring to the debate in the sense of what links they had to different types of communities that we might be trying to reach, like perhaps ethnic minority communities, particularly vulnerable low-income communities, disabilities—those sorts of things. And we asked when they applied for them to give us information about what links they already had.[32]

The connections with different communities are important for the organization, not least because the FSA in some aspects reverses the traditional communication strategy about food risks. Part of its communication starts with commissioning research in order to find out what the concerns of consumers

---

[31] The Consumer Committee is not the only permanent body for consumer consultation within the FSA; in November 2003 the agency establishes the Consumer Stakeholder Forum. This forum is meant to give stakeholders the opportunity to discuss the current issues and upcoming plans, to function as an informal communication vehicle, and explore possibilities for partnerships.

[32] Interview FSA Je_02_#1, Barbara Richardson.

are; annual consumer surveys, formal consultation with stakeholders, focus groups, and specific research into consumer issues (e.g. how to communicate with teenagers about nutrition).[33] The concerns of consumers do not always correspond to what the agency itself regards as food-safety issues, but this is no reason for not starting a communication campaign on the topic:

> traditionally what's happened is that the policy people have said, 'Oh, I'm doing a piece of work on animal feed to salmon, or whatever. We should communicate about it.' And you say, 'Why? What's the purpose? What are you going to achieve? And does anyone care?' So what we tend to do now is start from the other end and say, 'OK, what are consumers really worried about?' Because quite often what they're worried about—for example, in food safety terms, radiated food is a good example. Consumers are worried about radiated food. The fact of the matter is, in the UK there is virtually no radiated food. It's spices that are radiated. And there are no food safety issues at all. But actually, that doesn't matter because consumers are saying 'I'm worried about it.' So we're saying, 'OK, we need to communicate about it then. If that's the reality, we need to say what the facts are.'[34]

This approach is not taken to its maximum. Some stakeholders argue that the agency should expand the remit for its safety assessments, and take into account the broader range of factors that might be important for consumers (e.g. sustainability; cf. Dean of Thornton-le-Fylde 2005: 40). Although this latter critique is uttered only by a small cross-section of stakeholders, it links up to a more frequently heard criticism that the FSA frames consumer interest exclusively as the safety and compositional quality of food, excluding the wide range of ethical and economical issues that also might be of interest to the public (Wales 2004: 4).

Leaving aside the complex normative choices that are hidden behind the slogan 'putting the consumer first', it is clear that sending out uniform food-safety messages simply will not do in a modern, fragmented society like the United Kingdom. Nor can the FSA rely solely on contacts with consumer organizations like *Which?* (Henderson 2005):

> In an interview with *The Times*, Sir John [Krebs] said that the agency found their views [of non-profit organisations] useful for 'tensioning the debate' as a counterweight to those of big companies but considers their campaigns neither representative nor reliable. Sir John said: 'I see pressure groups as

---

[33] The policy of engaging with consumers also includes cooperation with other bodies, like training seminars for FSA staff run by consumer groups and secondment to the National Consumer Council (NCC) to work on food policy.

[34] Interview FSA Je_02_#7, Neil Martinson.

businesses—they have a constituency of people who pay their subscriptions or buy their magazines. That is not the same as reflecting the views of the wider public. They are reflecting the views of their constituency.

This brings up one of the seemingly eternal issues in deliberative governance: who are to participate in a deliberation? Can we really just do away with interest groups as 'businesses' or should we, rather, see them as informed spokespersons of a wider constituency? But if we open this latter procedure, how do we account for the strength of the relation between the people at the table and their supposed constituencies?

In terms of legitimacy, it remains important to check whether those at the table really represent the public for whom they claim to speak. This applies, for instance, to the topic of GM food—a subject on which the agency (and John Krebs in particular) had an unfortunate start, being portrayed in the media as having a pro-GM agenda. However, according to the FSA, the perspective of consumer organizations does not reflect the views of the wider public:

> And indeed the UK government on advice of the FSA opposed what the European Union did [the GM moratorium]. Now of course all the consumer organizations in the UK strongly favoured what the European Union did. And one of the things we did in the FSA quite deliberately was we held, we conducted quite a few opinion polls to see whether the views of the consumer organizations were in fact the views of the public. And in relation to GMOs they were not. Which again is not to criticize consumer organizations, but it's to recognize that you have this dilemma, and that whilst you seek to involve consumer organizations, you may at times simply decide that you don't agree with them, and there are better routes for dealing with them. I think the truth is that the consumer organizations were not prepared to move from the point they held, and they held their point not for scientific reasons but for theological reasons, if I could use that term.[35]

Yet such an approach is at odds with the idea that it is a continued deliberation, the repeated interaction of actors from a variety of backgrounds (scientific, lay people, activists, regulators) that creates the better insights. Reverting back to opinion polls on such complex issues as GM seems to be stepping back from the more advanced search for a new deliberative practice.

Whereas the agency tries to keep some distance from pressure groups, reaching different constituencies and target groups of consumers can be of crucial importance either to gather or to spread information about food risks. As most policy divisions of the FSA regularly consult with stakeholders, they

---

[35] Interview FSA #8, Sir Geoffrey Podger.

usually have their own lists of organizations and people to contact. However, when a policy is issued or a safety concern discovered that will affect one sector or community more than another, these regular lists are insufficient.

The FSA in practice—The soy sauce story

A good example of such an issue is the discovery of a potentially cancer-causing chemical in soy sauce in June 2001. The foot-and-mouth crisis has made its first appearance in February 2001 and Chinese restaurants—whose waste food is collected for pigswill—are thought to be the original source of the epidemic. Newspapers publish stories about the smuggling of Asian meat, leading to a fall in trade for Chinese restaurants of about 40% (Burrell 2001). In response to the rumours—which are considered to originate from MAFF—Chinese-restaurant owners in Manchester and London organize marches that are attended by hundreds of people, and announce they intend to sue the government.

In this politically sensitive situation, the FSA has to publish the results of its survey of soy sauces. Knowing that the affected brands are mainly sold in South East Asian shops, and that there are many high consumers on a daily basis among South East Asians, the FSA contacts the National Chinese Community Organizations. Direct contact is sought with Chinese community leaders and with representatives of the Chinese media in the UK:

> We said, 'Look, we've come across this problem, this is going to be our advice, can you help us communicate it to the Chinese communities? And we want to do this before we do it to the English-language media.' Quite deliberately. And we could have been criticized for that. Why should they get special treatment?[36]

The reason for the FSA to give the Chinese community this special treatment is the complexity of its message. The chemicals involved only have an effect if consumed on a daily basis over a long period of time, and that would be an unlikely consumption pattern for non-Chinese Britons. And so, for about four days, the FSA directs all its communication about the sauces to the Chinese community, before informing the general public. At this point, the careful communication strategy fails. Tabloids publish headlines like 'Chinese food can kill you' or 'Shock ban on Chinese foods' (Walton 2001; Marsh and Ingham 2001) and Chinese chefs accuse the FSA of scaremongering (Sherwin 2001):

> The thing we learned from that exercise is that it's as important to say what you don't mean as well as what you mean. So what we do now, for example, is we did a similar one which could have affected the Chinese community, and we said 'This does not affect Chinese restaurants or Chinese food from takeaways. It will not affect...' You know, very very explicit. So we do that now with almost any communication we do. We say, 'This is what it affects; this is what it doesn't affect.'[37]

Nevertheless, the Agency also receives praise from the Chinese community for the way in which the incident is handled, and particularly for the usability of the provided information.

---

[36] Interview FSA Je_02_#7, Neil Martinson.   [37] Ibid.

The Soy Sauce Case is probably the most conspicuous multilingual campaign, but it proves a starting point for further cooperation with cultural ethnic minorities. The agency draws on the lessons learnt from the Soy Sauce Case to inform the Turkish community about microbiological hazards in halva (NAO 2003: 59). Furthermore, it cooperates with the Jewish community (when a kosher baby instant formula is recalled), the Japanese community (when high levels of arsenic are discovered in hijiki seaweed), the Nigerian and West African community (on the subject of calabas chalk), and the Muslim community (to inform them on the risk of BSE in sheep and goats). For this last group the agency establishes a Muslim Organisations Working Group, both to ensure that the information of the agency reaches the Muslim community, and to gather knowledge about the concerns of this community in relation to food.[38] This topic also shows the difficulties of the FSA's strategy. The agency obviously does not want to interfere in religious requirements, and considers the question whether or not Halal meat is prepared according to Islamic standards as outside its remit. However, the working group expresses concerns that this aloofness also prevents the agency from noting large-scale violations of legal requirements—indeed, all members of the group believe that a large proportion of the meat sold as Halal does not meet the criteria (Dean of Thornton-le-Fylde 2005: 42).

Enacting the principle of 'Putting the Consumer First'

The agency perceives its partnerships as important successes, but this approval does not extend to the Consumer Committee. On the contrary; even the consumer representatives on the committee itself are sceptical about their actual influence. There seems to be a tension between the FSA's declared intention to listen to the voices of consumers and the way in which actors perceive their actual influence in decision-making (Wales 2004: 43).

To a certain extent, this might be unavoidable. The FSA promises to put the consumer first, but it is an essential part of its task to *balance* consumer safety against commercial and national interests. The organization's guiding principles explicitly state that 'the Agency's decisions and actions should be proportionate to the risk; pay due regard to costs as well as benefits to those affected by them; and avoid over-regulation' (Ministry of Agriculture

[38] FSA (2005*b*: Annex A: 9).

1998). It implies that all options are open, and that the choices about trade-offs within the commitment to 'putting the consumers first' will have to be made in the concrete enactment of regulatory moments. Balancing health risks against health benefits is a case in point. As Neil Martinson puts it:

> I think that what often you get, or sometimes you can get —because the other big issues is balancing risk against benefits. So you could have a risk assessment that says, 'Hmmm, bit of a problem here.' An example, which is one that crops up time and time again, is consumption of oily fish. Oily fish are potentially very beneficial in terms of helping to prevent heart attacks. The downside is that they contain very high levels of dioxins, right? Now, you've got a clear benefit, and a clear risk. And there will be lots of foods like that, where you can say, 'Well, hmmmm, bit of a risk here.' But actually, how do you weigh that against the benefits? And with the oily fish it's pretty clear-cut because the benefits you can't get from any other food in a diet at all. There's no way you can get it. So you can say, 'Well, actually, in terms of the benefits, there are [sic] always a risk.' But in some cases it won't be as clear-cut as that.[39]

The weighing of risks is the weighing of interests, and thus potentially detrimental to the legitimacy of the agency. Wales's (2004: 43) judgement is harsh:

> The Agency is still in the exploratory stages of accommodating the consumer as citizen. There is an evident asymmetry of power, where the power to set and steer the food policy agenda rests firmly with the institution; consumer representative groups express a frustration at their powerlessness....The expectation of some groups that the Agency would be more sectoral in its decision-making have clearly been dashed. Such confusion over this core value means that the Agency may be running the risk of losing the trust of some groups claiming representative consumer status.

This risk is even more aggravated when a restructuring in June 2004 moves the responsibility for the 'Consumer Branch' from the Corporate Resources and Strategy Group into the Communications Division. Stakeholders worry that the Consumer Committee has lost its strategic status and fear that the committee does not have sufficient resources and communication with the rest of the organization to be truly effective. Moreover, there are questions about the membership of the committee, the problem of identifying 'the consumer', and the appropriate method to reconcile the needs of different groups of consumers. As representative bodies have

---

[39] Neil Martinson, interview FSA Je_02_#7.

varying strengths of voice, the stronger lobbying-groups could influence the agency's policies in a disproportionate way—whereas it is not always clear whom these groups represent. It is felt that the agency does not always take into account the needs of minority ethnic groups and low-income consumers, and that it fails in effectively disseminating information to this latter group (Dean of Thornton-le-Fylde 2005). Members of the committee agree that there is confusion about who they represent (FSA 2005*d*: 37). The structure of the committee (six individual members, six representatives from consumer organizations) causes difficulties as well. Representatives of organizations often promote the policy of their own organization, whereas the individual members tend to be more open, more committed to deliberation. Yet the latter do not have the same depth of knowledge as the organization members, who often take part in discussions about the topics concerned outside the meetings. Individual members therefore find it hard to participate in the debate (ibid. 36):

> This was evident when the Consumer Committee were observed at their December meeting. Much of the discussion was dominated by members from organizations (one independent member only spoke once during the meeting) and although the Chair looked round the table seeking comments, these were not forthcoming from the independent members. On more than one occasion less vocal Committee members were interrupted by those who were more vocal.

Staff of the agency consider the Consumer Committee mainly as another route for the consumer organizations to promote an agenda that they feel already familiar with. They find that the committee fails in providing advice on consumer concerns; the views of the committee are predictable and not necessarily representative of issues that consumers in general are worried about. In turn, the committee members feel that their advice is not being heard and that they do not receive sufficient feedback from the agency, with the result that they do not know whether they are effective or not. An extra complication is the fact that none of those involved with the Consumer Committee seem to be sure about the role, purpose, membership, and effectiveness of the committee. It is even questioned whether all those involved in the committee understand the meaning of 'putting the consumer first' (ibid.).

The critique is shared by outsiders. A report prepared for the Council for Science and Technology regards the FSA's engagement activities merely as a form of PR (Wooding *et al.* 2004):

> The FSA does carry out engagement activities designed to engage the public, but these tend to be aimed at honing the messages for the FSA's campaigns

or assessing the effectiveness of those campaigns, rather than providing input into policy-making. The FSA's approach is particularly interesting, as it appears to have built a solid reputation of public trust despite not directly engaging the public in extensive dialogue. This may suggest that dialogue processes are not the key determinant in building public trust.

In December 2005 the FSA board decides to discontinue the Consumer Committee, following the advice of the committee itself. The committee concludes that (FSA 2005c: 3): 'the Agency should break away from rigid structures and make full use of networks to engage with individuals and groups who were currently not part of the FSA's consumer policy process.' The FSA then develops a new strategy for consumer engagement with the help of DEMOS, a 'think tank for everyday democracy' (Stilgoe and Wilsdon 2006). This report argues that there are two types of relevant public knowledge: *knowledge about the public* (the traditional results of sociological research, quantitative surveys about public opinion, etc.) and *what the public knows* (also known as local knowledge or lay expertise, and as such a test for the credibility of scientific advice). The latter type can again be divided in *questions* (as the public tends to focus on what science does not know, e.g. concerning long-term risks), *connections* (as the public tends to focus on the political context in which evidence is presented), and *suggestions* (fragments of knowledge or evidence that are often discarded as non-certified knowledge).

Following the DEMOS analysis, the FSA decides to split its consumer-engagement model in three parts: direct engagement with individual consumers, engagement with consumer stakeholders, and engagement with groups that are hard to hear or hard to reach. For the direct engagement with consumers, ten consumer panels are to be established in England, Scotland, Wales, and Northern Ireland and annually refreshed with respondents. For the engagement with consumer stakeholders, a 'head of External Affairs' is to be nominated and to function as one single point of contact for all key stakeholders. Further research is to be done as regards the engagement with groups that are hard to reach. In order to assure the quality of the FSA's consumer processes, a Social Science Research Committee and an Advisory Committee on consumer engagement are to be established. The latter consists of an independent chair and a senior representative of a leading think-tank, a senior representative of government with extensive experience of engaging with the public, possibly two additional members from an umbrella voluntary organization and a community food initiative, but also—and this is significant—a senior consultative relationship manager from the private sector. With this move the question 'how to reach the public(s)?' receives even more emphasis—giving the term 'public relations' a different meaning and strangely echoing Dewey's persuasion that the public will only be able to find its substance when communication is improved.

Conclusion

The inception and first steps of the Food Standards Agency provide a remarkable and illuminating experiment with deliberative governance. It shows a marked shift away from the previous 'first get the facts right' approach to issues pertaining to the broad domain of public health, food, and the environment (cf. Hajer and Loeber 2007; Hajer, Loeber, and Van Tatenhove 2007). Several authors have questioned whether the institutional response was as innovative as it was suggested to be. Forbes (2004: 354–5) argues that the BSE crisis only showed the major doubts of the public about the balance between consumer and industry interests, and about the truthfulness of statements about safety. A reorganization would not be able to overcome this; consumer groups, environmentalists, and other opponents of the existing agricultural practices were the winners of the BSE episode, but it was far from clear whether the public would now be better off. Millstone and Van Zwanenburg (2002: 605) criticized the ambiguity of the FSA, with unelected, unaccountable board members taking almost all policy decisions—allowing ministers to stay at arm's length. But this is an eternally disputed issue: is it better to have a minister in charge or is it better to organize controls at arm length? The former has the advantage of direct parliamentary accountability, but with the risk of politics influencing decision-making on issues of food safety; the latter has the advantage of autonomous decision-making putting consumers first, but with the risks of a less central embedding in classical-modern parliamentary accountability mechanisms.[40] Yet while these critics are quick to come up with their assessments, they fail to appreciate the struggle, the many moments and places where the FSA's history is determined in the very enactment of its own principles. My reading of the case is one in which a traumatic event, the BSE/CJD crisis, functions as a catalyst to introduce a new, deliberative genre of governance. Yet to no one is it clear what this means exactly, how to operationalize it, and what can remain of

---

[40] But note that the director of the FSA is not an invisible bureaucrat but does indeed make his own appearances in the various parliaments of the UK.

the old ways of doing food-safety governance and what is to go. It is that struggle, at the same time intellectual and institutional, that we see taking place in the first years of the FSA's history.

Looking back at the first years of its operational practice, the least one can say is that the FSA has so far performed better than most of the critics (including the stakeholders) expected. It might not always have been successful, but it has certainly tried to establish an experience of democratic, or at least trustworthy, governance from the day of its establishment. But as this chapter has shown, such an endeavour is not without its problems, paradoxes, and dilemmas. And it is in pointing these out that we can come to a better understanding of how an authoritative governance is possible in our mediatized age, and to what extent a deliberative genre can fulfil a role in this.

The FSA represents the most active enlistment of 'hard core' communication techniques in the sphere of environmental governance, broadly conceived, that I am aware of. This has been crucial for giving the new agency its image, but at the same time the prominence of its communication strategy causes conflicts with stakeholders. They acknowledge the difficulties of communicating complex messages in a way that will attract the media, but some of them suspect the agency of being too eager for media coverage and believe that the agency mainly seeks favourable publicity for itself, instead of accurately portraying information (Dean of Thornton-le-Fylde 2005). The high media profile urges the agency to 'keep people on message', creating the risk of silencing dissent or filtering out complexities that were important in the agency's deliberations. Consequently, stakeholders feel that their contributions in the policy-developing process are not always acknowledged in the public communication of the FSA. While the case study shows that the FSA does much more that 'simply stating the facts', it is this, in essence, classical-modernist 'the expert speaks' performance that lends itself best to mediatic representation. Nevertheless, the case also shows interesting crossovers, as for instance where communication techniques are used to support the authority of the FSA's statements that 'it does not know' what exactly is the case.

Arguably the most impressive part of the FSA's work, however, is the new involvement of stakeholders in food-safety regulation. Most prominent is the multitude of ways in which consumers, producers, and other stakeholders are now integrated in the various internal practices, such as in the FSA board and forums, but also as consumer representatives on the scientific committees. We here see an institutional uptake of other, non-scientific 'ways of knowing' (cf. Ingram and Schneider 2007). This obviously creates all sorts of tensions, and we can read the FSA's early history as a struggle to try and act on its commitment to break through the classical-modernist control of regulatory policy by expert advice. In much of the FSA's case it is evident that the BSE crisis cast a long shadow over the choices that were made. After all, the catastrophic misjudgements that led to the contamination of the public with CJD had to do with the fact that the recommendations following the expert reports on whether or not BSE was a health risk were basically impractical, and were therefore not respected in the everyday treatment of meat and bone in UK slaughterhouses. Bringing the stakeholders into the internal proceedings will, most likely, help to prevent this from happening again. Yet such an innovation comes with conflicts and frictions.

Deliberative governance is always going to be a multifaceted endeavour. It requires a continued and repeated interaction among the variety of actors that together constitute the broader field of food regulation and food safety. It implies an institutional creativity in identifying and remedying institutional biases that are to be found in institutional practices. But it also requires a sharp eye for the role of concrete incidents in this process of searching for the right mode of deliberation. Policy-making in the mediatized age is a process in which conflicts and incidents are the windows to communicate policy goals and strategies and, ultimately, to create an authoritative governance. The incident becomes a narrative, a storyline that is subsequently used to make sure that the old routines do not resurface but are held in check.

The FSA case shows not only how difficult it is to break through established institutional routines, but also that it is often an emotional moment that helps to really secure a shift in thinking. The direct discursive confrontation, where families of victims basically point out the nasty consequences of a particular way of reasoning, is what resonates in the FSA and informs a change of institutional routines. The fact that this incident was reported to be an eye-opener in many of the interviews we conducted, suggests that this was a 'critical moment' in the young institutional history of the FSA, a moment constitutive of its new identity, one in which people realized what it really meant to 'put consumers first'. Basically, it is through incidents like these (and all the less 'charismatic' moments where consumer representatives argued for a new mode of discourse in the scientific committees of the FSA) that new institutional routines emerge, are enacted, and become routinized that do indeed differ from their predecessors. The FSA shows that there are procedures that do in fact combine different ways of knowing in a deliberative process. These practices, well hidden within the FSA as an institution, we may understand as 'boundary practices' (cf. Jasanoff 1990) that perform a function across publics.

The functioning of a deliberative governance alternative to the old classical-modernist logic of food-safety regulation can be illustrated by the FSA's handling of the carcinogenic substances in soy sauce. Defining characteristics are the alarm-bell ringing from scientific findings, which are then contextualized to attain the most precise assessment of which groups are potentially affected. By then pointing out the findings to the group, and relating the experts directly to the people who can explain how the sauce is used, the FSA avoided a fully mediatized spectacle causing unnecessary social unrest. Confined as the story may be, it shows an important reorientation in the way in which the government seeks to perform food-safety policies, allowing for a more mature role of societal actors.

The importance of such intelligent cooperation with societal actors is underlined by the FSA's difficulties in acting on the apparently simple commitment of 'putting consumers first'. The FSA is a regulatory agency and works with stakeholders as diverse as consumers, producers, retailers, and enforcing authorities, whose demands often conflict with each other. Constructive relations with industry and enforcing authorities are indispensable if the agency is to do its work effectively, while at the same time its responsibility (and credibility) as watchdog may ask for publicly naming-and-shaming these same stakeholders. The agency still struggles to keep the balance between its remit and responsibilities as an advisory agency and its tendency to be perceived as a campaigning agency acting in the interest of consumers (e.g. on the theme of nutrition).The slogan 'putting the consumer first' hides a reality of fragmented publics that can only be reached by targeted communication. Much of what we have seen in this chapter is evidence of the continued struggle of the FSA to find the appropriate means to deliver on this commitment to putting the consumer first.

This endeavour is in turn related to the ambiguities of openness and transparency, often mentioned as obvious goals of a new deliberative governance. The open board meetings, the broadcasting on the website, and the various communication strategies are all part of the FSA's endeavour to convey an image of itself as an open and honest organization. But making all the existing information easily available does not necessarily mean that the various audiences can easily gather the specific information they need. Consequently, the FSA is criticized for publishing such a huge amount of information that it is difficult to identify the relevant issues. Moreover, transparency can conflict with the complexity of the message and the need for balanced policy-making. Stakeholders see a trade-off between openness and the quality of decision-making in the FSA's policy of open board meetings, and the FSA communication strategy towards consumers seems to hinder important relations with stakeholders. Paradoxically, practices of openness and dialogue with stakeholders may even lead to a loss of trust when stakeholders feel they should be consulted but are not, or when they feel that the consultation process is unfair. This threatens to damage the relations between the FSA and industry actors (as could be seen in the case of the Nutrient Profiling Model), and this can in turn lead to confusion and uncertainty among consumers.

In Warren's 1996 account, a true democratic authority 'comes from a set of institutionalized protections and securities within which the generative force of discursive challenge is possible. More specifically, authority operates when the possibility of discursive justification exists and is occasionally exercised, but is not brought to bear on every authoritative decision, precisely because the critical background of attentive publics renews the authoritative status of the decision maker' (1996: 57). This is a subtle way of combining the commitment to more inclusive participation with a response to the critique, heard so often, that deliberative democracy sets unrealistic targets for public participation. The FSA seems to have created these preconditions: it allows for a discursive interpellation, has institutionalized many boundary practices that make sure that a variety of discourses are represented, while at the same using communication strategies that support the authority of the FSA leadership. Ironically, while its board meetings are open to the public and can all be watched over the internet, this turns out to have a neutralizing effect on the media: while one might have feared that exposure of internal deliberations might be to the detriment of the unified authority of the FSA, as the media could jump on issues discussed, this has not been the experience. Instead, the new openness has taken away the interest of the media, as they seem to believe that important topics will not be discussed publicly. It creates another paradox: the very practice of being open can depoliticize the issue.

6

The Paradox of Authority in a Mediatized Politics

The search for authoritative governance

Authoritative governance has to be achieved in a world marked by political fragmentation, where public problems often transgress the borders of existing political jurisdictions. In this context political utterances, however well intended, are all too often whispered down the lane like in the children's game 'Telephone' or 'Chinese whispers': constantly changing meaning, with political turmoil as a result. Such is the condition of what I called the politics of multiplicities. Trying to make sense of the current authority problem in its historical context, I have distinguished two rival 'genres' of trying to be authoritative: one related to the established classical-modernist way of governing, the other manifest in a new, more flexible approach, now widely known as network governance. The problem is, however, that neither form of governance has an automatic fit with today's politics of multiplicities.

I have sought to show that both forms of governance have to be performed, and that both genres have their own preferred way of doing so. Authority, in my view, is a function of this performance. The classical-modernist mode of governing mobilizes all the advantages related to its long historical record. It is a front-stage politics in which actors occupying established institutional positions mobilize the entire setting so as to be seen as authoritative: the architecture of its places of decision-making, the parliamentary rituals, and the bureaucratic routines. It has an obvious advantage over network governance, which has to do without the help of well-known stages that immediately invoke institutional routines and conventions. Network governance escapes the eye, a feature which is only enhanced by the fact that it is mostly performed by actors that see the shadows of the back-stage as a relief. The advantage of network

Table 6.1. Governance genre and authority mechanism

Genre of governance	Authority mechanism
Classical-modernist	Authority rooted in an established repertoire of performances and settings
Network governance	Authority rooted in interactions that create the potential for 'reasoned elaboration' and problem closure

governance, however, is its flexibility: networks can be adjusted so as to precisely achieve the scale and shape to match a particular problem. It can bring together the coalition of actors needed to really address a particular problem, cutting across jurisdictions, backgrounds, and hierarchy. Its scope can be tailored to problem-solving. Lacking the established context of classical-modernist institutions, network governance needs another authority mechanism. It builds up authority by organizing the interaction in such a way as to produce solutions that those affected see as legitimate; authority is to be derived from the characteristics of the interaction itself. These two genres of governance can be compared in a simple table (Table 6.1).

We have seen how both genres struggle with the question of authority. I see no theoretical or empirical grounds to argue that one mode of governing (classical-modernist) is on its way out, with the other (network governance) as an obvious successor. Indeed, the case studies confirm that in politics the making of authoritative claims often requires the employment of elements from both genres.

Even if network governance should not be seen as the 'successor model' to classical-modernist governance, there clearly is a growing recognition of network governance, both as an empirical phenomenon and as a strategy of problem-solving. Network governance is then seen as an emergent strategy originating in particular struggles with practical problems. However, the role of network governance in bringing about a new authoritative governance has hardly been studied. I will here turn to the understanding of network governance as an element in the development of democracy first, and then reconnect the findings to the broader issue of authoritativeness of governance.

Network governance can be democratic...

The concept of network governance clearly grew in importance because of its problem-solving capacities ('network follows problem'). Initially it was therefore a concept developed in the public-administration literature and public-policy literature (Heclo 1974; Marin and Mayntz 1991; Kooiman 1993). In the 1990s many theorists working as 'organic intellectuals' in particular policy fields started to use related terms (e.g. Rosenau and Czempiel 1992 in IR; Hooghe and Marks 2002 in European Studies). More recently several prominent democracy theorists have examined network governance in terms of its potential for a renewal of democracy.

John Dryzek was arguably one of the first to draw on the insights from the public-policy literature to develop his case for reinvigorating democratic governance (Dryzek 1990, 1996). His later work explicitly refers to examples where governance was practised to address public problems that would otherwise just remain unaddressed, such as in the case of whaling, the *maquiladoras*, and bio-piracy (Dryzek 2000). The appeal of his work was that he found a way to combine activity on solving pressing public problems with a normative notion of democratic governance, first under the label of discursive democracy, later as 'deliberative politics' (Dryzek 2006). For Dryzek, a deliberative politics refers to what one could describe as a normative 'code of conduct' for discussions and decision-making. As with most deliberative theory there is always the sound of an echo of Habermas's communicative ethics. There is, of course, no necessary confinement of the application of such a code of conduct to new non-parliamentary configurations. Deliberative norms can be applied to judge the democratic quality of decision-making in standard, classical-modernist political institutions. Yet crucial in Dryzek's later work is that he sees deliberative politics as an alternative that could guide discussion and decision-making that has to take place in an institutional void, that is, across different jurisdictions, in non-standard political spaces and by 'discursive representation' (Dryzek and Niemeyer 2007). Here his approach should be seen as an alternative to the call for a global institutional politics. So what Dryzek explores is the potential of configurations of network governance for a strengthening of democracy. Although his work deals with authority as the potential for reasoned elaboration, he does not address the issue in these terms.

In a similar vein Archon Fung (Fung 2004) has elaborated the notion of Empowered Participatory Governance (EPG), drawing on his fieldwork in Chicago inner-city politics. Brilliantly ignoring the divide between political theory and public administration, *Empowered Participation: Reinventing Urban Democracy* describes how the introduction of the combination of a devolution of power and sophisticated accountability mechanisms in the domains of educational politics and fighting crime produced remarkable results. Fung develops the notion of an 'accountable autonomy' which creates the conditions under which state agencies can successfully collaborate with non-governmental actors and, indeed, with loosely organized citizens. In earlier work Fung and colleagues empirically analysed the ways in which configurations that we would here label as network governance effectively collaborated in the sphere of environmental policy (Sabel, Fung, and Karkkainen 2000). Yet it is in his later work that he explicitly draws on the empirically observed possibilities to develop a new democratic theory (Fung 2006). Arguing that the three dimensions of legitimacy, justice, and effectiveness together constitute a space within which the various mechanisms of participation can be situated, he goes beyond the traditional idea of public participation as 'motherhood and apple pie' to acknowledge the more complex reality that 'specifying and crafting *appropriate* roles for participation...demands forward-looking empirical sensitivity and theoretical imagination' (ibid. 74, emphasis added).

Yet another example of a democratic theorist who has turned his attention to governance networks is Mark Warren, who recently proclaimed that 'policy and administration are increasingly front and centre to the project of democratization'. Anticipating the disbelief of many, Warren noted:

> Who would have thought that policy and policy-making—the province of technocrats and administrators—would move into the vanguard of democratization? And yet it is in this domain—not in electoral democracy—that we are seeing a rebirth of strongly democratic ideals, including empowered participation, focused deliber-ation, and attentiveness to those affected by decisions. (Warren 2008: 1)

Warren plays with the concept of 'governance-driven democratization' (GDD) to refer to this phenomenon wondering whether it signifies a 'third transformation of democracy'. After the introduction of mass democracy in the nineteenth century and the wave of advocacy and social-movement politics over the last four decades of the twentieth century, he now sees governance processes as potential drivers of a new wave of democratization. The crux in his thinking is that network governance does not only respond to the deficits of the formal democratic institutions that are incapable of producing solutions for public problems and have difficulty in organizing legitimacy. Warren also regards network governance as a configuration with the potential to organize dynamic constituencies of people in 'post-boundary contexts', that is, where problems spill over political jurisdictions. Democratic quality is not only a matter of representing the complexity of the wishes coming out of a plural society and a very dense civil society, it is also to be judged in terms of the 'all affected principle': all those groups that are potentially affected by particular policy choices should be part of the deliberation leading the definition of problem and solution.

Deliberative democracy for these authors is thus not only a set of norms that are to guide deliberation and decision-making to improve practices in existing institutional settings; they also see it as a response to the new political sociology of what I have called the institutional void. They come up with a normative theory that can guide and inspire the quality of democracy of the growing political 'in between': the politics taking place in between or beyond the jurisdictions of standing classical-modernist state institutions. In each case we see how the political theory of a deliberative democracy—as a practice of governing which focuses on the exchange of arguments in an atmosphere of equality, where the force of the better argument prevails over the force of numbers, money, or vested interests— is combined with the identification of real-life examples of governance in action. The interesting move we observe here is one of an *empirical political philosophy* in which it is not the deductive reasoning of the armchair that prevails, but that develops deliberative mechanisms in an iteration between empirical observation and theoretical reflection.

All three authors have an acute eye for changes in the political-sociological set-up. Hence where the classical parliamentary systems fail (or are absent!—cf. He and Warren 2008 on China, and Dryzek 2000 on environmental problems spilling over jurisdictions), they see this new logic of a deliberative governance providing new possibilities to address and resolve pressing public problems. There is a strong sense that a renewed classical-modernist answer to the political challenges will not do: the institutional void is, in that sense, not a temporary phenomenon. The strength of deliberative democracy is that it actually presents norms as to how to conduct politics in the context of network governance to govern the growing political 'in-between'.

The cases studies in this book suggest a slightly different angle. Characteristic for all three cases is the *fragility* of the deliberative processes. Indeed, in my cases it might be better to speak of 'deliberative moments in governance' instead of 'deliberative governance'. What is more, whereas the theoretical literature all too often sketches a dichotomy between on the one hand interest-based, highly political, bargaining-oriented governance, and on the other hand idealistic deliberation for the public good (cf. Papadopoulos 2002 for a critique), none of the cases in this book confirms this. Yet the cases do clearly support the idea that in certain situations a deliberative notion of network governance can indeed give a powerful new meaning to democratic government.

But can network governance be authoritative?

Network governance may thus be seen as a promising way of strengthening democracy in our age, but the key question here is whether network governance can also be authoritative. In Chapter 1 I have spelled out a way of conceptualizing authority that suggests that authority may be seen in terms of the possibility for a reasoned elaboration. Theoretically Mark Warren (1996) has most explicitly addressed the relationship of authority and deliberation. Warren observes that authority and deliberation are often juxtaposed; in the prevailing view people think of authority as involving the surrender of judgement, not the interactive deliberation among many (1996: 46). He cites Claus Offe, who noted that discussions of authority are marked by a neo-conservative bias which holds that authority can only be regained by restoring the classical-modernist repertoire. This repertoire, in which the political leader takes up the leading role, is then seen as providing the economic, moral, and cognitive foundations for a new way of effective governing (discussed in ibid. 48). Warren puts forward a deliberative alternative. In this model the deliberation is no threat to authority, but the mechanism that provides it: 'only because authorities are scrutinized critically do they come to possess authority' (ibid. 56). This questioning can come from experts and from 'concerned, attentive non-experts' alike. Hence, here authority depends on the institutionalized possibility of a discursive challenge and the related idea of improving both content and confidence via the discussion over how to address a problem.

How does this relate to the case-study findings? The cases in this book support Warren's thesis that 'democratic procedures, especially those that enable and protect critically attentive publics, serve to constitute and reproduce the boundaries of authority, and in so doing help generate the terms of trust and authorization' (ibid. 49). The advantage of the empirical investigations is, however, that they also show the complicated conditions under which the experimentation with and the enactment of this deliberative governance is taking place. *And here the mediatizedness of politics is an aspect which is ignored in the political-theoretical debate on deliberative democracy almost entirely.* This cannot be neglected if the account is to fulfil its ambitions. I have argued in this book that our politics and policy-making should be regarded as fundamentally mediatized. This affects the authority of particular forms of governance. It is why I think it makes sense to speak of an authority paradox.

The authority paradox

The authority paradox of a mediatized politics is that the phenomenon of 'media 24/7' multiplies the attention for the classical-modernist political centre at a time at which crucial problems often spill over jurisdictions, disempowering the political centre. While media attention gives a boost to the authority of the centre, actual problem-solving requires complex forms of network governance. What is more, the preoccupation with the simplest symbolic stagings of classical-modernist authority suggests that the media are themselves losing their grip on politics as well.

What are the repercussions of this paradox? Is there a potentiality for reasoned elaboration under these conditions of mediatized politics, or is mediatization in and of itself a force promoting a dumbing down? It is easy to understand why media have a preference for classical-modernist politics. For a start, look at network governance through the eye of the media: network governance is ephemeral, a politics without a centre. More importantly, it is politics without a face. A mediatized politics is all about events, occurrences, and about communicating news by giving things a recognizable story. Governance, on the other hand, is all about process and, in its present form, a non-entity for the media. A process of network governance resists mediatized appreciation.

Despite the evidence that much politics takes place elsewhere, the media continue to portray the staged moments of collective decision-making in parliament as the very essence of politics, thus helping to reproduce and replicate the classical-modernist politics of the 'decisive act'. The old classical-modernist order remains the strongest symbolization of political democracy. The power of this symbolization becomes easily understandable when you think of the architecturally sculptured spaces, the annual timetable of a parliamentary year, with recurring rituals and events, and the cast of self-important actors that tend to like to be seen in power, proactively turn to the media, and regard the media as the measuring-rod of the quality of their performance. Policy-makers and politicians use all the tools available to them, from the power of narrative to the employment of the context in which they speak, to give meaning to an unstructured and potentially unstable situation. The media call upon political actors to show their authority, also in situations where the classical-modernist practices from which their authority derives cannot deliver. Mediatized politics entices politicians to show that they matter, and the temptation is to try to perform authority in precisely the way that fits the preferred media format.

This symbolic appeal of the classical-modernist order has the result that the media—while often being critical—are at the same time attached and attracted to whatever performances take place within these clearly demarcated spaces. Hence, while the autonomous power of the centre to change events diminishes, its press coverage soars. Press conferences of governmental figureheads are now attended by a multitude of television channels that each try to use the footage to create their own particular story. Mediatized politics creates new symbolic realities based on the staging of power of the centre. It is an offer that political elites can hardly refuse.

The second part of the explanation of the paradox of authority is that network governance resists easy representation. It might be able to bring together the formations that do have the capacity to generate authority and create coalitions of collaboration, but it is weak in the symbolic representation of the legitimacy of intervention. The performance perspective helps to explain this side of the paradox. While in the modernist repertoire there are clear settings for performing politics, network governance is notoriously weak in this respect. It lacks both drama and dramaturgy. This is deeply problematic in a society in which politics has come to be inherently mediatized (cf. Bennett and Entman 2001; Crozier 2007). Classical-modernist politics is characterized by a wealth of ceremonies, emotional debates, the personal dramas and charismatic legitimacy of celebrity politicians, or of decision-making moments that come to symbolize an entirely policy process. Network governance, on the other hand, thrives on quiet negotiation. Reports on classical-modernist politics in effect focus on Weber's ideal type actors: risk-taking, passionate, seeking responsibility (or, if they are not there, this absence of 'real' politicians is the story). Network governance features those who know most about the substance, not those who like to be on stage. Should some enlightened spirit try to connect that round table to the mediatized politics, all that network governance can offer is a meeting room filled with administrators, some stakeholders, expert reports, and a folder with minutes and draft agreements. This can hardly be made into an interesting story, and is therefore neglected by journalists and remains invisible to the general public. This invisibility might contribute to the problem-solving capacity of the networks—after all, it is easier to come to a compromise or an agreement in the dark—but is of course highly problematic in terms of legitimacy and, importantly, in terms of generating a broader commitment for a particular line of action.

The lack of a recognizable face and place is not 'merely' a matter of communication. It also has a democratic significance. Network governance fails in being representative (cf. Hajer and Versteeg 2008). While the term representation or representative is mostly understood in the cognitive context of an individual defending (or pretending to defend) the political interests of a larger group, it has a second, equally political meaning, namely the portrayal of something abstract or absent (cf. Latour 2005: 6). Parliament both literally and physically *re-presents* the demos, even if it is in an imperfect and by citizens (often rightly) criticized way. After all, how would we be able to understand 'democracy' when we could not engage in experiential practices—rituals of decisive acts such as voting or the passing of a bill? What would we make of parliamentary democracy if we were not able to witness and experience it: to see or enter our parliamentary buildings, the site where important decisions are made (cf. Mumford 1952; Goodsell 1988), to watch parliamentary proceedings? Parliamentary rules and procedures seem so self-evident that one might easily forget that they are themselves the product of endless thinking and rethinking of how political decisions are best enacted. This is what the study of the parliaments of the French Revolution by Jean-Philippe Heurtin brings out so nicely, and that is why I made that an element of the argument in Chapter 2. What now appears a quasi-natural procedure is in fact a dramaturgy of political decision-making that was established after many rehearsals and try-outs, and readjusted over the course of the many social conflicts that were fought out in this setting thereafter.

So one type of governing is strong in its mediatized representation but weak in problem closure (classical-modernist), the other is potentially strong in problem closure but weak in representation (network governance). Now the background of the paradox has been cleared, the question is, of course, if there is a way out. Can we come any closer to answering the question of if and how an authoritative governance is possible in our mediatized age?

A way out

Politics is now often to be made on new political stages, and political actors need to experiment with new political repertoires to be able to speak to the diversity of publics. In this book I have introduced the term 'politics of multiplicities' to capture the challenges facing political leaders and policy-makers. It is a condition in which meanings bounce, reflect, and refract; where the particular circumstances and lead-ups of statements are easily lost and politics all too often seems to be only about semantic damage control. Authority based on some foundational source, whether institutional position or inheritance or similar, is often ineffective in generating widespread authoritativeness. In our mediatized age two types of Weber's sources of authority thus seem to have diminished relevance: neither traditional authority ('resting on an established belief in the sanctity of immemorial traditions') nor legal authority ('based on the belief in the legality of enacted rules') can help to understand how to achieve authoritative governance in the complicated situation of institutional voids where the task of politics is to first establish a relationship between problems, publics, and political decisions (cf. Weber 1978: 215–51). Yet this does not mean that all we are left with is his 'charismatic authority' ('resting on devotion to the exceptional sanctity, heroism or exemplary character of an individual person...'). On the contrary, this book has shown how we should always understand the authority of the acts of political leaders in their contexts. We need another understanding of authority, not in terms of systems or persons, but in terms of the string of enactments that create and sustain authority.

The media love the setting of the castle of classical-modernist politics, they exploit the theatrical element and add the interaction between protagonists and antagonists to present politics in a way that fits their particular medium. The cases in this book present some examples of this. In a mediatized politics, political acts made in the 'appropriate' classical-modernist settings are sometimes almost ignored, as in the case of Mayor Cohen's speech to the Amsterdam City Council described in Chapter 3, while more spectacular 'staged' meetings get all the attention.[1] But politics responds. We can discern three trends.

A first trend is a move from an authority based on institutional conventions towards a more personified politics of style. Stardom is a polit-ical possibility, allowing for some authority based on personified politics (cf. e.g. Street 2004). A second trend is the move to try to generate authority using a different mode of interaction. This leads to

---

[1] Despite the fact, as in this case, that what is said is less radical in terms of content. Clearly, it was not the content that was determining what was news; it was content-in-setting which made the speech in the Al-Kabir mosque by the new Moroccan-Dutch alderman news at the cost of the other, more radical, discursive shift.

a discursive authority which is generated by an extended and explicitly staged practice of deliberation. This is what Dryzek, Fung, Sabel, Warren, and others find in some examples of network governance. It is a form of governing which seeks to develop an interaction with publics drawing on discursive interaction within a well-defined setting. Here the authority of governance is not a derivative of the institutional rules and conventions, but is actively created in the joint experience of being political between policy-makers and publics. Thirdly, we see a field of political techniques, staging an extended form of reasoned elaboration between stakeholders, outside the classical-modernist order and often removed from the view of 'the general public'. However, it should be said explicitly: these three trends are what can be observed; they are not meant to underpin a normative theory of a new authoritative governance.

The case studies in this book give us insights into the effect and meaning of these three trends for authoritative governance. In fact they allow us to turn our earlier table (6.1) into a more complex table of ways of performing authority, to step beyond the literature on governance and take the mediatizedness of politics fully into account (see Table 6.2). In compliance with the theoretical discussion of Chapter 1, I here focus specifically on the ways in which modes of governing seek to establish a relationship with the public(s).

My argument is that the classical-modernist way of performing authority becomes rare. A passive audience is only passive until it switches on. Or, using the language of Chapter 1, Manin's audiences have made way for Schudson's monitorial citizens or my own idea of 'citizens-on-standby'. These concepts explain the mechanisms that can change a seemingly passive audience into active and politically astute publics that want to be part of the representation of politics.

Table 6.2. Ways of performing authority

	Authority based in institutional setting	Authority based in characteristics of interaction
Classical-modernist	1. Authority generated following institutional rules and conventions / acceptance by a passive audience	2. *Personified politics of style*: authority dependent on *in situ performances* / judged by monitorial citizens
Network governance	4. Authority generated by enactment using particular stagings of deliberation / based on the joint experience of politics, creating a relationship between policy makers and publics	3. Authority generated by extended practice of reasoned elaboration / based on the discursive interaction in the network, but without involvement of public

The above discussion implies that an authoritative governance in the mediatized age now has to draw primarily on a combination of the authority mechanisms of boxes 2, 3, and 4, always appreciating the requirements of the context. In some regards this requires a shift in thinking. We are now looking towards a politics that starts with the fact that publics are now active judges of performances. It also appreciates the discursiveness of politics: the fact that meanings are not fixed but should be seen as growing, evolving. I therefore conceive of governance in terms of a string of performances, at a variety of settings, which 'enlist' authority through this sequence of enactments. These settings will often include those of the classical-modernist politics.

Last but not least, it allows for governance to be a joint experience which, ultimately, creates the authority of a reasoned elaboration. Authoritative governance in a mediatized politics requires more than a reasoned exchange of arguments among those affected. The strength of a network governance depends on its capacity to fit the scope of problems, and its appreciation of reason, but now in its broader, performative understanding. What is needed is, to use the terms of William James, the reflection on the conditions under which we develop the 'will to believe' and lend authority to a particular way of acting on the world (James 1956).

Mark Warren has pointed to the fact that even in a system of deliberative governance there remains a need for what he calls 'authority as trust': there will always be many decisions that citizens just have to leave to officials or administrators (Warren 1996: 47). One can only agree. My argument is that this can work particularly well if politics is successful in dealing with crises and incidents, or what I have called dislocations. If one is able to enact a reasoned elaboration in those foregrounded situations then more classical authority-as-trust will be the spin-off. And it is, of course, precisely those situations of crisis or incident that are often picked up by the media. To be authoritative in our day and age calls for an awareness of the crucial role of these dislocatory moments. Here the case studies give us insightful new material.

Understanding mechanisms of authoritative governance through the case studies

The case studies in this book help us to appreciate the importance of the perspective on politics as drama and performance for understanding authority in our day and age. They illustrate the sometimes bizarre interaction around moments of dislocation among acts of governing, but also the particular conditions under which an authority based on reasoned elaboration prospers, perhaps may even prevail. However, most of all they show the contradictions that this sometimes implies. In what follows I will discuss the cases, illuminating the four ways of performing authority shown in Table 6.2.

The Amsterdam case reveals some of the workings of a personified politics of style. Looking at the Amsterdam leadership, it was not simply that the 'multiculturalist' claim was rated as a better argument than its populist counterpart—far from it. Yet while the populists expressed themselves in a style described in Chapter 3 as satirical cynicism, the Moroccan-Dutch alderman Ahmed Aboutaleb counteracted that with a performance of what we might call an 'authority of authenticity'. While defending a—at the time deeply unpopular (!)—'multiculturalist' claim, it was his authenticity that gave his arguments authority and created, in terms of Alexander (2004a), a 'fused', seemingly natural performance. It was not simply what was said; it was very much about who said it, how, and where.

Wherever the role of style popped up, it reinforced the importance of what I have called situational credibility (cf. King 1987). A particular act has to meet the requirements of a particular scene. Political authority requires the ability to 'read' a situation and come up with recognizable political style that 'weaves together matter and manner, principle and presentation, in an attractively coherent and credible political performance', as Dick Pels put it (2003: 57).

Thus, just as interesting as where actors got it right are those situations where they got it wrong, the most striking example thereof being the way in which the situatedness of their performance was misjudged by some of the actors in the Ground Zero case. Skidmore, Owings & Merryl (SOM), a long-time developer-friendly and almost default corporate architect, did not read the signs and lost the competition in the eye of the public. Performing a presentation to the 'client', they missed the significance of the fact that the presentations were a mediatized event. Instead, Libeskind, who had never built a skyscraper before, captured the public imagination with his emotional narrative, and created new political facts.

The identification of the importance of a personified politics of style is central to an understanding of policy-making in an age of mediatization. In nearly all situations it was impossible to make a hard differentiation between policy-making on the one hand and media reporting on the other. Susan Herbst was already struck by the fact that news and entertainment media seemed to be able to 'imbue' certain individuals with authority (2003: 481), arguing that authority can be media-derived. Arguably the most striking example thereof in this book concerns the role of the 'Friends of Theo' in the Van Gogh case. At first non-existent, they became the 'official' antagonist within hours of his murder, and were given air-time whenever the official political leadership gave its opinion on the issue. This is not incidental. Mediatized politics has given a boost to the phenomenon of self-imposed leaders. This is particularly evident in those fields in which established institutions are lacking. For instance, both the United Kingdom and the Netherlands had their own experiences with media performances of self-imposed quasi-religious Islamic leaders who later turned out to have no following at all. Here it was their eloquence and style that paved the way for a media career, not the hard work of becoming an authoritative leader within a particular community. The fact is that the media can bestow authority on political leaders (cf. Herbst 2003: 495–8), but in order for those media figures to remain authoritative they will have to continue to successfully enact their role.

While the employment of style is an obvious element in performing authority, I have suggested that it does not make sense to pick up on this and try to coach political actors to 'change political style'. The notion of 'performative habitus' (cf. Hajer and Uitermark 2008) puts the possibilities of such a strategy into perspective: it is not as if everyone can just 'pick and choose' a style for a particular moment. On the contrary, one of the findings of the empirical chapters is the extent to which the performance of political and administrative leaders should be understood taking their 'performative habitus' into account. For most leading politicians, operating effectively requires having a repertoire of acts available. For those who are not political 'naturals' this is something which can only be acquired over a period of time. It is this learned capacity to act that explains, for instance, the remarkable role that Alderman Ahmed Aboutaleb could play in performing authoritative governance in the turmoil after the murder of Theo Van Gogh in the Netherlands.

Another set of findings relates to the conditions under which a mediatized politics can work for reasoned elaboration. The rebuilding of Ground Zero was obviously always going to be a media event. The scale and approach of the 'Listening to the City' event fitted very well with the media format; indeed, it was consciously designed to be so big as to be news. Hence this was a performance that got reported, and by virtue of having been reported, it also fulfilled a role in the subsequent process.

The rebuilding of Ground Zero provides an important contrast to the Amsterdam case. Unlike there, we see how in the Ground Zero case the emerging possibilities for joint elaboration between the classical-modernist institutions and the ad hoc practices of network governance are no longer appreciated in the later phases of the political process. The potentiality for reasoned elaboration is ignored or actively destroyed, and in its place we get a classical 'front-stage/back-stage' politics, reproduced and reinforced by its mediatized representations, with a general loss of authority and legitimacy as a result. The case of rebuilding of Ground Zero is a powerful illustration of how an old-style politics can work like an oyster: it opens up when this is opportune, but surely and slowly closes again when the situation allows it to do so.

Then there is the role of settings and staged performances in gaining authority. The Van Gogh case showed the need to sometimes perform authority outside the sphere of institutional rules and conventions. In this case the politico-administrative leadership did indeed manage to impose its definition of reality on the situation, but only by actively engaging in political work elsewhere. Mediagenic moments of a speech in a mosque, or venturing into the lion's den of a populist talk show, were crucial in imposing storylines on the situation. At the same time the Amsterdam leadership performed in good classical-modernist fashion: the front-stage rhetoric was one of representatives of a classical strong state that was imposing its will. The public was judging the messages it received. Surely sometimes we simply see this type of authority, mixing the institutional powers with those related to personal capabilities (conditioned under the concept of performative habitus—political actors cannot be expected to persuasively employ just any repertoire at any moment in time).

The case study on the handling of the Van Gogh crisis also reveals that the successful performance of authority drew not only on a politics of style, but also on a network-governance approach: having the governance network with the key players in migrant communities in place before the event allowed for the successful discursive interaction and facilitated the staging of the Amsterdam leadership as strong and decisive. And, as the moment of dislocation waned, it was this network-governance approach that took priority again. In this sense the Van Gogh case illustrates both the vulnerability of an instrumental communication strategy in times of crisis and the difficulty of communicating collaboration in a mediatized politics. Collaboration was simply not a credible story in the context of the handling of the murder of Van Gogh. Yet the analysis reveals that performing authority after the murder relied on an interplay between two ways of performing authority. While the need for 'decisive acts' was crystal clear, the effectiveness of this classical-modernist performance was informed by the network governance that had created the informed trust that allowed political leaders to be outspoken. Finally, it shows the crucial role of reiteration: storylines that stick are those that evolve and develop through a period of intense mediatized politics.

An important question in this book was how to conceive of the relationship between the well-known and strongly institutionalized genre of classical-modernist politics on the one hand and a more flexible form of network governance on the other. In this regard it is instructive to compare the Amsterdam case with the case study of rebuilding Ground Zero. The case of Ground Zero shows a tough confrontation between an old elitist politics and the employment of more open, participatory interaction. Initially the latter, governance-type of strategies conquered some political space, primarily because of the insensitivity of the old-style politics in New York. Yet here too the mediatizedness of politics made itself felt. While officers at the LMDC wanted to open up, they were nonetheless unprepared to mediate between, on the one hand, the active public showing agency reordering messages and meanings, and on the other hand the various bureaucratic agencies. The presentation of the initial plans for the rebuilding of Ground Zero proved to be a communications disaster. Officials conceived of authority in terms of 'type 4' (using Federal Hall as a stage), but the mismatch between a staging in Federal Hall and the six mediocre plans presented backfired on the process. Likewise, the staged deliberation of 'Listening to the City' and the following 'design study' seemed to show to the distrustful public how the LMDC was trying to deliver on its promise to rebuild 'as a democracy'—a promise that would be all the more reason for cynicism when the process had closed again. It is the very stagedness here that creates the power of the deliberative moments: by virtue of being staged they have generated a moment in the public consciousness. Ignoring it, or overruling it without good reason, then contributes to a loss of authority and legitimacy.

The third case study on the institutional recovery after the BSE fiasco in Great Britain is a powerful example of how the potentially opposing forces of governance on the one hand and mediatized politics on the other can be brought together to support an authoritative governance. The case of the British Food Standards Agency is unique in showing how a sphere prone to contentious politics actually transformed into a domain by and large ruled by deliberative mechanisms. Of course there are contradictory stories that can be told about the acts and practices of the FSA. Yet it is a truly remarkable case, standing out for its very proactive employment of new techniques of *both* network governance *and* mediatization and resulting in an authoritative governance in a policy field where the government had lost all its credibility beforehand.

Significantly, the analysis reveals how the authority of the FSA was performed using *both* discursive and dramaturgical means. First of all, the FSA case shows how authority can be based on practices of reasoned elaboration. The governance strategy encompassed the prominent involvement of stakeholders whereby many new institutional rules and routines were invented to make sure that stakeholders enhanced the quality of the deliberation and implementation, rather than simply promoting their own stakeholder interests. It included the conscious reordering of secluded classical-modernist spheres of expert advice, for example through the appointment of ordinary citizens on scientific panels—not always unproblematic, as the case study shows, but successful in terms of creating another institutional discourse. Likewise, the idea of bringing scientists into contact with user groups and to develop regulatory strategies in close cooperation with the people at risk is the sort of deliberative governance that shows the virtues of a break with the functionalist 'input–output' logic and separation of roles under the classical-modernist regime.

Secondly, the FSA stands out for the very active way in which it sought to generate authority using particular stagings of deliberation. The open board meeting, travelling through the country and accessible through the internet, was a way of creating the active experience of a relationship between policy-makers and the variety of publics involved. The FSA website is a less charismatic, but similarly interesting attempt to rethink ways in which government can perform authority. The study reveals a myriad of ways in which the FSA used dramaturgical means to enhance its authority. Deliberation was supported by rituals that keep interest-group bargaining at bay: the micro-practice of 'declaring an interest' at the FSA serves as a remarkable example thereof. In a different way the 'field trip' to a stakeholder community was another very clear illustration of the differentiated way in which the FSA sought to actively create a relationship with one of its key publics.

The analysis of FSA practices illuminates the role of the accompanying media strategy. This very professional and strategic communication effort was succinctly described by one of its inceptors as a 'spin of no spin'—in itself an illustration of the quality of their communication. The FSA case hints at how a mediatized political environment can be approached so as to overcome the suggested dichotomy between mediatized politics on the one hand and serious governance on the other. Of course, not all is hunky-dory with the FSA. It is continuously searching, adjusting, and readjusting. Some boundary practices work better than others, and obviously there is evidence of backlash and perhaps even restoration (cf. Rothstein 2004; Irwin 2006). But the FSA qualifies as a powerful example of a working strategy of governance which draws on all three new ways of performing authority.

The case study on the FSA is crucial to the findings of this book. The FSA is neither classical-modernist nor pure network governance. It surely is an example of the deliberative form of network governance, and I am certain that it is going to find its way into the empirical discussion among theorists of deliberative democracy. The FSA breaks with the prevailing logic of network governance, which is often about avoiding attention, staying in the shadow, having no face. But it is more than that: the FSA is mediatized governance in action. The media profile gave food-safety regulation a face—very consciously so, in fact. At the same time, it is a very instructive case in showing how authority is gained under very difficult circumstances, bringing in stakeholders, renegotiating the rules of the game, and communicating no (false) certainties but rather wisdom and considered judgement. Interestingly, it illustrates the paradox of authority in a mediatized politics in other ways: the FSA's strategy of openness and transparency simply took away the media's appetite, as if the media motto was: 'If it is open it cannot be news.' What is more, deliberative as many of its practices may be, the FSA was well aware that it also needed to be able to present a stern face to the media when this was appropriate. In fact, they reserved a face for precisely that.

The drama of authoritative governance

The above in one sentence: understanding authority requires an understanding of politics as drama. There is nothing necessarily frivolous about the latter claim. Paraphrasing Shakespeare, Erving Goffman once wrote: 'All the world is not, of course, a stage, but the crucial ways in which it isn't are not easy to specify' (Goffman 1959: 72). In Chapter 2 I showed, in discussing the work of Jean-Philippe Heurtin, how parliament and parliamentary proceedings, the capstone of modern democracy, were staged and staged again during the years of the French Revolution, at some point settling into a particular set of parliamentary routines. This wasn't meant to reduce politics to theatre but to enhance our appreciation of the role of the performatives in bringing about the authority of classical-modernist politics. If even classical-modernist politics was rehearsed and staged, then it makes sense to look at today's configurations in similar terms as well.

Using the open analytical languages of 'stages', I have sought to show the diversity of interconnected places where politics and policy-making takes place nowadays and what this means in terms of repertoires and practices of governance. Although I am sure that many others will be more creative in pushing this agenda further, I am satisfied if we have gained new insights as to where policies are made and how politics comes to be enacted outside the sphere of constitutional politics. Yet the combination of a political sociological argument and empirical case-study work also produced something of a twist to the argument. While writing, I grew more and more convinced that it is a mistake to conceive of the new realities in terms of a 'shift' from one form to the next. It seems more appropriate to conceive of it as a recombination. The difference is that network governance is the more encompassing notion; it now *includes* the particular classical-modernist enactments at a variety of levels. I have sought to illuminate how authoritative governance is possible; but our understanding of policy-making then must be a different one. Policy-making processes in our time should be conceived of as non-linear and meandering: policy-making is a sequence of staged performances that create a diversity of ways of representing, elaborating, and correcting meanings that have been brought to the fore. It is shared discourse that informs the decision-making that needs to take place at the variety of sites, and it is enactment that makes definitions stick. And it is this meandering that creates the basis for authoritative governance as it allows for the variety of stagings that relates many different publics to the political decision-making on our pressing political problems.

References

Abell, J. 2002. 'Mad cows and British politicians: the role of scientific and national identities in managing blame for the BSE crisis.' *Text*, 22 (2): 173–98.

Alexander, J. 2003. *The meanings of social life: a cultural sociology*. New York: Oxford University Press.

—— 2004*a*. 'Cultural pragmatics: social performance between ritual and strategy.' *Sociological Theory*, 22 (4): 527–73.

—— 2004*b*. 'From the depths of despair: performance and counterperformance on September 11th.' *Sociological Theory*, 21 (1): 88–105.

Anderson, A. 2005. 'John Krebs.' *Prospect*, 22 Dec.

Anonymous. 1996. 'Government turns a drama into a crisis: ministers failed totally to foresee public reaction to the possibility of humans catching BSE.' *Financial Times*, 10 Apr.

—— 2002. 'Six months later.' *Gotham Gazette*, 11 Feb.

—— 2004. 'Cohen wilde boycot Verdonk.' *De Telegraaf*, 12 Nov.

—— n.d. 'Job Cohen, burgemeester van Amsterdam: de boel bij elkaar houden!' *http://www.burgemeesters.nl/files/File/Crisisbeheersing/interviews/Cohen.pdf*.

Appardurai, A. 1996. *Modernity at large: cultural dimensions of globalisation*. Minneapolis: University of Minnesota Press.

—— 2006. *Fear of small numbers: an essay on the geography of anger*. Durham, NC: Duke University Press.

Arendt, H. 1961. *Between past and future: six exercises in political thought*. New York: Viking Press.

Arnold, T. 1935. *The symbols of government*. New Haven: Yale University Press.

Arnstein, S. 1969. 'A ladder of citizen participation.' *Journal of the American Planning Association*, 35 (4): 216–24.

Austin, J. 1962. *How to do things with words*. Oxford: Oxford University Press.

Bailey, J. 2007. 'Review of openness in the Food Standards Agency; an independent review carried out by J. A. Bailey.' *http://www.food.gov.uk/aboutus/how_we_work/copopenbranch/reviewofopenness*.

Bang, H. 2004. 'Culture governance; governing self-reflexive modernity.' *Public Administration*, 82 (1): 157–90.

—— (ed.). 2003. *Governance as social and political communication*. Manchester: Manchester University Press.

References

Bauman, Z. 1991. 'Modernity and ambivalence.' In M Featherstone (ed.), *Global culture: nationalism, globalization and modernity.* London: Sage, 143–70.

Beck, U. 1986. *Risikogesellschaft: auf dem Weg in eine andere Moderne.* Frankfurt am Main: Suhrkamp.

—— 1992. *Risk society: towards a new modernity.* London: Sage.

—— 2005. *Power in the global age.* Cambridge: Polity Press.

—— and E. Beck-Gernsheim. 2002. *Individualization: institutionalized individualism and its social and political consequences.* London: Sage.

Benford, R. and S. Hunt. 1992. 'Dramaturgy and social movements: the social construction and communication of power.' *Sociological Inquiry,* 62 (1): 36–55.

Benhabib, S. (ed.). 1996. *Democracy and difference: contesting the boundaries of the political.* Princeton: Princeton University Press.

Bennett, W. and R. Entman. 2001. *Mediated politics: communication in the future of democracy.* Cambridge: Cambridge University Press.

—— R. Lawrence, and S. Livingston. 2006. 'None dare call it torture: indexing and the limits of press independence in the Abu Ghraib scandal.' *Journal of Communication,* 56 (3): 467–85.

Berkey-Gerard, M. 2002. 'Rebuilding by consensus?' *Gotham Gazette,* 10 June.

—— and E. Pearson. 2002. 'The Six Rebuilding Plans.' *Gotham Gazette,* 22 July.

Berman, M. 1983. *All that is solid melts into air: the experience of modernity.* London: Verso.

Better Regulation Commission. 2006. *Risk, responsibility and regulation: whose risk is it anyway?* London: Better Regulation Commission.

Birtek, F. 2007. 'From affiliation to affinity: citizenship in the transition from empire to the nation-state.' In S. Benhabib, I. Shapiro, and D. Petranovic (eds.), *Identities, affiliations and allegiances.* Cambridge: Cambridge University Press, 17–44.

Blumler, J. and M. Gurevitch. 1995. *The crisis of public communication.* New York: Routledge.

Blythman, J. 2000. 'Following the recent damning report into BSE, the Food Standards Agency is once again under the spotlight. But is it delivering the goods?' *Guardian,* 4 Nov.

Bohman, J. 1996. *Public deliberation: pluralism, complexity, and democracy.* Cambridge, Mass.: MIT Press.

—— 1997. *Deliberative democracy: essays on reason and politics.* Cambridge, Mass.: MIT Press.

Boomgaarden, H. and C. De Vreese. 2007. 'Dramatic real-world events and public opinion dynamics: media coverage and its impact on public reactions to an assassination.' *International Journal of Public Opinion Research,* 19 (3): 354–66.

Boorstin, D. 1961. *The image: a guide to pseudo-events in America.* New York: Vintage.

Bourdieu, P. 1998. *Practical reason.* Cambridge: Polity Press.

Breed, I. 2005. 'Toespraak van burgemeester Job Cohen, November 3, 2004.' *http://amsterdam.nl/?ActItmIdt=2524*

—— 2007. 'Toespraak wethouder Aboutaleb in Alkabir Moskee.' *http://amsterdam. nl/gemeente/college/freek_ossel/aboutaleb/toespraak_wethouder*

Brookes, R. 1999. 'Newspapers and national identity: the BSE/CJD crisis and the British press.' *Media, Culture and Society*, 21 (2): 247–63.

Burke, K. 1969 (1945). *A grammar of motives*. Berkeley: University of California Press.

Burrell, I. 2001. 'Chinese to sue government over virus food scare.' *Independent*, 16 June.

Buruma, I. 2006. *Murder in Amsterdam: the death of Theo van Gogh and the limits of tolerance*. New York: Penguin Press.

Butler, J. 1999. *Gender trouble: feminism and the subversion of identity*. New York: Routledge.

Cardwell, D. 2001. 'In final address, Giuliani envisions soaring memorial.' *New York Times*, 28 Dec.

Castells, M. 1996. *The information age: economy, society and culture*. Oxford: Blackwell.

—— 1997. *The power of identity*. Oxford: Blackwell.

Chouliaraki, L. 2004. 'Watching 11 September—the politics of pity.' *Discourse and Society*, 15 (2–3): 185–98.

Civic Alliance. 2002. 'Listening to the City: report of proceedings.' New York: Civic Alliance.

Coalition of 9/11 Families. 2002. 'Recommendations of the Coalition of 9/11 Families to the LMDC regarding memorial and future of WTC Site.' *Tribute*, 1 (2): 3.

Cobb, R. and C. Elder. 1972. *Participation in American politics: the dynamics of agenda-building*. Boston: Allyn & Bacon.

Collins, R. 2004. *Interaction ritual chains*. Princeton: Princeton University Press.

Committee on Toxicity of Chemicals in Food, Consumer Products and the Environment (COT). 2002*a*. 'TOX 2002/49: proposal to hold COT meetings in open session.' *http://www.food.gov.uk/multimedia/pdfs/2002-49open.pdf*

—— 2002*b*. 'TOX/MIN/2002/06: minutes of the meeting held on Tuesday 10 December 2002.' *http://cot.food.gov.uk/pdfs/200206dec.pdf*

—— 2003. 'TOX/2003/06: procedure for holding COT meetings in open session.' *http://www.food.gov.uk/multimedia/pdfs/2003-06.pdf*

Cook, T. 2005 (1998). *Governing with the news: the news media as a political institution*, 2nd edn. Chicago: University of Chicago Press.

—— 2006. 'The news media as a political institution: looking backward and looking forward.' *Political Communication*, 23 (2): 159–71.

Cornelissen, J., M. Kafouros, and A. Lock. 2005. 'Metaphorical images of organization: how organizational researchers develop and select organizational metaphors.' *Human Relations*, 58 (12): 1548–78.

Corner, J. and D. Pels (eds.). 2003. *Media and the restyling of politics*. London: Sage.

Corona, V. 2007. 'Voices and visions of Lower Manhattan: organizing civic expression in post-9/11.' *Journal of Civil Society*, 3 (2): 119–35.

References

Crozier, M. 2007. 'Recursive governance: contemporary political communication and public policy.' *Political Communication*, 24 (1): 1–18.

—— 2008. 'Listening, learning, steering: new governance, communication and interactive policy formation.' *Policy and Politics*, 36 (1): 3–19.

Czarniawska, B. 2004. *Narratives in social science research*. London: Sage.

Dahrendorf, R. 1988. *The modern social conflict*. London: Weidenfeld & Nicolson.

Davies, B. and R. Harré. 1990. 'Positioning: the discursive production of selves.' *Journal for the Theory of Social Behaviour*, 20 (1): 43–63.

Dean of Thornton-le-Fylde, B. 2005. *An independent review of the Food Standards Agency conducted by The Rt Hon Baroness Brenda Dean of Thornton-le-Fylde*. London: Food Standards Agency.

De Fina, A., D. Schiffrin, and M. Bamberg (eds.). 2006. *Discourse and identity*. Cambridge: Cambridge University Press.

Dekker, P. and E. Steenvoorden. 2008. *Continu onderzoek burgerperspectieven: kwartaalbericht 2008–1*. Den Haag: Sociaal en Cultureel Planbureau.

Dewey, J. 1927. *The public and its problems*. New York: Holt.

DeYoung, K. 2006. *Soldier: the life of Colin Powell*. New York: Alfred A. Knopf.

Dillon, D. 2003. 'Brawny designs for WTC site scale new heights of ambition.' *Dallas Morning News*, 3 Feb.

Dixon, J. and K. Durrheim. 2004. 'Dislocating identity: desegregation and the transformation of place.' *Journal of Environmental Psychology*, 24 (4): 455–73.

Domke, D., D. Perlmutter, and M. Spratt. 2002. 'The primes of our times? An examination of the "power" of visual images.' *Journalism*, 3 (2): 131–59.

Dressel, K. 2002. *BSE—the new dimension of uncertainty: the cultural politics of science and decision-making*. Berlin: Sigma.

Dryzek, J. 1990. *Discursive democracy: politics, policy, and political science*. Cambridge: Cambridge University Press.

—— 1996. *Democracy in capitalist times: ideals, limits, and struggles*. Oxford: Oxford University Press.

—— 2000. *Deliberative democracy and beyond: liberals, critics, contestations*. Oxford: Oxford University Press.

—— 2006. *Deliberative global politics*. Cambridge: Polity Press.

—— and S. Niemeyer. 2007. 'Discursive representation'. Paper presented at the Rethinking Democratic Representation Workshop, University of British Columbia, May 18–19.

—— J. Farr, and S. Leonard. (eds.). 1995. *Political science in history*. Cambridge: Cambridge University Press.

Edelman, M. 1964. *The symbolic uses of politics*. Urbana: University of Illinois Press.

—— 1988. *Constructing the political spectacle*. Chicago: University of Chicago Press.

Edgley, C. 2003. 'Dramaturgy: a brief history of an idea.' In L. Reynolds and N. Herman-Kinney (eds.), *Handbook of symbolic interactionism*. Walnut Creek, Calif.: AltaMira Press, 141–72.

Edwards, R. 2000. 'Every bite you take, every trip you make, no one's watching out for you... BSE: When we were worried about the safety of British beef the government and civil servants assured us it was safe. If they were so wrong about that can we ever trust a word they say?' *Sunday Herald*, 29 Oct.

—— and S. Schneider. 2001. 'Self-governance and peer review in science-for-policy: the case of the IPCC second assessment report.' In C. Miller and P. N. Edwards (eds.), *Changing the atmosphere: expert knowledge and environmental governance*. Cambridge, Mass.: MIT Press, 219–46.

Entman, R. 2004. *Projections of power: framing news, public opinion, and U.S. foreign policy*. Chicago: University of Chicago Press.

Ewald, F. 1986. *L'État providence*. Paris: Gallimard.

Ezrahi, Y. 1990. *The descent of Icarus: science and the transformation of contemporary democracy*. Cambridge, Mass.: Harvard University Press.

Fairclough, N. 1992. *Discourse and social change*. Cambridge: Polity Press.

Fear, J. 2007. *Under the radar: dog-whistle politics in Australia*. Canberra: The Australia Institute.

Fernandez, J. 2002. 'A brief history of the World Trade Center towers.' In E. Kausel (ed.), *The towers lost and beyond: a collection of essays on the WTC by researchers at the Massachusetts Institute of Technology*. Boston: MIT, 5–12.

Fischer, F. 2003. *Reframing public policy: discursive politics and deliberative practices*. Oxford: Oxford University Press.

—— and J. Forester (eds.). 1993. *The argumentative turn in policy analysis and planning*. Durham, NC: Duke University Press.

Fiske, J. 1996. *Media matters: race and gender in US politics*. Minneapolis: University of Minnesota Press.

Food Standards Agency (FSA). 2002*a*. *The Food Standards Agency: the first two years*. London: Food Standards Agency.

—— 2002*b*. 'Report on the review of scientific committees.' *http://www.food.gov. uk/science/researchpolicy/commswork/scicomrev*

—— 2002*c*. 'Criteria for the use of fresh, pure, natural, etc. in food labelling.' *http://www.food.gov.uk/consultations/ukwideconsults/2001/criteriaforfreshpure-natural*

—— 2005*a*. 'Action taken to remove illegal dye found in wide range of foods on sale in UK.' Press release, 18 Feb.

—— 2005*b*. 'FSA 05/12/03: Consumer engagement.' Open Board Meeting Agenda Item 6, Annex A, 8 Dec.

—— 2005*c*. 'FSA 05/12/03: Consumer engagement.' Open Board Meeting Agenda Item 6, 8 Dec.

—— 2005*d*. 'FSA 05/07/04a5: Consumer engagement strategy: advice to the Board from the Consumer Committee. Annex 5: summary of the stakeholder review.' Open Board Meeting Agenda Item 6, 14 July.

—— 2006. 'FSA 06/06/07: Openness.' Closed Board Meeting Agenda Item 3.5, 15 June.

References

Food Standards Agency 2007. 'FSA 07/03/04: Conflicts of Interests.' Open Board Meeting Agenda Item 3.5, 15 Mar.

Forbes, I. 2004. 'Making a crisis out of a drama: the political analysis of the BSE episode.' *Political Studies*, 52 (2): 342–57.

Forester, J. 1999. *The deliberative practitioner: encouraging participatory planning processes*. Cambridge, Mass.: MIT Press.

Franklin, B. 1994. *Packaging politics: political communications in Britain's media democracy*. London: Arnold.

—— 1998. *Newszak and News media*. London: Arnold.

Fraser, N. 1992. 'Rethinking the public sphere: a contribution to the critique of actually existing democracy.' In C. Calhoun (ed.), *Habermas and the public sphere*. Cambridge, Mass.: MIT Press, 109–42.

Friedman, R. 1990. 'On the concept of authority in political philosophy.' In J. Raz (ed.), *Authority*. New York: New York University Press, 56–91.

Friedrich, C. 1958. *Authority*. Cambridge, Mass.: Harvard University Press.

—— 1972. *Tradition and authority*. London: Pall Mall.

Fung, A. 2004. *Empowered participation: reinventing urban democracy*. Princeton: Princeton University Press.

—— 2006. 'Varieties of participation in complex governance.' *Public Administration Review*, 66 (1): 66–75.

Futrell, R. 1999. 'Performance governance: impression management, teamwork, and conflict containment in city commission proceedings.' *Journal of Contemporary Ethnography*, 27 (4): 494–529.

Gamson, W. 1992. *Talking Politics*. Cambridge: Cambridge University Press.

Geertz, C. 1981. *Negara: the theatre state in nineteenth-century Bali*. Princeton: Princeton University Press.

Gillmor, D. 2004. 'The crystal method: iconic architecture à la Daniel Libeskind has produced some extraordinary buildings. But what kinds of cities will it create?' *The Walrus*, 2: 56–65.

Gittrich, G. and E. Herman. 2001. 'Many visions for WTC site: plans lacking a consensus.' *New York Daily News*, 17 Dec.

Glanz, J. and E. Lipton. 2003. *City in the sky: the rise and fall of the World Trade Center*. New York: Times Books.

Godlee, F. 1997. 'Food safety, from plough to plate: both public and industry need a food agency with clout.' *British Medical Journal*, 315: 619–20.

Goffman, E. 1959. *The presentation of self in everyday life*. Harmondsworth: Penguin.

Goldberger, P. 2001. 'The "new" New York City skyline.' Lecture delivered at the Gotham Center Symposium, New York, 29 Oct.

—— 2002a. 'Groundwork: how the future of Ground Zero is being resolved.' *New Yorker*, 20 May.

—— 2002b. *RPA regional assembly keynote speech*. New York, Regional Planning Association.

—— 2004. *Up from zero: politics, architecture and the rebuilding of Ground Zero*. New York: Random House.

Gomart, E. and M. Hajer. 2003. 'Is that politics? For an inquiry into forms in contemporary politics.' In B. Joerges and H. Nowotny (eds.), *Social studies of science and technology: looking back, ahead*. Dordrecht and Boston: Kluwer Academic Publications, 33–61.

Goodin, R. 1978. 'Rites of rulers.' *British Journal of Sociology*, 29 (3): 281–99.

—— and H. Klingemann. 1996. *A new handbook of political science*. Oxford: Oxford University Press.

Goodsell, C. 1977. 'Bureaucratic manipulation of physical symbols: an empirical study.' *American Journal of Political Science*, 21 (1): 79–91.

—— 1988. *The social meaning of civic space: studying political authority through architecture*. Lawrence: University Press of Kansas.

Gotham Gazette. 2002. 'Live chat events: a conversation with Lou Tomson, July 24, 2002.' http://www.gothamgazette.com/rebuilding_nyc/chat/tomsontranscript.shtml#

Graber, D. 2003. *The power of communication: managing information in public organizations*. Washington, DC: CQ Press. As quoted in Cook 2006.

Gumperz, J. 1982. *Discourse strategies*. Cambridge: Cambridge University Press.

Gusfield, J. 1981. *The culture of public problems: drinking-driving and the symbolic order*. Chicago: Chicago University Press.

—— and J. Michalowicz. 1984. 'Secular symbolism: studies of ritual, ceremony, and the symbolic order in modern life.' *Annual Review of Sociology*, 10: 417–35.

Gutmann, A. and D. Thompson. 1996. *Democracy and disagreement*. Cambridge, Mass.: Belknap Press.

Hajer, M. 1995. *The politics of environmental discourse: ecological modernization and the policy process*. Oxford: Oxford University Press.

—— 2003*a*. 'Policy without polity? Policy analysis and the institutional void.' *Policy Sciences*, 36 (2): 175–95.

—— 2003*b*. 'A frame in the fields: policymaking and the reinvention of politics.' In Hajer and Wagenaar 2003: 88–110.

—— 2006. 'The living institutions of the EU: analysing governance as performance.' *Perspectives on European Politics and Society*, 7 (1): 41–55.

—— and D. Laws. 2003. 'Food for thought: organizing deliberative governance.' Paper presented at the ECPR Joint Workshops, European Consortium for Political Research, Edinburgh, 28 Mar.–2 Apr.

—— —— 2006. 'Ordering through discourse.' In M. Moran, M. Rein, and R. Goodin (eds.), *The Oxford handbook of public policy*. Oxford: Oxford University Press, 249–66.

—— and A. Loeber. 2007. *Paganini Work Package 5—Learning after the event: assessing the institutional role of civic participation after food scandals and food scares*. Amsterdam: Amsterdam School for Social Science Research.

Hajer, M. and J. Uitermark. 2005. 'Performing authority in the "multicultural drama": building bridges after the assassination of Theo van Gogh.' Paper presented at the ECPR general conference, Budapest, September 9–11.

References

———— 2008. 'Performing authority: discursive politics after the assassination of Theo van Gogh.' *Public Administration*, 86 (1): 5–19.

—— and W. Versteeg. 2005. 'A decade of discourse analysis of environmental politics: achievements, challenges, perspectives.' *Journal of Environmental Policy and Planning*, 7 (3): 175–84.

———— 2008. 'The limits of deliberative governance.' Paper presented at the APSA 2008 Annual Meeting, Boston, 28–31 Aug.

—— and H. Wagenaar (eds.). 2003. *Deliberative policy analysis: understanding governance in the network society*. Cambridge: Cambridge University Press.

—— A. Loeber, and J. van Tatenhove. 2007. *Paganini Final Report—Theory and method: investigating new participatory practices of the 'politics of life' in a European context, participatory governance and institutional innovation*. Amsterdam: Amsterdam School for Social Science Research.

—— D. Sijmons, and F. Feddes. (eds.). 2006. *Een plan dat werkt: ontwerp en politiek in de regionale planvorming*. Rotterdam: Nai Publishers.

Hannerz, U. 1996. *Transnational connections: culture, people, places*. London: Routledge.

Hariman, R. 1995. *Political style: the artistry of power*. Chicago: University of Chicago Press.

Harré, R. and G. Gillett. 1994. *The discursive mind*. Thousand Oaks: Sage.

Harris, P. and N. O'Shaughnessy. 1997. 'BSE and marketing communication myopia: Daisy and the death of the sacred cow.' *Risk, Decision and Policy*, 2 (1): 29–39.

Hay, C. 2007. *Why we hate politics*. Cambridge: Polity Press.

He, B. and M. Warren. 2008. 'Authoritarian deliberation: the deliberative turn in Chinese development.' Paper presented at APSA annual meeting, Boston, 28 Aug.

Heclo, H. 1974. *Modern social politics in Britain and Sweden: from relief to income maintenance*. New Haven: Yale University Press.

Heilbron, J., L. Magnusson, and B. Wittrock (eds.). 1997. *The rise of the social sciences and the formation of modernity*. Dordrecht: Kluwer Academic Publishers.

Hellebø, L. 2004. *Food safety at stake: the establishment of food agencies*. Bergen: Stein Rokkan Centre for Social Studies.

Helms, L. 2008. 'Governing in the media age: the impact of the mass media on executive leadership in contemporary democracies.' *Government and Opposition*, 43 (1): 26–54.

Henderson, M. 2005. 'Friends of the corporate earth: the outgoing food watchdog chief takes ecology groups with a pinch of salt.' *The Times Online*, 12 Apr.

Herbst, S. 2003. 'Political authority in a mediated age.' *Theory and Society*, 32 (4): 481–503.

Heurtin, J.-P. 2005. 'The circle of discussion and the semicircle of criticism.' In B. Latour and P. Weibel (eds.), *Making things public*. Boston: MIT Press, 754–69.

Hilgartner, S. 2001. *Science on stage: expert advice as public drama*. Stanford: Stanford University Press.

—— 2004. 'The credibility of science on stage.' *Social Studies of Science*, 34 (3): 443–52.

—— and C. Bosk. 1988. 'The rise and fall of social problems: a public arenas model.' *American Journal of Sociology*, 94 (1): 53–78.

Hindson, P. and T. Gray. 1988. *Burke's dramatic theory of politics*. Aldershot: Avebury.

Hirschkom, P. 2002. 'Six options offered to rebuild Ground Zero.' New York: CNN. *http://archives.cnn.com/2002/US/07/16/wtc.site.plans/*

Hobsbawm, E. J. 1977. *The age of revolution*. London: Abacus.

Holbert, R. 2004. 'Book review of Matthew A. Baum. *Soft news goes to war: public opinion and American foreign policy in the new media age.*' *Public Opinion Quarterly*, 68 (4): 644–8.

Holzer, B. 2001. 'Transnational subpolitics and corporate discourse: a study of environmental protest and the Royal Dutch/Shell Group.' Unpublished Ph.D. thesis. London: LSE, Department of Sociology.

Hooghe, L. and G. Marks. 2002. *Multi-level governance and European integration*. Lanham, Md.: Rowman & Littlefield.

House of Commons. 2004. 'Minutes of evidence taken before Science and Technology Committee: the use of science in UK international development policy, public questions 212–289', 26 Apr.

House of Commons, Select Committee on Science and Technology. 2006. 'Minutes of evidence: examination of witnesses, questions 640–659', 10 May.

Howarth, D. 2000. *Discourse*. Buckingham: Open University Press.

Ilie, C. 2001. 'Semi-institutional discourse: the case of talk shows.' *Journal of Pragmatics*, 33: 209–54.

Ingram, H. and A. Schneider. 2007. 'Ways of knowing: implications for public policy.' Paper presented at the annual APSA meeting, Chicago, 30 Aug.

Innes, J. 2002. 'Improving policy making with information.' *Planning Theory and Practice*, 3 (1): 102–4.

Inns, D. 2002. 'Metaphor in the literature of organizational analysis: a preliminary taxonomy and a glimpse at a humanities-based perspective.' *Organization*, 9 (2): 305–30.

Iovine, J. 2003. 'Turning a competition into a public campaign; finalists for the Ground Zero design pull out the stops.' *New York Times*, 26 Feb.

Irwin, A. 2006. 'The politics of talk: coming to terms with the "new" scientific governance.' *Social Studies of Science*, 36 (2): 299–320.

James, P. 1997. *Food Standards Agency: an interim proposal by Professor Philip James*. London: Cabinet Office.

James, W. 1956. *The will to believe*. New York: Dover.

Jasanoff, S. 1990. *The fifth branch: science advisers and policy makers*. Cambridge, Mass.: Harvard University Press.

—— 1997. 'Civilization and madness: the great BSE scare of 1996.' *Public Understanding of Science*, 6 (3): 221–32.

Jasper, J. 1997. *The art of moral protest: culture, biography, and creativity in social movements*. Chicago: Chicago University Press.

Jensen, K. 2004. 'BSE in the UK: why the risk communication strategy failed.' *Journal of Agricultural and Environmental Ethics*, 17 (4–5): 405–23.

Johnson-Cartee, K. 2005. *News narratives and news framing; constructing political reality*. Lanham, Md.: Rowman & Littlefield.

Joll, J. 1978. *Europe since 1870*. Harmondsworth: Penguin.

Jones, S. 2000. 'Scientists gang up on organics.' *New Statesman*, 11 Dec.

Jong, W. and R. Johannink. 2005. *Als dat maar goed gaat: bestuurlijke ervaringen met crises*. Enschede: Bestuurlijk Netwerk Crisisbeheersing.

Jordan, A. and I. Lorenzoni. 2007. 'Is there now a political climate for policy change? Policy and politics after the Stern Review.' *Political Quarterly*, 78 (2): 310–19.

Kertzer, D. 1988. *Rituals, politics and power*. New Haven: Yale University Press.

Kiesling, S. 2006. 'Hegemonic identity-making in narrative. 'In A. De Fina, D. Schiffrin, and M. Bamberg (eds.), *Discourse and identity*. Cambridge: Cambridge University Press, 261–87.

King, A. 1987. *Power and communication*. Prospect Heights: Waveland Press.

Kishan Thussu, D. and D. Freedman (eds.). 2004. *War and the media: reporting conflict 24/7*. Thousand Oaks: Sage.

Kjaer, A. 2004. *Governance*. Cambridge: Polity Press.

Kooiman, J. (ed.). 1993. *Modern governance: new government–society interactions*. London: Sage.

—— 2003. *Governing as governance*. London: Sage.

Kuo, M. 2003. 'Testimony before the New York city council.' New York: Imagine New York.

Kuper, S. 2004. 'Trouble in paradise: once a bastion of liberal values, the Netherlands is struggling to accept its large Muslim population. And the whole world is watching.' *Financial Times*, 4 Dec.

Laclau, E. 1996. 'The death and resurrection of the theory of ideology.' *Journal of Political Ideologies*, 1 (3): 201–20.

Lakoff, G. 2004. *Don't think of an elephant! Know your values and frame the debate*. White River Junction: Chelsea Green Publishing.

—— and M. Johnson. 1980. *Metaphors we live by*. Chicago: Chicago University Press.

Lane, F. 1979. *Profits from power: readings in protection rent and violence controlling enterprises*. Albany, NY: SUNY Press.

Lang, T. 1999. 'The complexities of globalization; the UK as a case study of tensions within the food system and the challenge to food policy.' *Agriculture and Human Values*, 16 (2): 169–85.

Latour, B. 1987. *Science in action*. Cambridge, Mass.: Harvard University Press.

—— 1994. *Pasteur: une science, un style, un siècle*. Paris: Perrin.

—— 2005. *Making things public: atmospheres of democracy*. Karlsruhe: ZKM Karslruhe.

—— and P. Weibel. 2005. *Making things public*. Boston: MIT Press.

Laws, D. 2001. 'Enacting deliberation: speech and the micro-foundations of deliberative democracy.' Paper presented at the EPCR Joint Sessions Grenoble, 6–11 Apr.

—— 2009. 'Enacting deliberation: speech and the microfoundations of deliberative governance.' *Planning Theory and Practice*, 10 (4). Forthcoming.

—— and M. Hajer. 2006. 'Policy in practice.' In M. Moran, M. Rein, and R. Goodin (eds.), *The Oxford handbook of public policy*. Oxford: Oxford University Press, 407–22.

Leary, K. 2004. 'Critical moments as relational moments: the Centre for Humanitarian Dialogue and the conflict in Aceh, Indonesia. '*Negotiation Journal*, 20 (2): 311–38.

Lenzer, G. (ed.). 1975. *Auguste Comte and positivism: the essential writings*. Chicago: University of Chicago Press.

Loeber, A. and K. Paul. 2005. 'The aftermath of BSE: reordering food safety discourse in the UK and the Netherlands.' Paper presented at the ECPR general conference, Budapest, 9–11 Sept.

Low, S. 2004. 'The memorialization of September 11: dominant and local discourses on the rebuilding of the World Trade Center site.' *American Ethnologist*, 31 (3): 326–39.

Lower Manhattan Development Corporation (LMDC). 2002*a*. 'Press release: Port Authority and Lower Manhattan Developent [*sic*] Corporation unveil six concept plans for World Trade Center Site, adjacent areas and related transportation.'*http://www.renewnyc.com/displaynews.aspx?newsid=b3aa6fb4-ebb6-48e3-ba62-c92bce75a647*

—— 2002*b*. 'Press release: Lower Manhattan Development Corporation and Port Authority open public exhibit at Federal Hall for World Trade Center Site concept plans and design elements.' *http://www.renewnyc.com/displaynews.aspx?newsid=9e7b8291-c2d2-492b-982f-61bf22fe0f71*

—— 2002*c*. 'Press release: Lower Manhattan Development Corporation announces Design Study for World Trade Center site and surrounding areas.' *http://www.renewnyc.com/displaynews.aspx?newsid=da800006-c35b-4f1c-a9ec-ff53cfe45ae2*

—— 2002*d*. 'Request for qualifications; innovative designs for the World Trade Center Site.' New York: Lower Manhattan Development Corporation. *http://www.renewnyc.com/content/rfps/RFQInnovativeDesignStudy.pdf.*

—— 2004. 'Press release: Governor Pataki, Governor McGreevey, Mayor Bloomberg lay cornerstone for Freedom Tower.' *http://www.renewnyc.com/displaynews.aspx?newsid=3b1e0426-eb70-481d-b0a8-ba1583081ffb*

Lynch, M. 1991. 'Laboratory space and the technological complex: an investigation of topical contextures.' *Science in Context*, 4 (1): 51–78.

McGeveran, T. 2002. 'Port Authority reasserts grip on powers site.' *New York Observer*, 5 May.

References

—— 2003. 'Beauty contest: two firms vie at W.T.C. site.' *New York Observer*, 9 Feb.

MacIntyre, A. 1981. *After virtue: a study in moral theory*. Notre Dame, Ind.: University of Notre Dame Press.

McLaughlin, A. 2005. 'Call for shake up after Sudan1 crisis.' *Sunday Herald*, 27 Feb.

McLeod, J. 1999. 'The sociodrama of presidential politics: rhetoric, ritual and power in the era of teledemocracy.' *American Anthropologist*, 101 (2): 359–73.

McNair, B. 2003. *An introduction to political communication*. London: Routledge.

Manin, B. 1997. *The principles of representative government*. Cambridge: Cambridge University Press.

March, J. and J. Olsen. 1984. 'The new institutionalism: organizational factors in political life.' *American Political Science Review*, 78: 734–49.

—— —— 1989. *Rediscovering institutions: the organizational basis of politics*. New York: Free Press.

Marcus, G. 2000. 'Emotions in politics.' *Annual Review of Political Science*, 3: 221–50.

Marin, B. and R. Mayntz. 1991. *Policy networks: empirical evidence and theoretical considerations*. Boulder, Colo.: Westview Press.

Marsh, G. and J. Ingham. 2001. 'Restaurants and shops clear out soy sauce after cancer warning; shock ban on Chinese food.' *Daily Express*, 21 June.

May, R., L. Donaldson, and J. Krebs. 2000. *Review of risk procedures used by the government's advisory committees dealing with food safety*. London: Department of Trade and Industry.

Mazmanian, D. and P. Sabatier. 1989. *Implementation and public policy*. Lanham, Md.: University Press of America.

Mead, G. 1938. *The philosophy of the act*. Chicago: University of Chicago Press.

Merelman, R. 1969. 'The dramaturgy of politics.' *Sociological Quarterly*, 10 (2): 216–41.

Meyer, T. and L. Hinchman. 2002. *Media democracy: how the media colonize politics*. Cambridge: Polity Press.

Meyrowitz, J. 1985. *No sense of place: the impact of electronic media on social behaviour*. New York: Oxford University Press.

Miles, A. and H. Rumbelow. 2007. 'The Weight-Watcher general who wants us to eat her words.' *The Times*, 24 Feb.

Millstone, E. and P. van Zwanenberg. 2000. *BSE: risk, science and governance*. Oxford: Oxford University Press.

—— —— 2001. 'Politics of expert advice; lessons from the early history of the BSE saga.' *Science and Public Policy*, 28 (2): 99–112.

—— —— 2002. 'The evolution of food safety policymaking institutions in the UK, EU and Codex Alimentarius.' *Social Policy and Administration*, 36 (6): 593–609.

Ministry of Agriculture, Forestry and Fisheries. 1997. 'MAFF Press Release (251/97): new group to set up Food Standards Agency', 31 Aug. *http://www.foodlaw.rdg. ac.uk/news/uk-97-35.htm*.

—— 1998. *The Food Standards Agency: a force for change*. London: Stationery Office.

Minnis, J. 2002. 'Between remembrance and rebuilding: developing a consensus process for memorialization at the World Trade Center site.' MA Thesis. Cambridge, Mass.: MIT Department of Urban Studies and Planning.

Mollenkopf, J. 2005. *Contentious city: the politics of recovery in New York City*. New York: Russell Sage Foundation.

Mouffe, M. 2000. *The democratic paradox*. London: Verso.

Moynihan, D. 2004. 'Public participation after 9/11: rethinking and rebuilding Lower Manhattan.' *Group Facilitation: A Research and Applications Journal*, 6 (1): 117–26.

Mumford, L. 1952. *Art and technics*. New York: Columbia University Press.

Murphy, C. 2004. 'What it says on the tin.' *Marketing*, 15 Apr.

Nasr, J. 2003. 'Planning histories, urban futures, and the World Trade Center attack.' *Journal of Planning History*, 2 (3): 195–211.

National Audit Office. 2003. 'Improving service delivery; the Food Standards Agency.' *http://www.nao.org.uk/whats_new/0203/0203525.aspx*.

Newman, J. 2001. *Modernising governance: new labour, policy and society*. London: Sage.

—— 2003. 'New Labour, governance and the politics of diversity.' In J. Barry, M. Dent, and M. O'Neill (eds.), *Gender and the public sector*. London: Routledge, 15–26.

Newton, K. 2006. 'May the weak force be with you: the power of the mass media in modern politics.' *European Journal of Political Research*, 45 (2): 209–34.

Nobel, P. 2003. 'The fix at Ground Zero.' *The Nation*, 27 Jan.

Norris, P., M. Kern, and M. Just (eds.). 2003. *Framing terrorism: the news media, the government, and the public*. New York: Routledge.

Norval, A. 2007. *Aversive democracy: inheritance and originality in the democratic tradition*. Cambridge: Cambridge University Press.

Norwegian Nobel Committee. 2007. 'The Nobel Peace Price for 2007.' *http://nobelprize.org/nobel_prizes/peace/laureates/2007/*.

Offe, C. 1997. 'Micro-aspects of democratic theory: what makes for the deliberative competence of citizens?' In A. Hadenius (ed.), *Democracy's victory and crisis*. Cambridge: Cambridge University Press, 81–104.

Oosterveer, P. 2002. 'Reinventing risks politics: reflexive modernity and the European BSE crisis.' *Journal of Environmental Policy and Planning*, 4 (3): 215–29.

Papadopoulos, Y. 2002. 'Is "Governance" a form of "Deliberative Democracy"?' Paper presented at the ECPR Joint Sessions of Workshops, Workshop 'The Politics of Metropolitan Governance', Turin, 22–7 Mar.

Pels, D. 2003. 'Aesthetic representation and political style: re-balancing identity and difference in media democracy.' In Corner and Pels 2003: 41–66.

Petersen, A. 2009. 'Climate simulation, uncertainty and policy advice.' In G. Grandsberger and J. Feichter (eds.), *Climate Change and Policy*. Berlin: Springer. Forthcoming.

References

Pierre, J. (ed.). 2000. *Debating governance: authority, steering, and democracy*. Oxford: Oxford University Press.

Polletta, F. and L. Wood. 2003. *Public Deliberation After 9/11*. New York: Center on Organizational Innovation Columbia University.

Porter, T. 1995. *Trust in numbers: the pursuit of objectivity in science and public life*. Princeton: Princeton University Press.

Postman, N. 1985. *Amusing ourselves to death*. New York: Penguin.

Potter, J. 1996. 'Discourse analysis and constructionist approaches: theoretical background.' In J. Richardson (ed.), *Handbook of qualitative research methods*. Oxford: Blackwell, 125–40.

—— and M. Wetherell. 1987. *Discourse and social psychology: beyond attitudes and behaviour*. London: Sage.

Pressman, J. and A. Wildavsky. 1984. *Implementation: how great expectations in Washington are dashed in Oakland; or, why it's amazing that federal programs work at all, this being a saga of the Economic Development Administration as told by two sympathetic observers who seek to build morals on a foundation of ruined hopes*. Berkeley: University of California Press.

Price, J. and M. Shildrick. 1999. *Feminist theory and the body: a reader*. London: Routledge.

Purnick, J. 2002. 'Metro matters; who can part the red tape? Who knows?' *New York Times*, 4 Feb.

Putnam, R. 1995. 'Tuning in, tuning out: the strange disappearance of America's social capital.' *Political Science and Politics*, 28 (4): 664–83.

—— 2000. *Bowling alone: the collapse and revival of American community*. New York: Simon & Schuster.

Randerson, J. 2006. 'Sir John Krebs: high standards at high table, the former head of the food watchdog tells James Randerson that scientists should admit their limitations. *Guardian*, 21 Feb.

Raz, J. 1979. *The authority of law*. Oxford: Oxford University Press.

Reich, R. 1991. *The work of nations: preparing ourselves for the 21st century*. New York: Vintage.

Rentoul, J. 1996. 'Beef crisis: Ashdown backs change to Maff.' *Independent*, 25 Mar.

Revill, J. and M. Townsend. 2005. 'Lifting the lid on a recipe for disaster.' *Observer*, 27 Feb.

Rhodes, R. 1997. *Understanding governance: policy networks, governance, reflexivity, and accountability*. Buckingham: Open University Press.

—— 2005. 'Is Westminster dead in Westminster? (And why should we care?)' Inaugural lecture in the ANZSOG-ANU Public Lecture series. Academy of Science, Canberra, 23 Feb.

Roe, E. 1994. *Narrative policy analysis: theory and practice*. Durham, NC: Duke University Press.

Rosegrant, S. 2003. *Listening to the city: rebuilding at New York's World Trade Center site*. Cambridge, Mass.: Harvard University. *http://www.ksgcase.harvard.edu/case-Title.asp?caseNo=1687.0*.

Rosenau, J. 2007. 'Governing the ungovernable: the challenge of a global disaggregation of authority.' *Regulation and Governance*, 1 (1): 88–97.

—— and E. Czempiel 1992. *Governance without government: order and change in world politics*. Cambridge: Cambridge University Press.

Rothstein, H. 2004. 'Precautionary bans or sacrificial lambs? Participative regulation and the reform of the UK food safety regime.' *Public Administration*, 82 (4): 857–81.

—— 2005. 'Escaping the regulatory net: why regulatory reform can fail consumers.' *Law and Policy*, 27 (4): 520–48.

Sabel, C., A. Fung, and B. Karkkainen. 2000. *Beyond backyard environmentalism*. Boston: Beacon Press.

Sagalyn, L. 2005. 'The politics of planning the world's most visible urban redevelopment project.' In J. Mollenkopf (ed.), *Contentious city: the politics of recovery in New York City*. New York: Russell Sage Foundation, 23–72.

Schattschneider, E. 1961. *The semisovereign people: a realist's view of democracy in America*. New York: Holt, Rinehart & Winston.

Schechner, R. 1988. *Performance theory*. New York: Routledge.

—— 1993. *The future of ritual: writings on culture and performance*. London: Routledge.

Schofield, R. and J. Shaoul. 2000. 'Food safety regulation and the conflict of interest: the case of meat safety and E. Coli 0157.' *Public Administration*, 78 (3): 531–54.

Scholz, J. and B. Stiftel. 2005. *Adaptive governance and water conflict: new institutions for collaborative planning*. Washington, DC: Resources for the Future Press.

Schön, D. and M. Rein. 1994. *Frame reflection: toward the resolution of intractable policy controversies*. New York: Basic Books.

Schrope, M. 2001. 'Consensus science, or consensus politics?' *Nature*, 412: 112–14.

Schudson, M. 1989. 'How culture works: perspectives from media studies on the efficacy of symbols.' *Theory and Society*, 18 (2): 153–80.

—— 1992. *Watergate in American memory: how we remember, forget, and reconstruct the past*. New York: Basic Books.

—— 1998. *The good citizen: a history of American civic life*. Cambridge, Mass.: Harvard University Press.

—— 2002. *The sociology of the news*. New York: W. W. Norton & Co.

Schulte, A. 2005*a*. 'Ik vraag: bent u bereid naar uzelf te kijken?' *Het Parool*, 8 July.

—— 2005*b*. 'Word dus niet boos op ons.' *Het Parool*, 7 July.

Schutz, A. 1997. 'Self-presentational tactics of talk-show guests: a comparison of politicians, experts and entertainers.' *Journal of Applied Social Psychology*, 27 (21): 1941–52.

Select Committee on European Communities. 1998. Minutes of evidence, examination of witnesses: question 603–619. *http://www.parliament.the-stationery-office.co.uk/pa/ld199899/ldselect/ldeucom/11/8102102.htm*.

Sheller, M. 2004. 'Mobile publics: beyond the network perspective.' *Environment and Planning D: Society and Space*, 22 (1): 39–52.

Sherwin, A. 2001. 'Top chefs condemn agency for soy sauce cancer fear.' *The Times*, 21 June.

Smith, A., J. Young, and J. Gibson. 1999. 'How now, mad cow? Consumer confidence and source credibility during the 1996 BSE scare.' *European Journal of Marketing*, 33 (11/12): 1107–22.

Smith, J. and G. Meade. 2000. 'Consumer groups "disappointed" at new food safety chief.' *Press Association*, 12 Jan.

Soderstrom, E., J. Sorensen, E. Copenhaver, and S. Carnes. 1984. 'Risk perception in an interest group context: an examination of the TMI Restart issue.' *Risk Analysis*, 4 (3): 231–44.

Sörensen, E. and J. Torfing. 2005. 'Network governance and post-liberal democracy.' *Administrative Theory and Praxis*, 27 (2): 197–237.

Sorkin, M. 2003. *Starting from zero: reconstructing downtown New York*. New York: Routledge.

—— and S. Zukin. 2002. *After the World Trade Center: rethinking New York City*. New York: Routledge.

Sparrow, B. 1999. *Uncertain guardians: the news media as a political institution*. Baltimore: Johns Hopkins University Press.

Stanley, A. 2001. 'A nation challenged; the real estate: Trade Center leaseholder pledges to rebuild.' *New York Times*, 5 Oct.

Stark, D. and M. Girard. 2006. 'Socio-technologies of assembly: sense-making and demonstration in rebuilding Lower Manhattan.' Paper presented at the annual meeting of the American Sociological Association, Montreal Convention Center, Montreal, August 11.

—— and V. Paravel. 2008. 'Powerpoint in public: digital technologies and the new morphology of demonstration.' *Theory, Culture and Society*, 25 (5): 30–55.

Steiner, B. 2007. 'Al Gore, Nobel peace laureate.' *New York Times*, 13 Oct.

Stern, N. 2006. 'Gains from greenhouse action outweigh the cost.' *Financial Times*, 8 Nov.

Stilgoe, J. and J. Wilsdon. 2006. *Engagement, evidence and expertise; balancing different forms of knowledge in regulatory decision-making, a discussion paper for the Food Standards Agency*. London: Food Standards Agency.

Stoker, G. 2006. *Why politics matter: making democracy work*. Basingstoke: Palgrave MacMillan.

Street, J. 2004. 'Celebrity politicians: popular culture and political representation.' *British Journal of Politics and International Relations*, 6 (4): 435–52.

—— 2005. 'Politics lost, politics transformed, politics colonised? Theories of the impact of mass media.' *Political Studies Review*, 3 (1): 17–33.

Szerszynski, B., W. Heim, and C. Waterton. 2003. *Nature performed: environment, culture and performance*. Oxford: Blackwell.

Taylor, J. 2007. 'Values are food for thought.' *The Times*, 12 June.

Torgerson, D. 1985. 'Contextual orientation in policy analysis: the contribution of Harold D. Lasswell.' *Policy Sciences*, 18 (3): 241–61.

—— 1986. 'Between knowledge and politics: three faces of policy analysis.' *Policy Sciences*, 19 (1): 33–59.

—— 2002. 'Policy as performance.' Paper presented at the NOB Conference, Rotterdam, 30–1 Oct.

—— 2003. 'Democracy through policy discourse.' In Hajer and Wagenaar 2003: 113–38.

Uitermark, J. 2005. 'Anti-multiculturalism and the governance of ethnic diversity.' Paper presented at the ECPR general conference, Budapest, 9–11 Sept.

—— and J. Duyvendak 2008. 'Civilising the city: populism and revanchist urbanism in Rotterdam.' *Urban Studies*, 45 (7): 1485–503.

Ungoed-Thomas, J. and J. Leake. 2005. 'The bungles that put poison on our plates.' *Sunday Times*, 27 Feb.

Van Zoonen, L. 2005. *Entertaining the citizen: when politics and popular culture converge*. Lanham, Md.: Rowman & Littlefield.

Wacquant, L. 2004. *Body and soul: notebooks of an apprentice boxer*. New York: Oxford University Press.

Wagner-Pacifici, R. 1986. *The Moro morality play*. Chicago: University of Chicago Press.

Wales, C. 2004. *Consumer trust in food—a European study of the social and institutional conditions for the production of trust. Country report: United Kingdom*. Manchester: University of Manchester.

Walker, P. 2000. 'Quick mind and thick skin essential for food safety chief.' *Press Association*, 12 Jan.

Walton, A. 2001. 'Chinese food can kill you.' *Daily Star*, 21 June.

Warren, M. 1996. 'Deliberative democracy and authority.' *American Political Science Review*, 90 (1): 46–60.

—— 2008. 'Key note address: governance-driven democratization (GDD): Opportunities and Challenges.' Third Interpretive Policy Analysis Conference, University of Essex, Essex, June 19.

Waterton, C. 2003. 'Performing the classification of nature.' In B. Szerszynski, W. Heim, and C. Waterton (eds.), *Nature performed: environment, culture and performance*. Oxford: Blackwell, 111–29.

Wax, A. 2001. 'Developer proposes 4 buildings at WTC.' *Newsday*, 21 Sept.

Weber, M. 1978. *The theory of economic and social organization*. Berkeley: University of California Press.

Webster, J. 2002. 'The UK Food Standards Agency: putting the consumer first.' *International Journal of Consumer Studies*, 26 (3): 210–16.

Weick, K.1988. 'Enacted sensemaking in crisis situations.' *Management Studies*, 25 (4): 305–17.

Wenger, E. 1998. *Communities of practice: learning, meaning, and identity*. Cambridge: Cambridge University Press.

Whelan, E. 2005. 'Why the Fuss about Sudan I?' *The Grocer*, 28 May.

References

White, J. 1999. *Taking language seriously: the narrative foundations of public administration research*. Washington, DC: Georgetown University Press.

Wiegman, M. 2004. 'Aboutaleb heeft zichzelf overtroffen: Ahmed Aboutaleb: "Wie niet mee wil doen, moet zijn koffer pakken".' *Het Parool*, 6 Nov.

Wildavsky, A. 1979. *Speaking truth to power: the art and craft of policy analysis*. Boston: Little, Brown & Co.

Williams, R. 1961. *The Long Revolution*. London: Chatto & Windus.

—— 1981. *Culture*. London: Fontana.

Winnett, R. and J. Ungoed-Thomas. 2005. 'Stores face fines in toxic scandal.' *Sunday Times*, 20 Feb.

Wolfsfeld, G. 2001. 'Political waves and democratic discourse: terrorism waves during the Oslo Peace Process.' In W. Bennet and R. Entman (eds.), *Mediated politics: communication in the future of democracy*. Cambridge: Cambridge University Press, 226–51.

Wooding, S., A. Scoggins, P. Lundin, and T. Ling. 2004. *Talking policy: an examination of public dialogue in science and technology policy, prepared for the Council for Science and Technology*. Cambridge: RAND Corporation.

Wrong, M. 2000. 'Inside track: playing piggy in the middle: Science food safety: Sir John Krebs' diplomacy will be tested as he asserts the independence of the new foodstuffs watchdog, says Michela Wrong.' *Financial Times*, 31 Mar.

Wyatt, E. 2002. 'Further designs are sought in rebuilding of downtown.' *New York Times*, 15 Aug.

Yanow, D. 1995. 'Practices of policy interpretation.' *Policy Sciences*, 28 (2): 111–26.

—— 1996. *How does a policy mean? Interpreting policy and organizational action*. Washington, DC: Georgetown University Press.

—— and P. Schwartz-Shea. 2006. *Interpretation and method: empirical research methods and the interpretive turn*. Armonk: M.E. Sharpe

Zürn, M. 1999. *Regieren Jenseits des Nationalstaates*. Frankfurt am Main: Suhrkamp.

Index